Disruptive Technology, Legal Innovation, and the Future of Real Estate

Amnon Lehavi • Ronit Levine-Schnur
Editors

Disruptive Technology, Legal Innovation, and the Future of Real Estate

Springer

Editors
Amnon Lehavi
Harry Radzyner Law School
Interdisciplinary Center (IDC)
Herzliya, Israel

Gazit-Globe Real Estate Institute
Interdisciplinary Center (IDC)
Herzliya, Israel

Ronit Levine-Schnur
Harry Radzyner Law School
Interdisciplinary Center (IDC)
Herzliya, Israel

Gazit-Globe Real Estate Institute
Interdisciplinary Center (IDC)
Herzliya, Israel

ISBN 978-3-030-52386-2 ISBN 978-3-030-52387-9 (eBook)
https://doi.org/10.1007/978-3-030-52387-9

This Springer imprint is published by the registered company Springer Nature Switzerland AG
The registered company address is: Gewerbestrasse 11, 6330 Cham, Switzerland

blockchain
estate
real
technology
disruption
contracts
smart
governance
Invest
law
commercial
innovation
energy
economic
agenda
management
Notary
public
registry
finance
information
Electoral
Law
land
ethics
Data
contract
vision
invest
digital
mortage
study
Smart
power
cryptography
Shareholders
Distributed
Transactions
crowd-sourcing
intelligence
education
opportunities
electronics
technological
valuations
solutions
distributed
construction
technologies
transparency
revolution
advisory
ledger
organizing
transaction
model
Danger
renewable
learning
Demand
crypto
centralized
types
social
planning
disrupted
Peer-to-peer
industry
currencies
processing
building
Health
cyber
computing
corporate
diligence
Individualization
customization
processing
portfolio
markets
Game
Impact
changer
notary
Fintech
Governance
Democracy
Financial
bitcoin
urban
Manufacturing
data
system
Case
mortgage
democracy
Blockchain
ledgers
durability
businessmodels
legal
cost
city
grids
economics
rental
Mass
advising
signal
theory
risk
due
grid

Introduction

This book addresses challenges that new technologies and the big data revolution pose to existing regulatory and legal frameworks. The volume attempts to address issues such as blockchain and its implications for property transactions and taxes, three (or four) dimensional title registration, land use and urban planning in the age of big data, and the future of property rights in light of these changes. This collection brings together an interdisciplinary set of papers that revolve around the potential influence of disruptive technologies on existing legal norms and the future development of real estate markets. It follows an international conference hosted by the Gazit-Globe Real Estate Institute at the Interdisciplinary Center (IDC) Herzliya, Israel, with additional contributions.

The book is organized into five parts. Part I presents a literature survey conducted by Jan Veuger. His chapter provides an overview and analysis of all blockchain-related scientific publications in the Netherlands and thus offers an exploration of international research, experts, and products of their work.

Part II concerns theoretical aspects and contains two contributions. Ronit Levine-Schnur's chapter asks how blockchain technology has already impacted and will further affect the basic underpinnings of the way we understand and capture property law theory. Some writers already suggest that blockchain is a new institution of property, or even, under a wider implementation of it, can lead to the disappearance of property rights. In order to assess these claims, this chapter considers whether property, as understood by William Blackstone in the eighteenth century, is still relevant in the current times of blockchain technology.

Benito Arruñada's contribution argues that recurrent difficulties are delaying, if not killing off, what for the time being are still modest applications of blockchain. His chapter identifies what value this new technology adds to contractual and proprietary processes, exploring its potential and analyzing the main difficulties it is facing. Paying particular attention to the distinction between contract (personal or *in personam*) rights and property (real or *in rem*) rights, this chapter examines, first, the difficulties with trading contractual rights through blockchain-based applications, mainly these designed to complete contracts ex ante without relying on third-party enforcers. Second, it explores the difficulties faced by blockchain to enable trade in property rights.

Part III deals with the changing landscapes of property rights. Amnon Lehavi's chapter contends that digital technology can open new frontiers in the formation, registration, and enforcement of property rights in land. His chapter explores the prospects—but also the limits—of digital technology in streamlining efficient land use and land markets. In particular, it asks whether the digital production and dissemination of information can enhance a more optimal use of land, such as by the three-dimensional (3D) delineation of real estate into distinct segments and specific rights thereto, including for subsurface infrastructure, or by the digital pooling of non-adjacent assets for purposes such as creating collective security interests in them.

Part III also includes Rebecca Leshinsky's and her coauthors' chapter on legal innovation in real estate. Specifically, they look at how drone-based land survey is disrupting tenure. In their chapter, Leshinsky, Ho, and Choudhury argue that ownership of most land globally is unrecorded. Recent sophistication in geospatial and drone technologies has provided for unmapped land to be recorded in ways that do not reflect traditional surveys. Such disruption is challenging established land law and creating novel opportunities for individual land certification—rattling indefeasibility and tenure. In some jurisdictions, such as Odisha, India, such disruption has triggered legislation to create new, but limited, possessory rights for those who would not have dreamed of security of tenure. The authors explore an understanding of the nature of this social innovation, which in turn has spurred legal innovation for land rights. They explore how the disruption of traditional real estate methods may lead to transformational outcomes for cities and urban dwellers, providing for greater democratization of land rights.

Part IV of the book includes two chapters on the potential effect of blockchain on land registration, one by Georg von Wangenheim, offering an economic perspective, and the other by Benjamin Verheye, focusing on legal issues from a European law perspective. Von Wangenheim's contribution rests on the assertion that both land registration and blockchain pursue the production of immutable information, and thus blockchain-based land registration systems should be widely advanced. However, only a very small number of successful large-scale applications exist. The chapter aims to explain this gap. It argues that trading shares of real estate investment funds on blockchain has little to do with land registration. This allows us to concentrate on the benefits that the blockchain technology may provide for land registration in a proper sense. The chapter shows that "anchoring" a land register in public blockchains by regularly writing hash values of their content in one or several of those blockchains can overcome lack of trust in the immutability of digitized land registers without affecting the latter's rules and organization. In contrast, implementing the entire land registration system on blockchain and changing rules of governance, accordingly, may result in high efficiency and effectiveness. This may be a big leap forward for many jurisdictions. In jurisdictions with already well-functioning land registration systems, the gain from a transition to the blockchain technology tends to be small for both deed recordation and title registration systems—in fact, often too small to outweigh the costs of transition. The major reason is that many inevitable links between real estate reality and its blockchain representation require human decisions, balancing the interests of affected parties.

Verheye's chapter notes that few things seem so opposite to each other as the highly innovative blockchain technology and the ancient land registration sector, in which one traditionally feels thrown back into the pre-digital era. However, for some advocates this unlikely pair might be on its way to form one of the world's new power couples. His contribution aims at analyzing blockchain technology in land registration matters from a material legal point of view. Verheye discusses some blockchain land registration initiatives and evaluates the possibilities of blockchain technology for land registration on the basis of two variables: the lacunar or complete nature of a land register and its negative or positive nature. In doing so, Belgian, French, and German law are taken into account, offering a thorough civil law perspective on the matter.

Part V is devoted to new technological applications that are relevant to real estate. Catalina Goanta's chapter focuses on Decentraland as a virtual world where LAND, a non-fungible token, is traded in order to allow users to build their own spaces on the virtual plots. This inquiry into Decentraland classifies LAND as digital content, and thus asks the question of which compliance issues may arise out of the application of Directive 2019/770 (the Digital Content Directive) to Decentraland in general, and LAND in particular. While much literature has focused on the legal implications of cryptocurrencies from a banking perspective, not the same can be said about the consumer protection angle necessary to tackle the hype that has affected users who spent valuable financial resources on investing, playing on, or using blockchain-based platforms. The chapter aims to make a contribution to fill this research gap, and to shed light on some of the considerations that platforms such as Decentraland ought to pay close attention to when creating consumer content or services.

Closing this volume, Kat Grimsley and Cody Pennetti discuss the effect of technology on business and development industries. They argue that these industries must prioritize investments in order to be prepared for disruptive technologies. They contend that within the real estate industry, the influence of new technologies is readily apparent in areas such as design and construction with Building Information Modeling (BIM), the incorporation of smart and sustainable/energy-efficient systems into new buildings, and a shared economy approach to space use (e.g., AirBnB). However, there is an extensive network of critical interrelated institutions connected to real estate that is often overlooked, making the effects of disruption less transparent in the context of the larger system. Their chapter emphasizes the complexity of the system that supports real property and its relevance for infrastructure, humanitarian, and market interests. The chapter then proposes a system-engineering approach as the appropriate lens through which to view the "real estate system" to ensure that projects are holistically envisioned and that disruptions can be anticipated.

We hope that the book's variety of topics and perspectives will serve and encourage a rigorous debate among experts and students interested in disruptive technologies and real estate regulation. Lastly, we are grateful to Dr. Efrat Tolkowsky, CEO of the Gazit-Globe Real Estate Institute at IDC Herzliya, and Michal Amir, the Institute's content manager, for their assistance with the book and the conference.

Amnon Lehavi and Ronit Levine-Schnur
Harry Radzyner Law School
and Gazit-Globe Real Estate Institute
Interdisciplinary Center (IDC)
Herzliya, Israel

Contents

Contributors

Benito Arruñada Pompeu Fabra University and Barcelona GSE, Barcelona, Spain

Pranab Choudhury NRMC Center for Land Governance, Bhubaneswar, Odisha, India

Catalina Goanta Maastricht Law & Tech Lab, Faculty of Law, Maastricht University, Maastricht, Netherlands

Serene Ho RMIT University, VIC, Melbourne, Australia

C. Kat Grimsley Center for Real Estate Entrepreneurship, George Mason University, Fairfax, VA, USA

Amnon Lehavi Harry Radzyner Law School, Interdisciplinary Center (IDC) Herzliya, Israel

Gazit-Globe Real Estate Institute, IDC Herzliya, Israel

Rebecca Leshinsky RMIT University, VIC, Melbourne, Australia

Ronit Levine-Schnur Harry Radzyner Law School, Interdisciplinary Center (IDC) Herzliya, Israel

Gazit-Globe Real Estate Institute, IDC, Herzliya, Israel

Cody A. Pennetti Department of Engineering Systems and Environment (ESE), Center for Risk Management of Engineering Systems, University of Virginia, Charlottesville, VA, USA

Benjamin Verheye Institute for Property Law, KU Leuven, Leuven, Belgium

Jan Veuger Saxion University of Applied Sciences, Schools of Finance and Accounting, Creative Technology and School of Governance, Law and Urban Development, Enschede, Netherlands

Georg von Wangenheim Faculty of Economics, University of Kassel, Kassel, Germany

Part I
Literature Survey

A Database Exploring Blockchain and Real Estate

Jan Veuger

Abstract The Foundation for International Blockchain and Real Estate Expertise (FIBREE) was founded in Amsterdam in 2018 with the aim of bringing together real estate professionals and blockchain specialists from all over the world to exchange expertise. FIBREE is aware of the current hype about blockchain technology, which does not always contribute to getting to know it better. FIBREE's mission is to help create a realistic expectation pattern that will allow the real estate market, step by step, to discover and exploit the true potential of blockchain technology. By bringing together the expertise of pioneers in this field and sharing knowledge and insights already gained, FIBREE wants to make an important contribution to the adoption and implementation of this technology in the real estate market in the coming years. This article provides an overview and analysis of all relevant scientific publications in the Netherlands, and does so within a context of a first small international exploration of international research, experts and products.

Keywords Blockchain · Real estate · Database · Research · Products · Experts

1 Introduction

There are some arguments for development the foundation as an international platform of professionals for professionals which is objective, neutral and integrity as core values. There is a growing network of 2000+ professionals who share an interest in blockchain and real estate with partnerships with relevant professional business organizations and platforms. FIBREE works in a decentralized structure: participants set the agenda by regional representatives. Together they create a realistic perspective on the applicability of blockchain in the real estate industry. In this

J. Veuger (✉)
Saxion University of Applied Sciences, Schools of Finance and Accounting, Creative Technology and School of Governance, Law and Urban Development, Enschede, Netherlands
e-mail: j.veuger@corporaterem.nl

A. Lehavi, R. Levine-Schnur (eds.), *Disruptive Technology, Legal Innovation, and the Future of Real Estate*, https://doi.org/10.1007/978-3-030-52387-9_1

article I look at a study that was carried out in 2018 to give an idea of the state of affairs regarding blockchain in real estate across five continents and 63 regions to the extent that this was public at the end of 2018.

2 Covering and Regional Chairs

Since the beginning of 2018 FIBREE has been developing a global network regarding blockchain and real estate on three different perspectives: research, experts and products. In total FIBREE is working on covering 63 regions and 5 continents: Eurasia (consisting of the continents of Asia and Europe), Africa, America (North and South America), Antarctica and Australia. On the reference date 31 December 2018, 24 regions—38% of the target number of 63 regions—are represented in this study, in which Europe is strongly represented with 14 regions or 58% of the participating regions (Table 1).

Table 1 Covering country, continent and region

Target country	Continent	Region
Austria	Europe	Vienna
Austria	Europe	Graz
Brazil	America	Sao Paulo
Croatia	Europe	Zagreb
Georgia	Europe	Tibilisi
Germany	Europe	Berlin
Germany	Europe	Stuttgart
Germany	Europe	Frankfurt
India	Asia/Pacific	Bangalore
Israel	Middle East	Tel Aviv
Italy	Europe	Milano
Netherlands	Europe	Amsterdam/Enschede
Poland	Europe	Warsaw
Slovenia	Europe	Ljubliana
Switzerland	Europe	Zug
Taiwan	Asia/Pacific	Taipeh
The Netherlands	Europe	Amsterdam
United Kingdom	Europe	London
USA	America	New York
USA	America	North America
USA	America	Seattle
USA	America	Chicago
USA	America	New York
USA	America	Silicon Valley

3 Methodology Worldwide and The Netherlands in Particular

The Regionals Chairs (RC) were asked to collect data on (1) which blockchain and real estate product-suppliers or initiatives do you see, (2) which research-output on blockchain and real estate do you have and know and (3) who are the experts with which specific expertise in the field of blockchain and real estate that you see?

The research looked for the combination of blockchain and real estate in the output of the various universities for research. The data collection started in mid-2018 and ended in December 2018. In January and February 2019, the analyzes were carried out centrally and in co-ordination, with some checks being carried out at the RC. The data collection does not include the announcements and reports of seminars, conferences and meetings, as well as duplications in professional journals. It has also been observed with some regularity that publications were no longer available in the libraries and gave an error message. The data collection for research in the Netherlands took place at all universities (of applied sciences) to which a real estate course is linked or related. In the public or non-public libraries, the data collection took place whereby it should be noted that much was public, but not everything (Table 2).

Table 2 Overview of libraries of universities (of applied sciences) in the Netherlands with a real estate course or subject related thereto

University	City	Source	Hits
Amsterdam School of Real Estate	Amsterdam	Public	5
Delft University of Technology	Delft	Public	25
Eindhoven University of Technology	Eindhoven	Public	80
Fontys University of Applied Sciences	Eindhoven	Not public	0
Hanze University of Applied Sciences	Groningen	Not public	0
Maastricht University	Maastricht	Not public	0
Radboud University	Nijmegen	Not public	0
Rotterdam University of Applied Sciences	Rotterdam	Part Public	95
Saxion University of Applied Sciences	Enschede	Public	23
Tias Business School	Tilburg	Public	491
University of Groningen	Groningen	Public	24
University of Amsterdam	Amsterdam	Public	47
University of Twente	Enschede	Public	10
Utrecht University	Utrecht	Not Public	0
Wageningen University and Research	Wageningen	Public	29
Total Dutch universities			**829**

4 Conclusions Research The Netherlands

The database of the Netherlands has a scale of 131 virtually one hundred percent score on the parts author, title, company name or university, research—product—expert, level, subject, country, publication year, keyword and link. The accrued database thus amounts to 16% ($n = 131^{829}$) of the hits found that have been stripped of regular announcements of seminars, master classes, press releases, news items, opinions and columns. Within the database, a distinction has been made between General or Real Estate because a number of articles do contain material about blockchain and real estate, but most of them are about blockchain in general. From this perspective, 59% ($n = 77^{131}$) are fully focused on real estate and blockchain (Fig. 1)

If we fully analyze the database that has been built up, the following figures will be published on numbers of publications in company name of (applied) university, numbers of publications levels, number of publications by topic, number of publications by country, publication year, keywords and most common authors.

4.1 *Company Name or University*

Of all 131 publications, a total of 82 universities in the Netherlands, with several producing only one or two publications. When these are excluded from the analysis, it appears that much can be traced back to the libraries of Tilburg University (24 publications), Rotterdam University of Applied Science (18 publications), followed

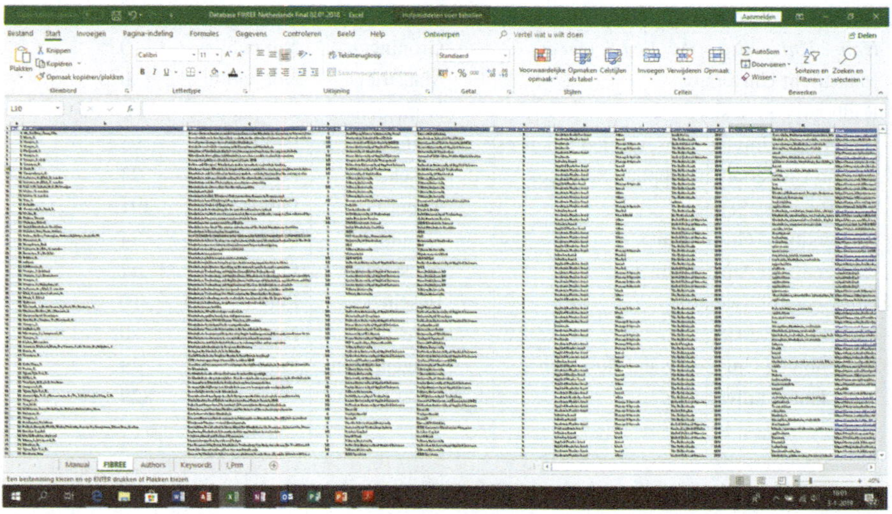

Fig. 1 Example of the database Research The Netherlands

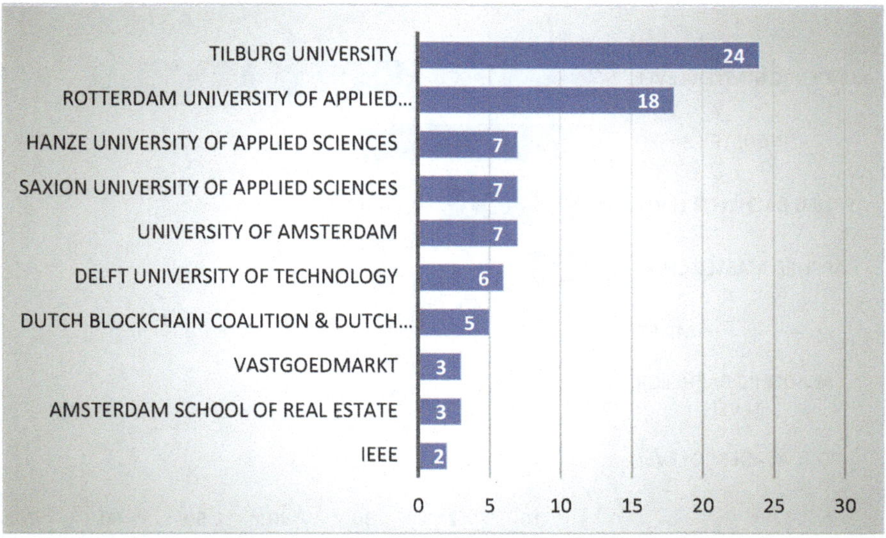

Fig. 2 Number of publications in company or (applied) university

by Saxion University of Applied Sciences (7 publications), Hanze University of Applied Sciences (7 publications) and University of Amsterdam (7 publications). As far as is known now, there is no PhD research in the Netherlands in the area of Blockchain and Real Estate in 2018 (Fig. 2).

4.2 *Levels*

The level of publications is high, especially at the academic master level (n = 64 [131]), followed by industry-based (n = 30 [131]), applied bachelor's (n = 21 [131]) and master's level (n = 10 [131]). This means that the academic level is high and the industry is also explicitly present in the field of publications (Fig. 3).

4.3 *Topics*

The topics are mainly in themes such as Manage and Operate, Invest and Work, together a share of 65% (n = 84 [131]). The topics of the publications are in sequential numbers: Manage and Operate 35% (n = 45 [131]), Other 25% (n = 32 [131]), Invest 17% (n = 22 [131]), Work 13% (n = 17 [131]), Market 9% (n = 12 [131]) and Plan and Build 2% (n = 3 [131]) (Fig. 4).

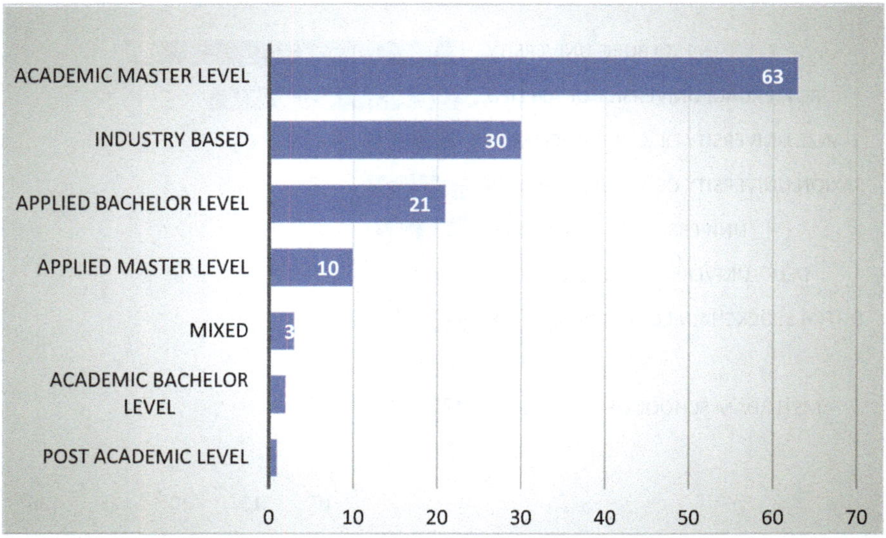

Fig. 3 Number of publications per level

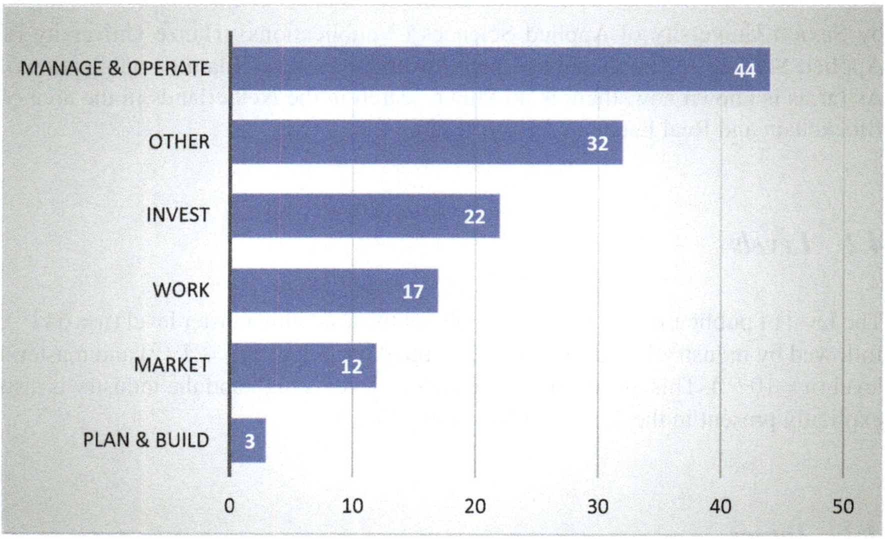

Fig. 4 Number of publications per Topic

4.4 Countries

The Netherlands is strongly represented in the number of publications, but in view of the demarcation of the working area of universities and applied universities in the Netherlands, this is not a special feature. However, the influence of the United

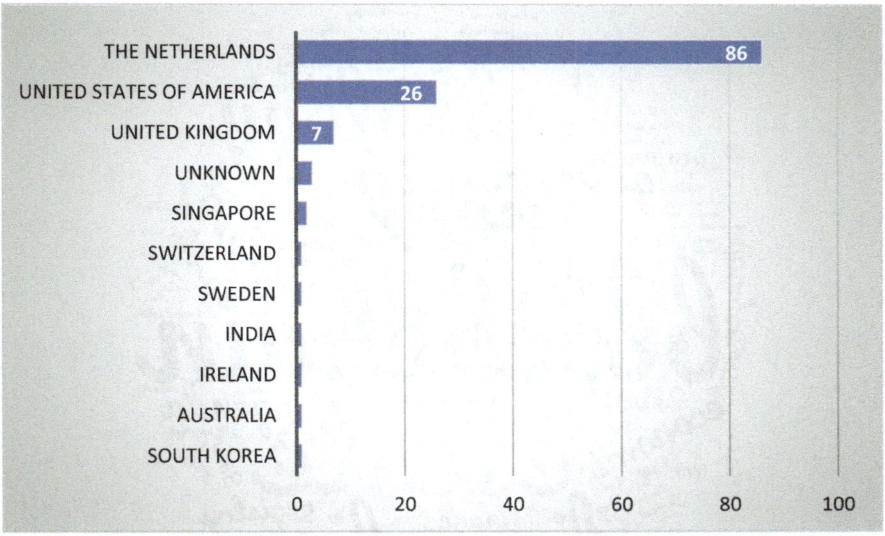

Fig. 5 Number of publications per Country

Kingdom and The United States of America compared to all other countries in the table below is clearly visible in this database (Fig. 5).

4.5 Publication Year

When we look at the Years in which the publications took place, in 2018 the number of explosives has risen in relation to the previous year 2015–2017. This study shows that 55% (n = 72 [131]) of the publications appeared in 2018 compared to 36% (n = 47 [131]) in 2017 and 4% (n = 5 [131]) in 2016 and 1% (n = 1 [131]) in 2015. At the start of 2019, a number of (4%) publications are already visible (n = 5 [131]). The attention in publications about Blockchain and real estate has mainly developed in 2017 and will continue in 2018. Given the upward trend, it is interesting for a follow-up study into how 2019 will develop in this area.

4.6 Keywords in a Word Cloud

The 131 databases from which this research is based have been added as far as possible. When these are included in a word cloud and the most common words in size of the word become visible, the following figure and image will appear. This shows that besides blockchain, technology, estate and disruption, the words governance, public, energy, economic, management, invest, finance and registry are very common (Fig. 6).

Fig. 6 Keywords in a cloud

4.7 Most Common Authors

The database shows that the most common authors are Veuger and co-authors 10% (n = 15 [131]), Tjong Tjin Tai 5% (n = 7 [131]), Lafarre and van der Elst 3% (n = 4 [131]) and Dutch Blockchain Coalition and Dutch Digital Delta together are 4% (n = 5 [131]). A substantive analysis of these authors shows that their focus is on vision, agenda, organization meetings, notaries, contracts. Legal business application possibilities in general to real estate and blockchain. Specifically, this can be described per author in alphabetical order as follows.

The Dutch Blockchain Coalition (DBC) and Dutch Digital Delta, two affiliated organizations, mainly published their mission and vision (*Blockchain for Good, the vision and mission of the DBC*, 2018), the knowledge and innovation agenda (*Knowledge and Innovation*, 2018), *Agenda ICT 2016–2019* (2017), in anticipation of further elaboration of its plans in the *Legacy Coalition* (2017) and smart contracts as a specific application of Blockchain technology in 2017–2018. The Dutch Blockchain Coalition is a public-private partnership of partners from financial services such as banks and insurance companies, the logistics, energy, security and ICT sectors, ministries, the knowledge world, supervisory parties such as the Netherlands Authority for the Financial Markets (AFM)) and the Royal Dutch Notarial Association (KNB) and organizations such as TNO, NWO and ECP |

Platform for the Information Society. The coalition is an initiative of the Ministry of Economic Affairs and Climate. Dutch Digital Delta is the meeting place to connect and create. It is a national platform, intended for everyone involved in technological innovation.

All publications of dr. A.J.F. Lafarre LLM MSc (professor of law Tilburg University with the expertise on corporate governance, law and economics and shareholder meetings) en prof. dr. C.F. van der Elst (professor of law and management of Tilburg University with the expertise business transactions, corporate governance, enterprises, law and economics, and legal persons law) were published in 2018 and are mainly about the organization around the application of Blockchain for meetings: *Blockchain and smartcontracting for the shareholder community* (2018), *Blockchain and the 21st century annual general meeting* (2018), *Blockchain maakt vergaderen efficiënt* [Blockchain makes meetings efficient] (2018) en *Blockchain for corporate governance and shareholder activism* (2018).

Publications of Prof. T.F.E. Tjon Tjin Tai (professor at Tilburg University with private law, law of civil law and IT law) mainly has Invest topics with attention to notary, contracts and law: *The blockchain as an alternative to the notarial practice* (2018), *The reasonable third and Blockchain* (2015), *Formalization of contract law for smart contracts* (2017), *Legal aspects of blockchain and smart contracts* (2017), *Legal Issues or Blockchain and contract* (2017), *Smart contracts and the law* (2018) and *The reasonable third party and the Blockchain* (2018).

In 2017 the research *A viable real estate economy with disruption and blockchain* has done by dr. ing. J. Veuger MRE FRICS (professor Blockchain of the School of Finance and Accounting, School of Creative Technology and School of Governance, Law and Urban Development of the Saxion University Enschede and therefore from 2012 to 2019 professor Real Estate Hanze University) which submitted other new publications and presentations: *A viable real estate economy with disruption and Blockchain* as a book (2017), *Attention to disruption and Blockchain creates a viable real estate economy* in the Journal of USA-China Public Administration (2017), *Blockchain: kantelpunt in de vastgoedsector* [Blockchain: turning point in the real estate sector] (2017), *Blockchain: vertrouwen in een wendbare vastgoedeconomie* [Blockchain: confidence in a maneuverable real estate economy] (2017), *Een wendbare vastgoedeconomie met disruptie en Blockchain* [An agile real estate economy with disruption and Blockchain] (2017), *Noordelijk Vastgoedcongres 2017: disruptie, blokchain en vastgoed* [North Real Estate Congress: disruption, blockchain and real estate] (2017) en *The true meaning of the Blockchain technology for real estate still needs to be investigated* in International Journal of Engineering and Sciences (2017). In 2018 is the before mention research presented on the American Real Estate Society (ARES) Congress 2018 with the title *A real game changer in real estate: blockchain* (2018)—and wins the Manuscript Prize Competition in category Property/Asset management American Real Estate Society (ARES) 2018—and on Barometer Maatschappelijk Vastgoedcongres [Barometer Social Real Estate Congress] (2018) in de publication *Barometer public real estate: special issue* (2018). In 2018 is also the article *Trust in a viable real estate economy with disruption and blockchain* published in the Journal Facilities, subject area Property Management and Build Environment. The full text of this document has been downloaded almost 2.000 times since 2018. In May 2019 the scientific peer reviewed book Blockchain Technology and Applications appeared by Veuger as editor of eight chapters and (co)writer of three articles: Blockchain technology looking for a problem in real estate (Veuger & Bronckers, 2019), Influence of blockchain applications and digitalization on real estate (Veuger, 2019a, b, c) and Start up GetaBrick in real estate (Veuger & Hulsebos, 2019). A publication of Nova Science Publishers New York was announced in May 2019 but has supposed to published in 2018.

5 Conclusions

5.1 Conclusion 1

Never before has an investigation been conducted on such a scale about the state of affairs of publicly available information about blockchain in combination with real estate. However, it should be noted that this is a snapshot on 31 December 2018 and is not necessarily exhaustive. This research should therefore also be seen as a first step for further (annual) research.

5.2 Conclusion 2

A follow-up study is necessary for further complementation and the best possible completeness of the database and the development and sharing of knowledge in the field of research, experts and products. The system and methodology of this study has shown that this method can provide the right information and can therefore be used to further broaden the scope of the study worldwide.

5.3 Conclusion 3

Finding innovative configurations for business models for the real estate sector is not easy when using blockchain technology. A distinction can be made between three platform generations: (1) Bitcoin, (2) blockchain platforms and (3) network of allowed participants. The first variant is not suitable for the real estate sector due to the fact that it is not possible to exchange assets other than token and currency than, for example, contracts. The second generation platform is mainly focused on improving exchange opportunities. This has led, among other things, to the development of smart contracts in an Ethereum network that is aimed at a global and public network where all transactions are visible. The third-generation platform is accessible to admitted participants and they are therefore the only ones who have insight into this network. Corda (www.corda.net) is an example of this.

5.4 Conclusion 4

Limited research has been done into the influence of blockchain technology in the real estate sector (Veuger, 2018, 2019a, b, c). Studies by Dijkstra (2017) and Gout (2017) provide an initial exploration (Veuger, 2017a, b, c, d, e, f, g, h). Dijkstra (2017) concluded that blockchain can add five values to real estate management (1) a building passport, (2) alternative financing options, (3) trading real estate by the blockchain, (4) smart leases and (5) sustainability applications. Gout (2017) concluded that a possible application of blockchain technology could be used when setting up Marketplace funding.

5.5 Conclusion 5

The real estate chain is a highly fragmented chain with many information exchanges between a large number of involved parties, as well as traditionally many data silos and a large diversity in standards and used software protocols. The real estate chain can be roughly divided into five information domains (Veuger and Bronckers, 2019), with the identity of the building or building part as connecting factor. If the various actors are then also projected, it should not come as a surprise that tedious communication and information exchange is among the top complaints. And that is exactly where blockchain shines, as we just discussed in being able to trust that everyone has the same information. In other words, many use cases are conceivable, but who will allow parties to not only communicate better, but also make them want to communicate? The real estate column lists various national or international, established or new standardisation initiatives, such as Oscre,[1] Redex,[2] Vastgoedtaxonomie,[3] BIMchain,[4] NEN,[5] ISO,[6] et cetera. These standards provide uniform definitions, data, protocols or IDs within the scope of the specific field of application, which is often still a silo. In other industries, such as the automotive[7] or

[1] http://www.oscre.org/oscreblockchaininitiative

[2] www.redex.nl

[3] Website SBR Banken

[4] www.bimchain.io

[5] Website smartindustries / NEN

[6] Website ISO

[7] www.dlt.mobi

the international transport industry,[8] the same issue is at hand. Broad consortia are now established to settle barriers, since they want to take maximum advantage of the blockchain potential. Why should this be different for the real estate column? Is it not time that parties who consider themselves trend setters to unify and take the initiative? As history as taught us, new technology for a broadly applicable administrative foundation can lead to revolutionary business models. L'Histoire se repète. Will time tell? (Veuger and Bronckers 2019).

5.6 Conclusion 6

The way in which disruption, Blockchain and real estate will develop in the coming years are not the only obvious characteristics of a particular era, but also its social impact and user behaviour. This also applies to how this real estate transition can best be tracked, guided and utilized in society at the international, national and regional level. Disruptive organizations clearly respond to the viability of the (built) environment and therefore determine competitive strength. This affects the current and future valuation of real estate. The value of the possible applications of Blockchain in real estate processes is reflected in more effective and efficient transactions, increasing transparency, a better foundation for investment and new development for the mortgage market. All of this will then grow into more trust in fundamental elements of an economy: land and real estate and from the 'internet of things' to an 'economy of things'.

Looking at the impact of Blockchain on real estate, we can draw a number of conclusions. First of all, the relationship between Blockchain and real estate has not yet been proven in practice. It is expected to develop further in the form of registering transaction processes and the DNA passport of a real estate object. Secondly, completeness and transparency are the basic ingredients for trust in the system. Third, real estate wants to remain viable. For this reason, taking the offense is necessary for real estate and management to connect with social demand. Behaviour also leads to new earnings models of the social and economic spin-off of disruptive real estate. If the Dutch real estate sector embraces Blockchain and is able to realize innovations, then there are opportunities for real estate entrepreneurs to exploit the disruptive character to provide those new services. Artificial intelligence through algorithmizing of Blockchain will increasingly play a role in the taking of decisions by learning organizations. It is good to realize that (thinking) processes and decisions are being outsourced by algorithms. This artificial intelligence cannot combine hard and soft factors to make considerations. The question is whether we will use the big-data models correctly and not inadvertently bring about inequality, discrimination and less vigilance. That technology develops faster than the adaptability of people is also not new: the parachute was invented before the first plane flew.

[8] www.bita.studio

Ethics for individuals and organizations remain important for judging and utilizing data.

Changes in value concepts affect the valuation of real estate and the thinking about it. The orientation of changing users and owners of real estate affects innovativeness, values and flexibility in managing that property. Orientation on disruption must be seen as proof that the real estate world is able to actually innovate the accumulated assets and consolidate this. The financial and real estate markets are markets that exaggerate through irrational behavior. Fear of 'eat or be eaten' determines people's behavior. Financial and thus real estate markets are always unstable and must always be regulated by people and organizations.

The question that remains is whether it is important to look at disruptive innovations in existing markets or newcomers in the real estate market and Blockchain. The question is whether Blockchain is only a technological disruption, or a real game changer, and whether the entire value chain of the real estate market will embrace it. No two disruptions are the same. Trust in Blockchain is a prerequisite for guiding the predictable form of that disruption where start-up companies use new technology to offer cheaper and inferior alternatives to real estate in the market (Veuger, 2017a, b, c, d, e, f, g, h).

5.7 Conclusion 7

Blockchain could have a huge impact on the value chain in our society. Examples are efficiency, transparency, ownership, value (transfer), automation and service provision. When we want to understand the world of blockchain, we need to understand the innovation of the currency Bitcoin in 2009 that is built on underlying technology called Blockchain. Bitcoin is a combination of four individual elements: (1) cryptography, (2) a peer-to-peer network, (3) an open source protocol and (4) a shared ledger. This makes it a phenomenon that people are enthusiastic about. The internet already makes it possible to transfer information quickly, cheaply without paper and without intermediaries being involved.

Blockchain gives the same benefits for transferring values. Internet is used to transfer word and image, blockchain for transactions. Blockchain is a combination of two elements: a shared and distributed ledger with synchronized data spread over multiple sites, countries and/or institutions and a cryptography: digital token with a monetary value. This book provides an overview of the latest developments on blockchain technology and its applications with the following themes and with the assistance of experts from Austria, Brazil, China, Croatia, Georgia, Germany, Italy, Netherlands, Slovenia, Spain and Switzerland: (1) *Blockchain and the Agenda 2030* by Danielle Mendes Thame Denny, (2) *Application of Blockchain Technology in the Field of E-Government Services* by Jiarui Zhang, (3) *Can the Cybersecurity of Smart Building be Improved Using Blockchain Technology?* by Ben van Lier, (4) *Influence of Blockchain Applications and Digitalization on Real Estate* by Jan Veuger, (5) *Blockchain: Technology Looking For a Problem in Real*

Estate? by Jo Bronckers and Jan Veuger et al., (6) *Start up 'Get a Brick' in Real Estate* by Wendel Hulsebos and Jan Veuger, (7) *Blockchain: An Efficiency Solution For Housing Associations?* by Michel Vonk, (8) *Blockchain Applications in Support of the Energy Transition* by Mieke Oostra and Jelle Rijpma, and (9) *Many Keys of Blockchain for Real Estate* by Esther Dekker (Veuger et al., 2018).

5.8 Conclusion 8

A question that remains is to continue to look at existing markets or to disruptive innovation newcomers in the blockchain market. The question is whether blockchain is only a technological disruption or a real game changer and whether the entire value chain of the market is going to embrace this. Confidence in blockchain is therefore a precondition for guiding that disruption where (new) companies use new technology to offer cheaper and superior alternatives in the market. But the big question is how quickly blockchain will develop as well as all its applications (Veuger et al., 2018).

6 Overall Conclusion

The way in which blockchain and real estate will develop in the coming years are not the only obvious. The true meaning of the blockchain technology for real estate still needs to be investigated. I am still curious to understand and clarify the value of Blockchain for real estate processes. Doubt continues to exist and is therefore a feeding ground for further research, because we do not know what we have not seen.

Bibliography

Anand, S. (2018). International property report: Europe: Test of blockchain for real estate is readied. *Wall Street Journal*. Retrieved from https://www.wsj.com/articles/a-pioneer-in-real-estate-blockchain-emerges-in-europe-1520337601

Asmoredjo, K. C., Hovanesyan, A., Tooo, S. M., & Sing, C. M. W. L. (2017). *Decentralized mortgage market: An open market for real-estate crowdsourcing*. Delft: Delft University of Technology. Retrieved from https://repository.tudelft.nl/islandora/object/uuid:a20fc94f-a959-44ec-9c29-0cae8ad831ce?collection=education

Bakker, S. (2017). *Niet de technologieën maar het gedrag. Omslagverhaal De Ware disruptie*. Het Financieele Dagblad. Retrieved from https://fd.nl/morgen/1197956/niet-de-technologie-maar-het-gedrag

Bessems, P., & Bril, W. (2017). *Blockchain organiseren*. Mijnmanagentboek. Retrieved from https://www.managementboek.nl/boek/9789463426572/blockchain-organiseren-paul-Bessems

Bhushan, R. (2018). *Five reasons why using blockchain technology can help overthrow the traditional real estate limitations*. Rotterdam University of Applied Sciences. Retrieved from https://hogeschoolrotterdam.on.worldcat.org/search?queryString=blockchain%20real%20estate&databaseList=2375,2572,3441,3837,1875,3018,1697,2268,3313,2267,4028,3633,638,10036,3834,2264,3551,2263,2262,3450,2261,1271,2260,2281,1941,3448,2259,2237,203,2277,1708,3841,3988,3967&sortKey=BEST_MATCH&clusterResults=true&scope=wz:60078&page=1#

Bikker, A. (2017). *Blockchain pilot in commercial real estate*. ABN Amro. Retrieved from https://www.abnamro.com/en/newsroom/press-releases/2016/Blockchain-pilot-in-commercial-real-estate.html

Blein, S. (2018). *A real estate coin has two sides: A study on the effects of tokenisation of real estate on the business model of the investment manager*. Retrieved from Amsterdam School of Real Estate. https://vastgoedbibliotheek.nl/#!/SingleDoc?find=BI:blockchain&hitnr=2

Blums, I., & Weigaard, H. (2017). *Financial reporting by a shared ledger*. Tilburg University. Retrieved from https://research.tilburguniversity.edu/en/publications/financial-reporting-by-a-shared-ledger

Breidbach, C., Ellway, B., Keating, B. W., Byron, W., Kormusheva, K., Kowalkowski, C., ···, Maglio, P. (2018). *Operating without operations: How is technology changing the role of the firm?* Emerald. Retrieved from https://www.emeraldinsight.com/doi/abs/10.1108/JOSM-05-2018-0127

Buisman, A. (2018). *Een betere cfo door blockchain*. Vastgoedmarkt. Retrieved from https://www.vastgoedmarkt.nl/data-en-technologie/nieuws/2018/08/verslaggeving-verslaglegging-een-betere-cfo-door-blockchain-101135572

Burazeri, A. (2018). *Blockchain is here to stay: An exploratory study upon blockchain technology in the Netherlands*. University of Amsterdam. Retrieved from http://www.scriptiesonline.uba.uva.nl/cgi/b/bib/bib-idx?type=simple;lang=nl;c=uvascript;sid=8d80e100620b75f76d424842fee998c6;rgn1=entire%20record;q1=blockchain;Submit.x=0;Submit.y=0;sort=publicationyear;cc=uvascript;view=reslist;fmt=long;page=reslist;start=7;size=1

Ceba Vega, J. (2018). *Creation and conveyance of real property rights on Blockchain Technology: A conciliation between real property principles and Blockchain functions?* University of Amsterdam. Retrieved from http://www.scriptiesonline.uba.uva.nl/cgi/b/bib/bib-idx?type=simple;lang=nl;c=uvascript;sid=8d80e100620b75f76d424842fee998c6;rgn1=entire%20record;q1=blockchain;Submit.x=0;Submit.y=0;sort=publicationyear;cc=uvascript;view=reslist;fmt=long;page=reslist;start=8;size=1

Cohen, L. R., Rinaudo, S., Samuelson, L., & Katz, H. (2017). How securitization can benefit from blockchain technology. *Journal of Structured Finance*. http://jsf.iijournals.com/content/23/2/51

Compton, S. H., & Schottenstein, D. (2017). *Questions and answer about using blockchain technology in real estate practice*. The practical real estate lawyer. Retrieved from http://files.alicle.org/thumbs/datastorage/lacidoirep/articles/PREL1709_Compton_thumb.pdf

Compton, S. H., & Schottenstein, D. (2018). *Questions and answer about using blockchain technology in real estate practice*. Retrieved from Rotterdam University of Applied Sciences. https://hogeschoolrotterdam.on.worldcat.org/search?queryString=blockchain%20real%20estate&databaseList=2375,2572,3441,3837,1875,3018,1697,2268,3313,2267,4028,3633,638,10036,3834,2264,3551,2263,2262,3450,2261,1271,2260,2281,1941,3448,2259,2237,203,2277,1708,3841,3988,3967&sortKey=BEST_MATCH&clusterResults=true&scope=wz:60078&page=1#

Couwenhoven, R. (2018). *Blockchain and its effect on business models: A study focused on the energy sector*. University of Amsterdam. Retrieved from http://www.scriptiesonline.uba.uva.nl/cgi/b/bib/bib-idx?type=simple;lang=nl;c=uvascript;sid=8d80e100620b75f76d424842fee998c6;rgn1=entire%20record;q1=blockchain;Submit.x=0;Submit.y=0;sort=publicationyear;cc=uvascript;view=reslist;fmt=long;page=reslist;start=10;size=1

CPB (2018). *CPB risicorapportage financiële markten 2018*. Centraal Planbureau (CPB). Retrieved from https://files.vastgoedbibliotheek.nl/Server/getfile.aspx?file=docs/publicaties/site/CPB/CPB_Notitie_29_mei_2018_CPB_Risicorapportage.pdf

Crosman, P. (2018a). *Better and Cheaper: Blockchain makes inroads in real estate lending*. Rotterdam University of Applied Sciences. Retrieved from https://hogeschoolrotterdam.on.worldcat.org/search?queryString=blockchain%20real%20estate&databaseList=2375,2572,3441,3837,1875,3018,1697,2268,3313,2267,4028,3633,638,10036,3834,2264,3551,2263,2262,3450,2261,1271,2260,2281,1941,3448,2259,2237,203,2277,1708,3841,3988,3967&sortKey=BEST_MATCH&clusterResults=true&scope=wz:60078&page=1#

Crosman, P. (2018b). *Could blockchains replace banks in real estate lending?* Rotterdam University of Applied Sciences. https://hogeschoolrotterdam.on.worldcat.org/search?queryString=blockchain%20real%20estate&databaseList=2375,2572,3441,3837,1875,3018,1697,2268,3313,2267,4028,3633,638,10036,3834,2264,3551,2263,2262,3450,2261,1271,2260,2281,1941,3448,2259,2237,203,2277,1708,3841,3988,3967&sortKey=BEST_MATCH&clusterResults=true&scope=wz:60078&page=1#

Dandapani, K. (2017). *Electronic Finance—Recent developments*. Florida International University. Retrieved from https://www.emeraldinsight.com/doi/abs/10.1108/MF-02-2017-0028

Davis, A. (2018). *Bringing the blockchain to Lethbridge*. Rotterdam University of Applied Sciences. Retrieved from https://hogeschoolrotterdam.on.worldcat.org/search?queryString=blockchain%20real%20estate&databaseList=2375,2572,3441,3837,1875,3018,1697,2268,3313,2267,4028,3633,638,10036,3834,2264,3551,2263,2262,3450,2261,1271,2260,2281,1941,3448,2259,2237,203,2277,1708,3841,3988,3967&sortKey=BEST_MATCH&clusterResults=true&scope=wz:60078&page=1#

de Boer, E. (2018). *o-evolution of disruptive technologies for sustainable transformation: Blockchain start-ups' interactions with incumbents in the energy sector.* University of Amsterdam. Retrieved from http://www.scriptiesonline.uba.uva.nl/cgi/b/bib/bib-idx?type=simple;lang=nl;c=uvascript;sid=8d80e100620b75f76d424842fee998c6;rgn1=entire%20record;q1=blockchain;Submit.x=0;Submit.y=0;sort=publicationyear;cc=uvascript;view=reslist;fmt=long;page=reslist;start=6;size=1

de Hert, P. (2018). *The future of privacy—Addressing singularities to identify bright-line rules that speak to us*. Tilburg University. Retrieved from https://research.tilburguniversity.edu/en/publications/the-future-of-privacy-addressing-singularities-to-identify-bright

de Kruijf, J., & Weigaard, H. (2017a). *Ontologies for commitment-based smart contracts*. Tilburg University. Retrieved from https://research.tilburguniversity.edu/en/publications/ontologies-for-commitment-based-smart-contracts

de Kruijf, J., & Weigaard, H. (2017b). *Understanding the blockchain using enterprise ontology*. Tilburg University. Retrieved from https://research.tilburguniversity.edu/en/publications/understanding-the-blockchain-using-enterprise-ontology

Deloitte (2018a). *Blockchain Centre of Expertise*. Deloitte. Retrieved from https://www2.deloitte.com/nl/nl/pages/over-deloitte/articles/deloitte-opens-blockchain-center-of-expertise.html

Deloitte (2018b). *Real Estate Predictions 2018*. Deloitte. Retrieved from https://www2.deloitte.com/nl/nl/pages/real-estate/articles/blockchain-technology-for-real-estate-rome-wasnt-built-in-a-day.html

Dijkstra, M. (2017). *Blockchain: Towards disruption in the real estate sector.* University of Delft. Retrieved from https://www.google.nl/search?q=on+the+impact+of+Blockchain+technology+in+the+real+estate+management+process.&ie=&oe=

Dutch Blockchain Coalition. (2018a). *Blockchain for Good. The vision and mission of the Dutch Blockchain Coalition.* Dutch Blockchain Coalition. Retrieved from https://visie.dutchblockchaincoalition.org/wp-content/uploads/2018/12/Visiedocument-brochure-Blockchain-For-Good-A4-ENGELS-WEB-031218.pdf

Dutch Blockchain Coalition. (2018b). *Smart contracts als specifieke toepassing van de blockchaintechnologie*. Dutch Blockchain Coalition. Retrieved from https://dutchdigitaldelta.nl/uploads/pdf/Smart-contract-rapport-DBC.pdf

Dutch Blockchain Coalition—Smart Contracts Werkgroep. (2018). *Smart contracts, als specifieke toepassing van blockchain-technologie*. Dutch Blockchain Coalition. Retrieved from https://search.saxionbibliotheek.nl/cgi-bin/koha/opac-detail.pl?biblionumber=22580

Dutch Digital Delta. (2017a). *Knowledge and innovation agenda ICT 2016–2019*. Dutch Digital Delta. Retrieved from https://www.dutchdigitaldelta.nl/uploads/pdf/PDF-Kennis-en-Innovatieagenda-ICT-2016-2019_2015-10-06_254.pdf

Dutch Digital Delta. (2017b). *Legacy Coalitie*. Dutch Digital Delta. Retrieved from https://www.dutchdigitaldelta.nl/uploads/pdf/ddd-Legacy-Flyer.pdf

Dutra, A., Tumasjan, A., & Welpe, I. M. (2018). *Blockchain is changing how media and entertainment companies complete*. Cambridge, MA: MIT. Retrieved from https://sloanreview.mit.edu/article/blockchain-is-changing-how-media-and-entertainment-companies-compete/

Edriouch, J., Bemelmans, R., Zoet, M., & Beumers, J. (2018). *Blockchain voor het hbo*. Zuyd Hogeschool. Retrieved from https://www.zuyd.nl/over-zuyd/nieuws/2018/07/verslag-zuyd-symposium-blockchain-in-het-hbo

El Hri, A. (2018). *De blockchain als pandregister: Kan de registratie van pandrechten in de blockchain dezelfde waarborgen bieden als het kadaster voor hypotheekrechten?* University of Amsterdam. Retrieved from http://www.scriptiesonline.uba.uva.nl/cgi/b/bib/bib-idx?type=simple;lang=nl;c=uvascript;sid=8d80e100620b75f76d424842fee998c6;rgn1=entire%20record;q1=blockchain;Submit.x=0;Submit.y=0;sort=publicationyear;cc=uvascript;view=reslist;fmt=long;page=reslist;size=1;start=13

Feng, Q., & Shanthikumar, J. G. (2017). *How research in production and operations management may evolve in the era of big data*. Purdue University. Retrieved from https://onlinelibrary.wiley.com/doi/abs/10.1111/poms.12836

Fischer, S. (2018). *Blockchain finances commercial real estate loan*. Idaho Business Review. Retrieved from https://idahobusinessreview.com/2018/07/02/blockchain-finances-commercial-real-estate-loan/

Gout, B. (2017). *Block mortgage: Blockchain inspired business model for mortgage funding marketplace*. Delft University of Technology. Retrieved from https://repository.tudelft.nl/islandora/object/uuid%3Abe64e8ed-6e28-489f-a84b-7661cae75e91

Grant, P. (2017). Real-estate industry explores use of 'blockchain' technology. *Wall Street Journal*. Retrieved from https://www.foxweek.com/news/real-estate-industry-explores-use-blockchain-technology

Henry, C. (2018). *Leadership and strategy in the news*. Emerald Publishing. Retrieved from https://www.emeraldinsight.com/doi/full/10.1108/SL-05-2018-139

Herian, R. (2018). *Legal recognition of Blockchain registries and Smart contracts*. Open University Law School. Retrieved from https://s3.amazonaws.com/academia.edu.documents/58014198/Legal_Recognition_of_Blockchain_Registries_and_Smart_Contracts_Final_Draft_Report___Appendix.pdf?AWSAccessKeyId=AKIAIWOWYYGZ2Y53UL3A&Expires=1546236789&Signature=VQkbjwrzOqk4vP3ceiRmBmk%2BBRg%3D&response-content-disposition=attachment%3B%20filename%3DLegal_Recognition_of_Blockchain_Registri.pdf

Hitesh, M. (2017). Blockchain for commercial Real Estate. *SSRN Electronic Journal*. Retrieved from https://sci-hub.tw/10.2139/ssrn.2922695

Hoogeboom, B. (2018). *Blockchain kan een informatievuist vormen tegen ondermijning*. NRC. Retrieved from https://www.nrc.nl/nieuws/2018/10/19/blockchain-kan-een-informatievuist-vormen-tegen-ondermijning-a2628340

JaeShup, O., & Song, L. (2017). *A case study on business model innovations using Blockchain: Focusing on financial institutions*. Emerald Publishing. Retrieved from https://www.emeraldinsight.com/doi/full/10.1108/APJIE-12-2017-038

Janssen, R., Stam, P., Visser, J., de Vries, D., & Wijnker, J. (2017). *Blockchaintechnologie in de gezondheidszorg*. Tilburg University. Retrieved from https://pure.uvt.nl/ws/portalfiles/portal/17518490/2017_08_09_Janssen_R.T.J.M.pdf

JLL. (2018). *How blockchain is reshaping the real estate industry*. JLL. Retrieved from https://hogeschoolrotterdam.on.worldcat.org/search?queryString=blockchain%20real%20est ate&databaseList=2375,2572,3441,3837,1875,3018,1697,2268,3313,2267,4028,3633,638,10036,3834,2264,3551,2263,2262,3450,2261,1271,2260,2281,1941,3448,2259,2237,203,2277,1708,3841,3988,3967&sortKey=BEST_MATCH&clusterResults=true&scope=wz:60078&page=1#

Jongeneel, M. (2018). *De mogelijke bijdrage van blockchain aan een transparante vastgoedsector.* Fontys University of Applied Sciences. Not public.

Karpook, D. (2017). Smart, connected and dangerous: Assessing the impact of digital business on real estate. *Corporate Real Estate Journal*. Retrieved from https://planonsoftware.com/us/articles-and-whitepapers/article-smart-connected-and-dangerous-assessing-the-impact-of-digital-business-on-real-estate/

Kleemans, J., & Jongeneel, M. (2017). *Blockchain: transparantiemotor of gehypte techtoepassing? Een onderzoek naar de mogelijke bijdrage van blockchain aan een transparantere vastgoedsector.* University of Eindhoven. Retrieved from https://www.service-studievereniging.nl/magazine/artikel/blockchain-transparantiemotor-gehypte-techtoepassing/

Lafarre, A., & van der Elst, C. (2018a). *Blockchain maakt vergaderen efficiënt*. Tilburg University. Retrieved from https://universonline.nl/2018/04/17/blockchain-maakt-vergaderen-efficient

Lafarre, A., & van der Elst, C. (2018b). *Blockchain technology for corporate governance and shareholder activism.* Tilburg University. Retrieved from https://research.tilburguniversity.edu/en/publications/blockchain-technology-for-corporate-governance-and-shareholder-ac

Lafarre, A., & van der Elst, C. (2018c). *Blockchain and smart contracting for the shareholder community*. Tilburg University. Retrieved from https://research.tilburguniversity.edu/en/publications/blockchain-and-smart-contracting-for-the-shareholder-community

Lafarre, A., & van der Elst, C. (2018d). *Blockchain and the 21st century annual general meeting*. Tilburg University. Retrieved from https://research.tilburguniversity.edu/en/publications/blockchain-and-the-21st-century-annual-general-meeting

Lafarre, A., & van der Elst, C. (2018e). *Blockchain technology for modernizing the shareholder dialogue*. Tilburg University. Retrieved from https://www.tilburguniversity.edu/upload/1413437f-2ccb-4fe9-bc01-60aa0c7ec657_BlockchaintechnologyformodernizingshareholderdialogueWP.pdf

Lavrijssen, S., van der Velde, F., Köpsel Sanz, P., & Heusschen, G. (2018). *Onderzoek naar de mogelijke juridische integratie van de Elektriciteits-, Gas- en Warmtewet.* Tilburg University. Retrieved from https://research.tilburguniversity.edu/en/publications/onderzoek-naar-de-mogelijke-juridische-integratie-van-de-elektric

Lifthrasir, R. (2016). *Blockchain platforms: Speeding up the money & assets transfer process.* RICS. Retrieved from http://www.rics.org/nl/news/het-latest-

Lipton, A. (2017). *Blockchains and distributed ledgers in retrospective and perspective.* Cambridge, MA: MIT. Retrieved from https://www.emeraldinsight.com/doi/full/10.1108/JRF-02-2017-0035?utm_source=TrendMD&utm_medium=cpc&utm_campaign=Emerald_TrendMD_0&WT.mc_id=Emerald_TrendMD_0

McClary, S. (2017). *Understanding blockchain for real estate.* Rotterdam University of Applied Sciences. Retrieved from https://hogeschoolrotterdam.on.worldcat.org/search?queryString=blockchain%20real%20estate&databaseList=2375,2572,3441,3837,1875,3018,1697,2268,3313,2267,4028,3633,638,10036,3834,2264,3551,2263,2262,3450,2261,1271,2260,2281,1941,3448,2259,2237,203,2277,1708,3841,3988,3967&sortKey=BEST_MATCH&clusterResults=true&scope=wz:60078&page=1#

Meijaard, J. (2018). *Adoption of blockchain digital asset management systems: An empirical study.* Retrieved from http://www.scriptiesonline.uba.uva.nl/622830

Mest, C. E. (2018). *Blockchain technology meets real estate investment at the St. Regis Aspen.* Retrieved from https://www.hotelmanagement.net/tech/blockchain-technology-meets-real-estate-investment-at-st-regis-aspen

Moerel, L., & Prins, C. (2016). *Privacy voor de homo digitali.* Tilburg University. Retrieved from https://pure.uvt.nl/ws/portalfiles/portal/11437684/Preadviezen_NJV_2016.pdf

Murtaza Haider, M., & Moranis, S. (2018). *Blockchain, AI will reshape real estate*. Rotterdam University of Applied Sciences. Retrieved from https://hogeschoolrotterdam.on.worldcat.org/search?queryString=blockchain%20real%20estate&databaseList=2375,2572,3441,3837,1875,3018,1697,2268,3313,2267,4028,3633,638,10036,3834,2264,3551,2263,2262,3450,2261,1271,2260,2281,1941,3448,2259,2237,203,2277,1708,3841,3988,3967&sortKey=BEST_MATCH&clusterResults=true&scope=wz:60078&page=1#

Navitas Capital. (2018). *Exploring blockchain & transformative applications in real estate*. Navitas Capital. Retrieved from https://navitascap.com/wp-content/uploads/2018/08/Exploring-Blockchain-Transformative-Applications-in-Real-Estate-Whitepaper-1.pdf

Nir, K., & Voas, J. (2018). *Blockchain in developing countries*. IEEE. Retrieved from https://www.computer.org/csdl/mags/it/2018/02/mit2018020011-abs.html

Noonan, L. (2018). Riding a new wave of deals. *Financial Times*.

Nordrum, A. (2017). *Govern by blockchain dubai wants one platform to rule them all, while Illinois will try anything*. IEEE Spectrum. Retrieved from https://www.semanticscholar.org/paper/Govern-by-blockchain-dubai-wants-one-platform-to-Nordrum/9829a48ad459dd1eb5f8e871d8c9d9098b376598

Pal, L. W. C. (2018). *Smart contracts: De juridische duiding van een smart contract naar Nederlands privaatrecht*. University of Amsterdam. Retrieved from http://www.scriptiesonline.uba.uva.nl/cgi/b/bib/bib-idx?type=simple;lang=nl;c=uvascript;sid=8d80e100620b75f76d424842fee998c6;rgn1=entire%20record;q1=blockchain;Submit.x=0;Submit.y=0;sort=publicationyear;cc=uvascript;view=reslist;fmt=long;page=reslist;size=1;start=22

Palavesh, S. (2018). *Top 5 industries that need blockchain development*. Rotterdam University of Applied Sciences. Retrieved from https://hogeschoolrotterdam.on.worldcat.org/search?queryString=blockchain%20real%20estate&databaseList=2375,2572,3441,3837,1875,3018,1697,2268,3313,2267,4028,3633,638,10036,3834,2264,3551,2263,2262,3450,2261,1271,2260,2281,1941,3448,2259,2237,203,2277,1708,3841,3988,3967&sortKey=BEST_MATCH&clusterResults=true&scope=wz:60078&page=1#

Peters, B. (2017). *Rental equipment/real estate/pot company is the latest to go blockchain*. Investor's Business Daily. Retrieved from https://www.investors.com/gdpr-agreement/?back_url=https%3A%2F%2Fwww.investors.com%2Fnews%2Findia-globalization-capital-latest-blockchain-bump%2F

Prins, C. (2018). *De Blockchain*. Tilburg University. Retrieved from https://pure.uvt.nl/ws/portalfiles/portal/13357217/NJB38_Vooraf.pdf

Puthal, D., Malik, N., Mohanty, S. P., Kougianos, E., & Das, G. (2018). *Everything you wanted to know about the blockchain: Its promise, components, processes, and problems*. University of Technology Sydney. Retrieved from https://ieeexplore.ieee.org/document/8386948

Razaghi, M., & Finger, M. (2018). *Smart governance for smart cities*. Lausanne: École polytechnique fédérale de Lausanne (EPFL). Retrieved from https://ieeexplore.ieee.org/document/8326767

Salmeling, M., & Fransson, C. (2017). *The land registry in the blockchain—Testbed*. Landshypotek Bank. Retrieved from https://chromaway.com/papers/Blockchain_Landregistry_Report_2017.pdf

Scheurwater, S. (2017). *The future of valuations; the relevance of real estate valuations for institutional investors and banks: Views from a European expert group*. Royal Institute of Chartered Surveyors. Retrieved from https://files.vastgoedbibliotheek.nl/Server/getfile.aspx?file=docs/publicaties/site/RICS/Future_valuations_relevance_real%20estate_valuations_institutional_investors_banks.pdf

Schols, F. W. J. M., & Waaijer, B. C. M. (2018). *Blockchain as alternative for the notary public*. Tilburg University. Retrieved from https://research.tilburguniversity.edu/en/publications/blockchain-as-alternative-for-the-notary-public

Seuren, F. F., (2018). *Introducing Blockchain to Commercial Real Estate: Exploring the applicability of blockchain technology in lowering transaction costs of the commercial real estate due diligence process*. Delft University of Technology. Retrieved from https://repository.tudelft.nl/islandora/object/uuid:e5266e5c-3c2c-45fe-a5df-5e9d1f5feec3?collection=education

Shedroff, N. (2018a). *Self-managing real estate*. IEEE Computer Society. Retrieved from https://ieeexplore.ieee.org/stamp/stamp.jsp?tp=&arnumber=8267594

Shedroff, N. (2018b). *Self-managing real estate*. Rotterdam University of Applied Sciences. Retrieved from https://hogeschoolrotterdam.on.worldcat.org/search?queryString=blockchain%20real%20estate&databaseList=2375,2572,3441,3837,1875,3018,1697,2268,3313,2267,4028,3633,638,10036,3834,2264,3551,2263,2262,3450,2261,1271,2260,2281,1941,3448,2259,2237,203,2277,1708,3841,3988,3967&sortKey=BEST_MATCH&clusterResults=true&scope=wz:60078&page=1#

Skinner, C. (2016). *Valueweb: How Fintech firms are using mobile and blockchain technologies to create the Internet of Value*. Saxion University of Applied Sciences. Retrieved from http://opcprod.utsp.utwente.nl/DB=20/LNG=NE/PPN?PPN=401131630

Suzuki, B., Taylor, T., & Marchant, G. (2018). *Blockchain: How it will change your legal practice*. Rotterdam University of Applied Sciences. Retrieved from https://hogeschoolrotterdam.on.worldcat.org/search?queryString=blockchain%20real%20estate&databaseList=2375,2572,3441,3837,1875,3018,1697,2268,3313,2267,4028,3633,638,10036,3834,2264,3551,2263,2262,3450,2261,1271,2260,2281,1941,3448,2259,2237,203,2277,1708,3841,3988,3967&sortKey=BEST_MATCH&clusterResults=true&scope=wz:60078&page=1#

Tan, W. K. (2018). *Dubai Land Department to conduct all transactions through blockchain*. Rotterdam University of Applied Sciences. Retrieved from https://hogeschoolrotterdam.on.worldcat.org/search?queryString=blockchain%20real%20estate&databaseList=2375,2572,3441,3837,1875,3018,1697,2268,3313,2267,4028,3633,638,10036,3834,2264,3551,2263,2262,3450,2261,1271,2260,2281,1941,3448,2259,2237,203,2277,1708,3841,3988,3967&sortKey=BEST_MATCH&clusterResults=true&scope=wz:60078&page=1#

Tjong Tjin Tai, E. (2015). *De redelijke derde en de blockchain*. Tilburg University. Retrieved from https://research.tilburguniversity.edu/en/publications/the-reasonable-third-party-and-the-blockchain

Tjong Tjin Tai, E. (2017a). *Formalization of contract law for smart contracts*. Tilburg University. Retrieved from https://research.tilburguniversity.edu/en/activities/formalization-of-contract-law-for-smart-contracts

Tjong Tjin Tai, E. (2017b). *Juridische aspecten van blockchain en smart contracts*. Tilburg University. Retrieved from https://research.tilburguniversity.edu/en/publications/legal-issues-of-blockchain-and-smart-contracts

Tjong Tjin Tai, E. (2017c). *Legal issues of blockchain and smart contracts*. Tilburg University. Retrieved from https://research.tilburguniversity.edu/en/publications/legal-issues-of-blockchain-and-smart-contracts

Tjong Tjin Tai, E. (2018a). *De blockchain als alternatief voor de notariële praktijk*. Tilburg University. Retrieved from https://www.tilburguniversity.edu/nl/webwijs/show/t.f.e.tjongtjintai_nl.htm

Tjong Tjin Tai, E. (2018b). *Smart contracts en het recht*. Tilburg University. Retrieved from https://research.tilburguniversity.edu/en/publications/smart-contracts-and-the-law

Tjong Tjin Tai, E. (2018c). *The reasonable third party and the blockchain*. Tilburg University. Retrieved from https://research.tilburguniversity.edu/en/publications/the-reasonable-third-party-and-the-blockchain

Tushar, W., Yuen, C., Mohsenian-Rad, H., Saha, T., Tapan, P., Poor, H., … Kristin, L. (2018). *Transforming energy networks via peer-to-peer energy trading: The potential of game-theoretic approaches*. Brisbane: University of Queensland. Retrieved from https://ieeexplore.ieee.org/document/8398582

University of Groningen. (2018). *Blockchain, public trust, law and governance*. University of Groningen. Retrieved from https://www.rug.nl/rechten/congressen/archief/2018/blockchain-public-law-public-trust/blockchain-conference-programme.pdf

Unknown. (2016). *Blockchain platform targets property financing opportunities in China*. Rotterdam University of Applied Sciences. Retrieved from https://hogeschoolrotterdam.on.worldcat.org/search?queryString=blockchain%20real%20estate&databaseList=2375,2572,3441,3837,1875,3018,1697,2268,3313,2267,4028,3633,638,10036,3834,2264,3551,2263,2262,3450,2261,1271,2260,2281,1941,3448,2259,2237,203,2277,1708,3841,3988,3967&sortKey=BEST_MATCH&clusterResults=true&scope=wz:60078&page=1#

Unkown. (2018a). *Latest blockchain real estate platform offers cashback and rewards*. Rotterdam University of Applied Sciences. Retrieved from https://hogeschoolrotterdam.on.worldcat.org/search?queryString=blockchain%20real%20estate&databaseList=2375,2572,3441,3837,1875,3018,1697,2268,3313,2267,4028,3633,638,10036,3834,2264,3551,2263,2262,3450,2261,1271,2260,2281,1941,3448,2259,2237,203,2277,1708,3841,3988,3967&sortKey=BEST_MATCH&clusterResults=true&scope=wz:60078&page=1#

Unkown. (2018b). *Leveraging blockchain technology to democratize the real estate industry*. Rotterdam University of Applied Sciences. Retrieved from https://hogeschoolrotterdam.on.worldcat.org/search?queryString=blockchain%20real%20estate&databaseList=2375,2572,3441,3837,1875,3018,1697,2268,3313,2267,4028,3633,638,10036,3834,2264,3551,2263,2262,3450,2261,1271,2260,2281,1941,3448,2259,2237,203,2277,1708,3841,3988,3967&sortKey=BEST_MATCH&clusterResults=true&scope=wz:60078&page=1#

van Bentum, J., Wiegerinck, E., Quispel, E., Veldhuizen, J., Santing, J. W., Nelson, E., & Oosting, W. (2017). *Slimme stenen*. Vastgoedmarkt. Retrieved from https://vastgoedbibliotheek.nl/#!/SingleDoc?find=TRF:blockchain&hitnr=10

van den Water, G. (2017a). *Blockchain ballot*. Tilburg University. Retrieved from https://www.tilburguniversity.edu/upload/57359745-a33a-4fe5-bf76-f645336d4887_Masterthesis%20Gijs%20van%20de%20Water.pdf

van den Water, G. (2017b). *Blockchain ballot. Electoral enhancement or danger to democracy?* Retrieved from https://www.tilburguniversity.edu/students/news/show/news-can-blockchain-contribute-to-combating-electoral-fraud.htm

van Leeuwen, G. (2018a). *The day after tomorrow*. Amsterdam School of Real Estate. Retrieved from http://files.vastgoedbibliotheek.nl/Server/getfile.aspx?file=docs/MRE/18/Leeuwen_GJ.pdf

van Leeuwen, G. (2018b). *The day after tomorrow: vastgoedbanken vandaag, morgen en de dag na morgen*. Amsterdam School of Real Estate. Retrieved from https://vastgoedbibliotheek.nl/#!/SingleDoc?find=BI:blockchain&hitnr=1

van Lier, B. (2018). *Thinking about ecologies of autonomous cyber-physical systems and their ethics*. Rotterdam University of Applied Sciences. Retrieved from https://www.hogeschoolrotterdam.nl/onderzoek/eventitem/openbare-les-ben-van-lier/112408/

van Os, V. H. M. (2017). *The emperor's new clothes: Smart cities, smarter contracts & smartest decisions*. Tijdschrift voor bouwrecht. Retrieved from https://vastgoedbibliotheek.nl/#!/SingleDoc?find=TRF:blockchain&hitnr=13

Veldhuizen, J., & Santing, J. W. (2017). *Meer transparantie en vertrouwen door blockchain*. Vastgoedmarkt. Retrieved from https://vastgoedbibliotheek.nl/#!/SingleDoc?find=TRF:blockchain&hitnr=10

Vermeend, S., & Smit, P. (2017). *Blockchain de technology die de wereld radicaal veranderd*. Einstein Books. Retrieved from https://www.managementboek.nl/boek/9789492460141/blockchain-de-technologie-die-de-wereld-radicaal-verandert-simone-vermeend

Vermeulen, E. P. M. (2018). *How blockchain will disrupt corporate organizations*. Harvard Law School Forum. Retrieved from https://www.tilburguniversity.edu/students/news/show/news-vermeulen-blockchanin-harvard/

Vermeulen, E. P. M., & Fenwick, M. (2018). *Technology and corporate governance: Blockchain, crypto, and artificial intelligence.* Tilburg University. Retrieved from https://www.tilburguniversity.edu/research/law/news/news-vermeulen-on-technology-and-corporate-governance/

Veuger, J. (2017a). Attention to disruption and blockchain creates a viable real estate economy. *Journal of USA-China Public Administration.* https://davidpublisher.org/index.php/Home/Article/index?id=33918.html

Veuger, J. (2017b). *A viable real estate economy with disruption and blockchain.* Hanze University of Applied Sciences. Retrieved from https://www.corporaterem.nl/wp-content/uploads/Blockchain-complete.pdf

Veuger, J. (2017c). *Blockchain: kantelpunt in de vastgoedsector.* Vastgoedmarkt. Retrieved from https://research.hanze.nl/ws/portalfiles/portal/16542880/Jan_Veuger_Blockchain_5245_pdf

Veuger, J. (2017d). *Blockchain: vertrouwen in een wendbare vastgoedeconomie.* VastgoedJournaal. Retrieved from https://vastgoedjournaal.nl/news/33425/blockchain-vertrouwen-in-een-wendbare-vastgoedeconomie

Veuger, J. (2017e). *Een wendbare vastgoedeconomie met disruptie en Blockchain, Real Estate in control.* Reasult. https://youtu.be/a91s_DP_ymw

Veuger, J. (2017f). *Noordelijk Vastgoedcongres 2017: disruptie, blockchain en vastgoed.* Hanze University of Applied Sciences. Retrieved from https://youtu.be/dg_PW_pyJik

Veuger, J. (2017g). *The true meaning of the blockchain technology for real estate still needs to be investigated. International Journal of Engineering and Sciences (IJES).*

Veuger, J. (2017h). Trust in a viable real estate economy with disruption and blockchain. *Journal Facilities.* Retrieved from https://www.emeraldinsight.com/doi/full/10.1108/F-11-2017-0106

Veuger, J. (2018). *A real game changer in real estate: Blockchain.* American Real Estate Society (ARES). Retrieved from https://www.etnpconferences.net/ares/ares2018/PaperSubmissions/Submissions2018/S-2018-233.pdf

Veuger, J. (Eds.). (2019a). *Blockchain technology and applications* (Editor 8 chapters). New York: Nova Science Publishers

Veuger, J. (2019b). Blockchain technology and applications: Influence of blockchain applications and digitalization on real estate. In *Blockchain technology and applications.* New York: Nova Science Publishers.

Veuger, J. (2019c). *Digitalization real estate on American Real Estate Society 2018.* Saxion University of Applied Sciences. Retrieved from https://www.corporaterem.nl/wp-content/uploads/Publicaties-Jan-Veuger.pdf#zoom=100

Veuger, J., & Bronckers, J. (2019). Blockchain technology and applications: Blockchain technology looking for a problem in real estate. In *Blockchain technology and applications.* New York: Nova Science Publishers.

Veuger, J., & Hulsebos, W. (2019). Blockchain technology and applications: Start up GetaBrick in real estate. In *Blockchain technology and applications.* New York: Nova Science Publishers.

Veuger, J., et al. (2018). *Barometer public real estate: Special issue 2018.* Spryg. Retrieved from https://www.corporaterem.nl/barometers/

Vos, J. (2016). *Blockchain based land registry: Panacea, illusion or something in between?* European Land Registry Association. Retrieved from https://www.elra.eu/wp-content/uploads/2017/02/10.-Jacques-Vos-Blockchain-based-Land-Registry.pdf

Vrielink, H. K., & ten Have, L. S. (2018). *De impact van Blockchain-technologie op business-modellen.* Saxion University of Applied Sciences. Retrieved from https://postit.saxion.nl/document/details?pid=EA24C9FA-37FD-4898-89ECCC32A0BE8752

Weihs, B. (2018). *Blockchain enabled asset management in the case of XDecks: Cooperation enhanced by decentralization in the building industry.* Delft University of Technology. Retrieved from http://files.vastgoedbibliotheek.nl/Server/getfile.aspx?file=docs/scripties/Delft/Weihs_B.pdf

Wilkinson, S., Halvitigala, D., Antoniades, H. (2017). *Educators, professional bodies and the future of the valuation profession.* Emerald. Retrieved from https://www.emeraldinsight.com/doi/abs/10.1108/PM-04-2017-0027

Windesheim en Hogeschool Rotterdam. (2018). *RAAK project: kansen en bedreigingen blockchain MKB.* Windesheim en Hogeschool van Rotterdam. Retrieved from https://www.windesheim.nl/over-windesheim/nieuws/2018/juli/onderzoekers-blockchain-biedt-kansen-voor-het-mkb/

World Banking. (2018). *International and national economies.* World Bank. Retrieved from https://onlinelibrary.wiley.com/doi/abs/10.1111/woba.5467

Wynder, E. (2018). *Real estate execs dismiss bitcoin frenzy.* Rotterdam University of Applied Sciences. Retrieved from https://hogeschoolrotterdam.on.worldcat.org/search?queryString=blockchain%20real%20estate&databaseList=2375,2572,3441,3837,1875,3018,1697,2268,3313,2267,4028,3633,638,10036,3834,2264,3551,2263,2262,3450,2261,1271,2260,2281,1941,3448,2259,2237,203,2277,1708,3841,3988,3967&sortKey=BEST_MATCH&clusterResults=true&scope=wz:60078&page=1#

Zaal, R. (2017). *TU-Delft heeft Blockchain-hypotheek werkend.* Delft University of Technology. Retrieved from http://agconnect.nl/artikel/tu-delft-heeft-Blockchain-hypotheek-werkend

Zlotowitz, I. (2018). *Way of the Future: Will blockchain disrupt established CRE processes?* Rotterdam University of Applied Sciences. Retrieved from https://hogeschool-rotterdam.on.worldcat.org/search?queryString=blockchain%20real%20estate&databaseList=2375,2572,3441,3837,1875,3018,1697,2268,3313,2267,4028,3633,638,10036,3834,2264,3551,2263,2262,3450,2261,1271,2260,2281,1941,3448,2259,2237,203,2277,1708,3841,3988,3967&sortKey=BEST_MATCH&clusterResults=true&scope=wz:60078&page=1#

Jan Veuger, MRE, FRICS, was appointed in 2019 as professor of Blockchain of the School of Finance & Accounting, School of Creative Technology and School of Governance, Law and Urban Development, Hospitality Business School and School of Commerce and Entrepreneurship of the Saxion University of Applied Sciences Enschede, The Netherlands. Previously, he was professor of Real Estate at the Hanze University of Applied Sciences, Groningen, Institute for Business, from 2012 to 2019. Jan graduated from the Erasmus University Rotterdam, one of Europe's top business schools for education and in the top three for research. Besides being a professor, Jan is co-promoter of several students, Chairman of the Committee of Quality Certificates (CKV) at Quality Center for Social Housing Corporations, and member of Supervisory Board of Commissioners for four different organizations (to 2000 employees) in the area of social housing and elderly care. Furthermore, he is member of the RICS Netherlands, Department of Research and Innovation, Fellow of the RICS, President of Academic Board FIBREE, and author of many books (chapters), international scientific and professional publications, syllabi, and research reports and has given many guest lectures.

Part II
Theoretical Aspects

From Blackstone to Blockchain: Theorizing Property Law in the Age of Cryptography

Ronit Levine-Schnur

Abstract In this concise introductory contribution I ask how blockchain technology has already and how it will in the future effect the basic underpinnings of property law theory. The chapter presents three main features of a blockchain cryptographic technique, and in addition, three features of property rights as acknowledged by the famous work of William Blackstone of the eighteenth century. The potential interaction between these features is briefly discussed.

Keywords Property theory · Property rights · Blockchain · Hard-fork

1 Introduction

This introductory chapter asks how blockchain technology has already and how it will in the future effect the basic underpinnings, the way we understand and capture, property law theory. Some writers already suggested that blockchain is a new institution of property (Ishmaev, 2017), or even, under wider implementation of it, can lead to the disappearance of property rights (Wright & De Filippi, 2015). In order to assess these claims, the paper considers whether property as understood by William Blackstone, of the eighteenth century, is relevant in times of Blockchain, of the current millennium.

The chapter is structured into three parts. First, I ask what characterizes "the age of cryptography"? Secondly, I attempt to explain what is a "Blackstonian" property law theory, and whether it remained relevant to property law theory over the centuries. Lastly, I address the core issue of the interaction between Blackstone and Blockchain and the effect this may have on democracy.

R. Levine-Schnur (✉)
Harry Radzyner Law School, Interdisciplinary Center (IDC) Herzliya, Israel

Gazit-Globe Real Estate Institute, IDC, Herzliya, Israel
e-mail: ronit.levineschnur@idc.ac.il

A. Lehavi, R. Levine-Schnur (eds.), *Disruptive Technology, Legal Innovation, and the Future of Real Estate*, https://doi.org/10.1007/978-3-030-52387-9_2

2 "The Age of Cryptography"?

Let me begin with putting a question-mark above the identification of these times as "the age of cryptography" and discuss the meaning of the term. Cryptography, as we all know, is not a recent invention, and encryption methods were used and developed since ancient days. However, the computer era has brought us significant advancements in cryptography, among which are the supplanting linguistic encryption with the operation on binary bit sequences, and additionally, the extended complexity and availability of cryptographic techniques.

With no doubt, the introduction of the public key or asymmetric key cryptography starting with Diffie and Hellman's (1976) paper, signifies a dramatic development for cryptography. Diffie and Hellman explain that a system with a large number of users who change allegiance frequently, such as in the business world, requires ways to preserve privacy of communication without assuming trust between users. The need for public key cryptography thus emerges from issues of trust and cooperation. It addresses the desire of each actor in a society to safely interact with others without relying on social commitments to secure one's interests. Where private relations are secured without reliance on familial and social bonds, the boundaries of interaction and benefiting cooperation are extended. Although cryptographic-based ledgers, such as Bitcoin, offer full public access to records (Ishmaev, 2017), public key cryptography does not mean the publicization of private relations by subjecting them to a centralized organization, such as the state's institutions. To the contrary, it is the decentralization of power and control that is at the basic of new cryptography.

Therefore, cryptographic techniques can be characterized by three important features that they possess, at least to a certain degree: they allow to overcome trust and cooperation setbacks among those who otherwise won't interact; they eliminate the need to rely on state or any third-party authority, and they offer universal, albeit anonymized, access to the knowledge they contain about rights. The extent to which new cryptography has changed the world, the extent to which it is justified to ask how to theorize property at the cryptographic age, depends on whether, to a significant measure, there are practical applications of cryptographic techniques that meet these criteria. There are reasons to suspect that at least in some cases, such as with "blockchained" systems of land recording, the reliance on intermediators and third-party enforcers will persist. So is even sometimes the case with cryptocurrencies, as Arruñada (2018) describes, that are still subject to third-party enforcement (such as in the DAO example). However, theoretically, we can ask whether these features, if exist, offer a novel understanding of property that amends our current one, and whether, if human discretion is maintained what effect that would have on our existing governmental institutions.

3 Blackstone and Property Law Theory

I will now turn to shortly explain what has come to be known as the "Blackstonian" theory of property and its place in modern property law theory. William Blackstone famously defined property, in his 1765 Commentaries on the Laws of England (1765, 1830, 2:*2), as "that sole and despotic dominion which one man claims and exercises over the external things of the world, in total exclusion of the right of any other individual in the universe." In this, three features of property right, ownership in particular, were identified. Firstly, property right as related to "external things of the world," i.e., things that can be separated from oneself (Penner, 1997). Secondly, property right as allowing "sole and despotic dominion" over a thing, i.e., the absoluteness of property holders power to exclude others, to disregard them, as an execution of one's right; thirdly, property as being a right over a thing, that avails against "any other individual in the universe." That is, the *in rem* character of property which allows a property right to be enforceable upon others without them knowing who the holder of that right is. This feature of property, the burden it puts on others, is vital for the understanding of property as distinctive from other types of rights.

Over the years these three features of property were under massive attack. As far as identifying what is a "thing," long way has gone since things were solely regarded as actual possessions. For instance, Charles Reich (1964) famously coined the term "new property" to reflect the propriety character of non-tangible assets such as regulatory benefits, licenses, subsidies, etc. The debates about the current definition of a thing are still prevalent (Wyman, 2017). With respect to the absoluteness of owners against others, it has been argued that the famous citation from the second Commentary presented above does not properly reflect Blackstone's himself rather much more balanced understanding of property law (Burns, 1985; Rose, 1998; Schorr, 2008). Furthermore, the "absolute dominion" view was used as a "red flag" for all those who asked to point at the social responsibilities of owners (Dagan, 2011; Munzer, 1990).

As regards to the *in rem* nature of property, legal realists following Hohfeld (1917) and economists such as Coase (1960), disregarded this unique character of property relations with a thing. Subsequently, the *in rem* notion of property was replaced with the metaphor of property as reflecting a bundle of rights, leading to an ongoing debates among legal scholars (Merrill & Smith, 2001). These debates were sometimes colored as "bundle of sticks" versus "the right to exclude," an approach according to which the power to exclude others, to set a boundary, is the ultimate virtue of ownership. But as Smith (2012) and others argued, exclusion is not an end but rather a means to allow us *using* things as we desire—to set agenda to them (Katz, 2012).

4 From Blackstone to Blockchain

We can therefore position one against the other three features for each of the systems. On the one hand, we have Blockchain, with its requirements for transparent records; decentralized enforcement mechanism; and the nature of allowing non-familiar parties means to communicate and cooperate without knowledge of who is "behind the block." On the other hand, we have Blackstone's theory of property, with the requirements for a separation between oneself and a thing; the granting of using powers—also limited and not absolute powers—that are subject to the social bonds an ownership status generates; and the nature of right that is applicable against all others, whether they know or do not know about the identity of the owner.

Are these two systems different one from each other? What are the issues raised by the interaction between the two sets of features characterizing each of them? One may think of it as a thought experiment: how would property theory developed if the cryptographic foundations have been there all along?

As this contribution is very limited in its scope and aspiration, I only want to suggest that there is a need to think of a variety property-related issues and consider whether there are important amendments to property theory intrigued by Blockchain.

For example, one of the issues that is most important for property rights theory is trust and cooperation among owners, users and third parties interrelated with a property, versus anonymity and the existence of massive amount of potential parties as characteristics of blockchain-based systems. Evolutionary theories of property such as those based on the works of Hardin (1968), Demsetz (1967), and Ostrom (1990), identify property rights as an answer to a tragedy of the commons, of over-using resources in societies that are not based on close-knit social relationships. Blockchain as a social development is coherent with this background of formalization of relationship as alternative to human-based interactions. The difference is that for Hardin and Demestz the assumption is that the problem is of limited resources, and that there is a fight over them. The proper and efficient investments or labour attached to assets, require confidence in the ability to capture the value created by these investments. For Blockchain, we can ask: what is the limited resource that we are fighting over? What are the investments that we wish to incentive? In other words—is it good to society to have Blockchain-based new resources such as cryptocurrencies? Are there any limitations on production, uses, or transfers, that should be accounted for?

Another key issue for property theories are the centrality of the *Nemo dat quod non habet* principle versus market overt, or the irreversibility of transactions. One of the main characteristics of a property right is that it is traceable. Meaning, an owner may trace her rights to whom and to where it has gone to if it was not under her consent. There are exceptions to this rule, which is also known as *nemo dat*, which can be combined under the title of market overt. Accordingly, regulative norms estop owners from reaching to their lost-to-others properties due to public interest such as the stability of the market. For Blockchain, irreversibility, or market overt, is mandatory, creating a potential clash between the systems (Lehavi, 2019, p. 213).

Market overt is usually dependent on conditions of open market, bone fide purchase, and consideration. In other words, market overt and other rules that eliminate rights such as adverse possession are justified on a balance between market and moral considerations. The irreversibility of Blockchain does not necessarily rely on moral justification—it can protect fraudulent actors. Should the stability of the market be granted such an absolute weigh to overcome all other considerations? Does the need to decisively identify the owner justify avoiding a more nuanced balance of interests approach, that considers issues such as who values the asset more, who is more blameworthy of the "accident" as is required under current understanding of property?

These are only two examples. In fact, the most basic building blocks of property such as possession, transaction, or ownership should be rethink. On the more organizational or political levels, the transition to a privatized model of ownership, that is handled and governed not by governments, raises important questions about discretion, power, and democracy. When the Soviet Union fell, many governments around the world privatized assets from political to private hands. Similar patterns occurred in recent years with the World Bank efforts to formalize land rights. Carol Rose argued that the transition to a privatized mode of private property and contract may fundamentally advance the growth of democratic institutions but that is only if there is a pre-existing accountable institutional infrastructure (Rose, 2005). Blockchain as a technology to govern property rights, may have the virtues of democratic governance that is global or borderless. But this depends on how the human aspect of a given system is set. Whether there are hard-forks or not, and who is there to decide, would have immense effect on the nature of the governance of property the future bears for us.

References

Arruñada, B. (2018). Blockchain's struggle to deliver impersonal exchange. *Minnesota Journal of Law, Science & Technology, 19*, 55.

Blackstone, W. (1830). *Commentaries on the laws of England* (Vol. 2). Collins & Hannay.

Burns, R. P. (1985). Blackstone's theory of the absolute rights of property. *University of Cincinnati Law Review, 54*, 67.

Coase, R. H. (1960). The problem of social cost. In *Classic papers in natural resource economics* (pp. 87–137). Springer.

Dagan, H. (2011). *Property: Values and institutions*. Oxford University Press.

Demsetz, H. (1967). Toward a theory of property rights. *The American Economic Review, 57*(2), 347–359.

Diffie, W., & Hellman, M. E. (1976). Multiuser cryptographic techniques. In *In Proceedings of the June 7–10, 1976, National Computer Conference and Exposition* (pp. 109–112). ACM.

Hardin, G. (1968). The tragedy of the commons. *Science, 162*(3859), 1243–1248.

Hohfeld, W. N. (1917). Fundamental legal conceptions as applied in judicial reasoning. *The Yale Law Journal, 26*, 710.

Ishmaev, G. (2017). Blockchain technology as an institution of property. *Metaphilosophy, 48*(5), 666–686. https://doi.org/10.1111/meta.12277

Katz, L. (2012). Governing through owners: How and why formal private property rights enhance state power. *University of Pennsylvania Law Review, 160*(7), 2029–2059.
Lehavi, A. (2019, January). Intellectual property, data, and digital assets. In *Property law in a globalizing world*. Cambridge University Press. https://doi.org/10.1017/9781108595391.006
Merrill, T. W., & Smith, H. E. (2001). What happened to property in law and economics essay. *The Yale Law Journal, 111*, 357–398.
Munzer, S. R. (1990). *A theory of property*. Cambridge University Press.
Ostrom, E. (1990). *Governing the commons: The evolution of institutions for collective action*. Cambridge University Press.
Penner, J. E. (1997). *The idea of property in law*. Oxford University Press.
Reich, C. A. (1964). The new property. *The Yale Law Journal, 73*(5), 733–787.
Rose, C. M. (1998). Canons of property talk, or, blackstone's anxiety. *The Yale Law Journal, 108*(3), 601–632.
Rose, C. M. (2005). Privatization—The road to democracy childress lecture. *Saint Louis University Law Journal, 50*(3), 691–720.
Schorr, D. B. (2008). How blackstone became a Blackstonian. *Theoretical Inquiries in Law, 10*(1), 103–126. https://doi.org/10.2202/1565-3404.1210
Smith, H. E. (2012). Property as the law of things. *Harvard Law Review, 125*(7), 1691–1726.
Wright, A., & De Filippi, P. (2015). Decentralized blockchain technology and the rise of lex cryptographia. *Available at SSRN 2580664*.
Wyman, K. M. (2017). The new essentialism in property. *Journal of Legal Analysis, 9*(2), 183–246.

Prospects of Blockchain in Contract and Property

Benito Arruñada

Abstract Recurrent difficulties are delaying, if not killing off, what for the time being are still modest applications of blockchain. This chapter identifies what value this new technology adds to the contractual and property processes, exploring its potential and analyzing the main difficulties it is facing. Paying particular attention to the distinction between contract (personal or *in personam*) rights and property (real or *in rem*) rights, it first examines the difficulties for trading contract rights through blockchain-based applications, mainly those to complete contracts ex ante without relying on third-party enforcers. Second, it explores the difficulties faced by blockchain to enable trade in property rights.

Keywords Property rights · Enforcement · Transaction costs · Impersonal exchange · Blockchain · Distributed ledgers · Smart contracts · Registries

1 Blockchain and Contract, In Personam, Rights

1.1 Contract Completion in Smart Contracts

Blockchain is now applicable not only to payments but to many types of contracts; thus, instead of exchanging digital tokens valuable by themselves and existing only in the blockchain ledger (such as Bitcoin), parties can exchange representations of claims in all types of physical or digital assets existing outside the ledger, even if the consequences of such exchange will often hinge, as we will see, on what courts consider the applicable law. Moreover, through systems with more flexible code-bases such as that of Ethereum, they can fully implement the decentralized "smart

B. Arruñada (✉)
Pompeu Fabra University and Barcelona GSE, Barcelona, Spain
e-mail: benito.arrunada@upf.edu

A. Lehavi, R. Levine-Schnur (eds.), *Disruptive Technology, Legal Innovation, and the Future of Real Estate*, https://doi.org/10.1007/978-3-030-52387-9_3

contracts" first proposed by Nick Szabo (1997) and featuring automatic execution. These contracts not only contain a fixed set of rules that trigger predefined responses corresponding to particular states of the world but also use blockchain's tokens as their enforcement mechanism, so that transactions are supposed to be perfectly enforced in a conclusive or "immutable" manner. Smart contracts therefore realize the "code is law" paradigm coined by Lessig (1999, 2006), according to which computer code itself provides conclusive enforcement.

Given this conclusiveness, smart contracts are often considered a fundamental innovation in the way economic transactions can be organized. According to this view, they would make obsolete many of the intermediaries and arrangements that now overcome the lack of trust between traders, including lawyers and judges.

Smart contracts are coded ex ante, at the time of commitment, and, in principle, exclusively by the intervention of (usually one of) their own parties. This may be enough for extremely simple transactions. However, once we move away from such simple trades, smart contracts are subject to the standard limitations that parties to contracts suffer to complete them ex ante and without relying on third parties. (I mean by contract "completion" the task of defining the content of the exchange—that is parties' mutual obligations. In principle, it is safe to assume that, ex ante, rational parties are generally inclined to complete their contracts using efficient terms.)

To be sure, writing contractual terms in computer code instead of legal language does open new opportunities such as greater precision (e.g., Surden, 2012). However, it also poses new challenges, mainly the likely presence of coding errors as well as greater rigidity. More fundamentally, it does not avoid a main difficulty for completing contracts ex ante: the cost of information on the infinite number of possible contingencies.

To solve this informational problem, parties often rely on relational contracts (Williamson, 1985), in which a variety of decisional mechanisms, from asymmetric allocation of rights between trading partners to boards of parties' representatives, are used to complete the contract ex post, once uncertainty disappears and parties discover the relevant circumstances in which the exchange will take place. However, completing the contract ex post poses serious problems of partiality and bargaining when ex post decision rights are allocated to one or all of the parties. For this reason, contracts often rely on third parties, mainly judges, to complete the contract ex post and enforce the terms of trade, often at the price of sacrificing informational advantages.[1]

[1] The situation implicit in the previous discussion is one of bilateral trade, which is closer to that of blockchain applications when dealing with users. In addition, contractual problems in blockchain networks often involve many diverse parties (e.g., miners, core and DApp developers, common and master nodes, application users, investors, etc.) with potentially diverging interests and asymmetric and limited information. Such situations are characterized by the presence of multiple potential equilibriums.

In principle, blockchain promised to make little use of specialized third parties for enforcement.[2] In particular, smart contracts were supposed to work without third-party intervention, avoiding the risk of ledger manipulation by governments or other third parties.[3] Instead, they must include automatic codified mechanisms for ex post completion and enforcement. This works for simple transactions such as escrow services (Gans, 2019), often relying on innovative third party intermediaries.[4] However, it faces serious limitations for more complex transactions. The most obvious solution, that of establishing ex ante automatic rules for ex post completion, confronts the cognitive limitations of foreseeing infinite contingencies and rightly coding the responses to all of them.

Implementing incentive structures may also help. For instance, Gans (2019) discusses how a simple commitment mechanism based on Moore's (1992) "simple sequential mechanism" could replace court adjudication, taking care of several enforcement risks in the trade of goods (seller's low quality and buyer's lack of payment). With blockchain immutability, it would provide parties' bonding with the commitment needed to ensure self-enforcement.[5] However, it is unclear to what extent the failure of this type of mechanism to become widespread in the past was due to parties lacking the commitment that blockchain is expected to add or, more plausibly, to some other reason which remains unaltered by the emergence of blockchain.

Moreover, the type of adjudication produced would tend to be limited to enforcing the terms of trade that parties agreed upon ex ante, without much ex post completion. Indeed, ex post contractual completion is not only a matter of enforcing

---

[2] In blockchain protocols, the distinction between two governance layers (e.g., Buterin, 2017) can be seen as corresponding to the separation between enforcement and completion. Freedom of individual nodes to run any software of their choice produces the bottom "enforcement" layer while coordinating institutions influencing the bottom layer play a "completion" function.

[3] To this extent, smart contracts could, therefore, be understood as a paradigm of pure private ordering (Tapscott & Tapscott, 2016, pp. 199–201; Narayanan et al., 2016, p. 285). However, even this effect or at least its importance is uncertain. Not only can states often defeat on-chain blockchain adjudication with off-chain measures but blockchain is in fact triggering substantial demand for court adjudication (Ortolani, 2019).

[4] For instance, blockchain applications usually require "oracles" to monitor off-blockchain information for conditions that trigger contractual execution (e.g., whether the market price of oil reaches a certain level when that level is specified in a conditional clause of the contract). Some smart contracts also require competitive arbitration implemented through "2-out-of-3 multisignature transactions" (Narayanan et al., 2016, pp. 278–279), a form of relatively conventional and primitive third-party enforcement (Ortolani, 2016). Moreover, the development of applications and, in particular, smart contracts, is increasingly relying on modules created and vetted by specialists. The supply side of the industry is increasingly based on a chain of multiple vertically-linked suppliers, as independent third parties seem to have an advantage in certifying and programming automatic contracts (Casey & Niblett, 2017).

[5] Similarly, Holden and Malani (2018) also try to solve the holdup problem using a commitment mechanism implemented through blockchain and based on penalty clauses resembling poison pills. However, courts could always set damages as an increasing function of blockchain damages, so that, at the limit, parties' blockchain assets would be exhausted and the mechanism would become ineffective.

well-defined terms of trade but also of defining their optimal content in the given state of nature, filling the gaps in the contract. This ex post completion ideally requires verifying the state of the world which has occurred, and applying a counterfactual hypothesis to guess what the parties would have explicitly contracted if they had considered that state ex ante. Assuming rational agents, this means finding and adjudicating the efficient terms of trade for that particular state (Cooter, Kornhauser, & Lane, 1979; Posner, 1973). Such type of completion requires judgment and, therefore, human intervention at least until artificial intelligence becomes much more effective. For now, artificial intelligence seems unable to provide the "self-driving contracts" that would "fill their own gaps and interpret their own standards," as envisioned by Casey and Niblett (2017), whose examples (self-pricing in insurance, short-term rentals and ridesharing) fall short of fulfilling such abilities. In particular, they seem unable to provide the degree of judgment often used by humans to fill the contractual gaps (Abramowicz, 2016), as illustrated by the DAO case (Arruñada, 2018).

1.2 Conclusions on Contract Rights

The failure of the DAO showed that implementing the code-is-law principle is harder than it seems, as a failure in the drafting of the original contract led to its subsequent revision, showing that its terms were not conclusive and the blockchain was not immutable. Blockchain is always open to ex post completion, at least in the form of a hard fork: whatever the intent of those promoting Ethereum Classic, even the community behind this purist blockchain could at some point implement a hard fork to reverse transactions. Even in the blockchain universe, code is law but not all the law is code.

More generally, the DAO fiasco showed that a presumed advantage of smart contracts—automatic enforcement—becomes a liability when it is efficient not to enforce the contract. In other words, automatic execution is detrimental to the extent that it precludes contractual breach, which is optimal in many uncontractible circumstances (Cooter & Ulen, 2016, p. 328; Shavell, 2004, pp. 304–314). This possibility therefore requires ex post decision mechanisms to achieve efficient trade.

These lessons hold some important consequences for blockchain initiatives in terms of which industries and types of contracts may benefit most from implementing them.

First, the presence of uncertainty emphasizes the need for adapting and completing the contract ex post, once more information is known about the relevant state of the world. Not only implementing smart contracts often requires new forms of ex post completion and third-party enforcement, based on new types of intermediaries, such as those mentioned in note 5. The DAO and similar cases show that blockchain systems may depart from the pure code-is-law paradigm by denying enforcement through hard forks. Understandably, many blockchain ventures are trying to reduce the risk of network splits caused by hard forks, by devising innovative governance mechanisms which facilitate formal and explicit ex post completion.[6] For instance, the EOS blockchain, relying on elected master-nodes, provides arbitration and judicial services designed to complete contracts, even enforcing subjective terms, as well as fixing code bugs, freezing misbehaving accounts and allowing users to designate key-recovery partners (Larimer, 2018).

Second, as in other attempts to enable impersonal exchange, it makes sense to argue in favor of contract simplicity. For instance, a root of the DAO problem was that smart contracts also face the traditional tradeoff between security and complexity (Shea, 2016). Errors in computer code are prevalent and impossible to eradicate, and they increase with complexity, as with conventional contracts.

Two practical consequences emerge from the limitations of ex ante completion and the prominent role of simplicity. On the one hand, they help to explain why blockchains—like computable contracts early on (Surden, 2012)—have been gaining more ground in the financial world and, in particular, in areas such as payments and derivatives trading (ISDA, 2016, p. 23): note that they are highly standardized, so that parties are able to contract legal commodities.

On the other hand, for low-value transactions, complex contracts are too costly to write and enforce, and low-value assets are not valuable enough to define multiple rights on them. To the extent that contractual and property simplicity are therefore negatively correlated to the value of transactions, blockchain and smart contracts also develop more easily in low-value contexts.

Third, blockchain clearly adds value by providing verifiability on the *content* of contractual documents (Catalini & Gans, 2016), with obvious competitive consequences for authentication services such as those provided by notaries. However, it is less clear to what extent or in which cases blockchain is able to make contractual *performance* verifiable. In particular, while blockchain likely makes contractual performance easier for parties to the contract to observe, it does not necessarily make it easier for third parties, including judges (Gans, 2019), to verify performance.

To the extent that blockchain provides parties' observability but does not enhance third-party verifiability, it should favor second-party over third-party enforcement. It should therefore favor "relational contracting," understood as the type of exchange that is safeguarded by parties' reputation and expected gains from trade (Klein & Leffler, 1981; Levin, 2003; Shapiro, 1983). This should affect the ability of parties not only to self-enforce the contractual terms without the intervention of third parties but also to complete the contract ex post, filling the gaps and adapting it to unforeseen contingencies (i.e., "relational" *à la* Williamson, 1985).

Moreover, applications enabling business-to-business (B2B) transactions could rely on "private" and/or "permissioned" systems, which are open for trade only to

---

[6] Arruñada et al. (2018) discuss the mechanisms designed by Dash, EOS, Tezos and Dfinity, which are based on different varieties of coin-holder voting.

preapproved users and/or in which the consensus may be driven by a previously established set of nodes. In this vein, private blockchains should expand rapidly in supply chain management, revamping the existing and mostly closely-knit networks of suppliers, manufacturers, and distributors, which are already characterized by phenomena such as "contract manufacturing," (Arruñada & Vázquez, 2006) as well as "virtual integration" (Arruñada, 2002b). Financial institutions are pioneers in this regard.

However, permissioned blockchains will face a basic contradiction: the smaller the network, the smaller the extent and the fewer the advantages of decentralization, and the easier it may be to manipulate it (Narayanan, Bonneau, Felten, Miller, & Goldfeder, 2016, pp. 34–38). They may therefore end up featuring little decentralization, causing little disruption, and even entailing some risk of collusion among incumbents.

In addition, the use of blockchain for tracking the flow of goods and services in supply chains could affect informal relational contracts which, on purpose, are not formalized in order to ensure self-enforcement and preclude third-party adjudication (Hadfield & Bozovic, 2016). In settings of repeated transactions (such as the typical interaction between consumer-goods manufacturers and large retailers), the blockchain would provide an immutable record of parties' actions, which courts could then use to ascertain the existence and content of the informal contract. In particular, disgruntled parties could now argue before the court that their counterparties have performed below the agreed terms, terms which they could ask the court to infer from their previous level of performance, now verifiable in the blockchain record.

Lastly, the comparative advantage of blockchain applications would be considerably enhanced if the technology fulfills its promise of enabling individual users to own and keep full control of their historical record of transactional data, which is now in the hands of third-party centralized data silos (such as Google, Facebook or Booking). Availability and ownership of transactional data would make it possible for individuals to, first, accumulate reputational capital; and, then, deploy such capital to safeguard their transactions across multiple markets and using different platforms and applications. Such a system would benefit from massive economies of scale and scope, and could achieve secure personal transactions with anonymous parties, therefore providing an effective alternative to impersonal (i.e., asset-based) exchange. This mobilization of reputational capital could eventually become even more valuable and transformative than the mobilization of land as collateral for credit (De Soto et al., 1986). Difficulties are numerous, however. For instance, reaching such economies without substantial centralization, and making the necessary investments without any possibility of capturing value in the future.

2 Blockchain and Property, In Rem, Rights

2.1 *The Need for a Public Interface Between Personal and Real Rights*

A public ledger currency platform is "a protocol for sending, receiving, and recording value securely using cryptographic methods" (Evans, 2014). In addition to exchanging *value*, to what extent are these systems capable of exchanging *property*? Exaggerated but conveniently imprecise claims are common—for instance, it is said that "[u]npermissioned ledgers can be used as a global record that cannot be edited: for declaring a last will and testament, for example, or *assigning property ownership*" (Taylor, 2016, p. 17, emphasis added).

These claims are valid for cryptocoins but note that these are very special assets: they exist only in blockchain and, more deeply, being a sort of bearer instrument—they work like cash—, their possession equates ownership. However, with the exception of assets for which possession is in fact the only property right, such as cryptocoins and cash, contracting property requires at least one intermediary (a registry or a court) between the world of mere claims (i.e., in personam rights) and the real world of in rem rights.[7] Blockchain applications in which parties trade claims on assets existing outside the blockchain ledger require interfaces between the digital and the real worlds.

At a minimum, these interfaces make it possible for claimants to get physical possession of the assets. But the key issue is to what extent they perform a legal transformation, a sort of second "public contract," through which mere claims against specific individuals are upgraded into property rights valid against the whole world (Arruñada, 2003). In this, they resemble the conventional legal institutions between contractual (in personam) and property (in rem) rights.[8]

The presence of such a legal interface is not new. In land law, two or more contradictory chains of title deeds often coexist. But upgrading one of the claims to a right in rem requires a third-party enforcer—a court and/or a register, or, in primitive legal systems, a communal decision—in any case, an independent adjudicator safeguarding the interests of all potential rightholders, including those outside the chains of title. Note that, in a sense, a chain of paper title deeds is also "virtual," as it is based on documentary possession and reflects mere claims; therefore, if parties to the contract agree, it can also support trade in claims without necessarily having in rem consequences for the traded assets.

This account is consistent with a salient feature in analyses of blockchain applications in "smart property" that use examples in which they are in fact describing transfers of possession instead of transfers of ownership. Note, for instance, how the

[7] On rights in rem, see Merrill and Smith (2000), and Hansmann and Kraakman (2002).

[8] Abadi and Brunnermeier (2018) make a somehow similar point, by distinguishing between mere "record-keeping"—which could be better seen as in personam claims—and "enforcement"—of, in my terms, in rem rights—, also misattributing the concepts of ownership and possession.

running example of a "car whose *ownership* is controlled through a block chain," used in chapter eleven of Narayanan et al. (2016, p. 272, emphasis added), immediately turns out to be a transfer of *possession*:

> The block chain transaction doesn't *merely* represent a change in ownership of the car: it *additionally* transfers actual physical control or possession of the car. When a car is transferred this way the earlier owner's key fob stops working and the new owner's key fob gains the ability to open the locks and start the engine. Equating ownership with possession in this way has profound implications. (Narayanan et al., 2016, p. 274).

The implications are indeed profound but they are achieved by degrading ownership into less than possession—that is, by enforcing at most only a single right in the asset.[9] The price being paid is huge because the modern economy is based on the specialization (or, some would say, separation) of ownership and control (that is, in its simplest sense, possession). If blockchain's smart property is limited to possessory rights, the word "merely" in the preceding quotation should be excised and the word "additionally" replaced by "only". In practical terms, this limits stand-alone (no trusted third parties) applications of smart property to bearer instruments and low-value assets, as Narayanan et al. themselves seem to conclude a few pages later (Narayanan et al., 2016, p. 284).

These are serious concerns for the common claim that all types of asset can be transferred in the blockchain. The legal effects of such transfers, at least, would be limited to the transferring parties. Indeed, property rights are in the sphere of public ordering, and pure "privacy" is only viable when parties trade in contractual claims. It therefore comes as no surprise that such concerns are also echoed in the caveats often introduced when foreseeing blockchain applications. For example, a prominent entrepreneur claimed that "Bitcoin gives us, for the first time, a way for one Internet user to transfer a unique piece of digital property to another Internet user" (Andreessen, 2014). Note, however, the "digital" adjective: one cannot send real property over the Internet or, more precisely, one cannot even transfer possession of real property over the Internet.[10]

For the same reason, it is understandable that enforcement of peer-to-peer decision systems is easier when they deal with digital resources being held in escrow. Not only is the losing party less effective in preventing enforcement but courts are unlikely to interfere because usually there are no claims by third parties. Even Nick Szabo, when implementing his idea of property clubs, also seems to be contemplating rights

[9] In fact, less than possession because having an active key fob does not give you physical possession or control of the actual car but merely the ability to exercise that control… if you actually have physical possession of the car. I thank Rod Thomas for this insight, which, as we will see, also has serious consequences for real estate.

[10] A somehow similar caveat is introduced by Abramowicz when he considers the limitations of bitcoin, also given a limited meaning to property rights: "Bitcoin can be seen not just as a currency, but more grandly as an institution that creates and enforces property rights. It is an institution, however, that can resolve only one type of decision: whether purported transfers of Bitcoins will be validated and added to a list of approved transfers, known as the block chain" (Abramowicz, 2016, p. 361).

in personam: "Actually getting end users to respect the property rights agreed upon by this system will be dependent on the specific nature of the property, and is beyond the scope of the current inquiry" (Szabo, 1998–2005).

The problem of relying on personal rights is that they offer weaker enforcement, reducing welfare (Arruñada, 2012, pp. 18–24). Understandably, for most durable and valuable assets, parties demand multiple in rem rights. And meeting this demand requires the intervention of a third party with a necessarily public function, as it must be impartial to all and prevail over the parties to any given contract (Arruñada, 2017). Such a third party is necessary at least to define the set of rights enforced in rem (often referred as the *numerus clausus* of rights) and the mechanisms and evidentiary requirements for rightholders to convey their consent with respect to intended transactions.

2.2 Blockchain-Enabled Peer-to-Peer in Property

In theory, if this gathering of the relevant consents were complete, blockchain could even sustain peer-to-peer (i.e., person-to-person, P2P) exchange and titling of property rights without relying on any private or public intermediary (assuming the blockchain platform is running and properly maintained).

In theory, such a peer-to-peer trading platform could even be capable of enforcing indefeasible title, as well-functioning registries of rights do. The reason is that even if it is their registrars who custody rights and gather rightholders' consents, it is individual rightholders who decide when granting or denying their consents. In principle, it is conceivable that these custody and gathering tasks could be governed by an automated system, including a decentralized one based on blockchain.

This would require several feats, however.

At the individual level, a truly peer-to-peer system for property exchange and titling would require the ability and willingness of individual rightholders to make their own decisions with respect to property rights, bearing the risks of such decisions. In a hypothetical, fully-decentralized property system, all individuals would therefore be granting or denying their consent to intended transactions affecting their property rights. Consequently, they would become the only custodians not only of their cryptographic keys (to receive notice and grant consent) but also of the legal integrity of their rights. In particular, with a pure peer-to-peer system, security of ownership (generally, of any right) would be limited to keeping the private cryptographic keys in the possession of the owner (generally, in the possession of the corresponding rightholder).

In addition, at the public level, blockchain registers would pose similar difficulties to those often faced when reforming property titling, such as, for example, when countries: (1) replace customary titling with a register-based system and have to ensure a smooth transition between both systems; (2) have several registries working in parallel and have to ensure that the law reduces the risks created by switching; or simply (3) want to reinforce the effects of a register with respect to overriding and possessory interests. In all these cases, if the law wants the new system to be effective, it must prevent individuals from abusing the exercise of choice of titling to the extent that titling kills preexisting property, in rem, rights. Legal cautions are most obvious in jurisdictions such as Massachusetts, which, having multiple land registers, tightly regulate switching (Arruñada, 2003, pp. 428–432), but are also present in other cases in which there are strict requirements for first registration and deregistration.

Implementing a blockchain register would face similar difficulties—e.g., adverse selection—and would have to meet similar demands—strict legal requirements for first registration, deregistration and switching registers—. It would also pose some specific additional problems. First, rightholders would be choosing not to be protected by registries and courts. This would probably require some safeguards to ensure that individuals are informed about possible consequences. Second, at least in theory, several blockchains could function in parallel, so that owners could choose in which one to register their property. In that case, any issues arising from blockchain ledger interoperability would have to be resolved to prevent the same asset from being registered in two blockchains (Cuomo, 2019).

Minimum necessary regulation would include: (1) defining the legal status of blockchain records to establish priority of claims and adjudicate property rights among conflicting claimants; (2) establishing a low and strict numerus clausus—exclusive of all unregistered rights—before coding a smart contract capable of handling property conveyancing and/or registration; (3) regulating the switch of title records or property rights to the blockchain register, a task which differs widely if mandatory or voluntary; if voluntary (as is likely inevitable in most cases), regulating any conflicts emerging from the resulting multiple sources of legal evidence, possible parallel sources of evidence and even overlapping registries; and (4) regulating the legal status of non-contractual property rights such as those derived from, e.g., judicial seizures, inheritance rights or even constraints rooted in land planning.

In practice, however, a peer-to-peer property system could not be universal and would instead rely on intermediaries for the majority of individuals. Decentralization is limited in the real world because individuals tend to misbehave with respect to security: "We were able to achieve decentralization only because we equated possession with ownership—owning [an asset] is essentially equivalent to knowing the private key corresponding to a designated transaction on a block chain" (Narayanan et al., 2016, p. 283). However, reducing ownership to securing the possession of private keys poses serious risks for nontechnical users, and any remedies lead us back to intermediaries.

Misbehavior with respect to security is only an instance of a broader and deeper phenomenon: individual freedom has a price in terms of individual responsibility that not all individuals are always willing to pay. Instead, knowing their own weaknesses, they often prefer to rely on centralized solutions based on private and public custodian agents who are motivated by making them liable for all sorts of failures, including security breaches. Such solutions include the strict liability of some registrars, indemnity funds in Torrens systems, and US title insurance.

This theoretical judgment is supported by empirical evidence from current blockchain systems. The fact is that most individual agents who are today trading bitcoin and other cryptocoins rely at least on intermediaries such as exchanges (digital marketplaces) and wallets (digital storage services) and, therefore, a fortiori, are even less likely to rely on peer-to-peer exchange without intermediation to trade their real property. Similarly, rightholders who to date have been shunning cryptocurrencies would be even less willing. This reluctance is present in all types of applications, but, understandably, it especially constrains those in which the stakes are higher, leading people to demand greater security.

In practical terms, blockchain applications in property are likely to demand that public authorities regulate the interaction between the two parts of a dual titling system (e.g., with intermediaries for most individuals and, at most, peer-to-peer systems limited to specialists such as traders in the secondary mortgage market), as well as regulating such intermediaries themselves.

This regulation is affected, in particular, by the possibility of hard forks, which makes reliance on public unpermissioned blockchains unsuitable for property rights and requires the system to be based on private permissioned blockchains.[11] (Note that a government-controlled blockchain is still "private" with respect to blockchain validation). States with weak bureaucracies may be happy to use unpermissioned blockchains to enhance the integrity of their title records (to some extent, this is the case of Georgia, to be discussed below). However, whatever the reliability of their bureaucracies, states will be unlikely to surrender their role as ultimate property adjudicator, which is what they would be doing with unpermissioned blockchain registers. Moreover, weak states are most unlikely to be able to credibly commit themselves in this direction.

2.3 *Blockchain-Enabled Intermediation in Property*

Intermediary-based systems face different possibilities, with more or less presence of blockchain in the two stages of the property contractual process (Arruñada, 2003): private conveyancing and public titling. In principle, blockchain could be implemented in either one or both of the two stages. These possibilities include (1) introducing blockchain to support conveyancing and/or registration, (2) relying on conventional conveyancers as intermediaries between individuals and blockchain-enabled systems, (3) enhancing conventional registries to act as blockchain-enabled

[11] See, for instance, the arguments in this regard of the Vermont Secretary of State: "It's unclear how a fork would affect the long-term reliance on blockchains as systems of record. Since there is not necessarily any long-term commitment to participation in any blockchain network, a fragmentation of a blockchain could pose a significant challenge: when verifying a record's authenticity in one of the above models, users would have to know which of the various different forks of any one blockchain are authoritative" (2019, p. 24).

conveyancers, and (4) keeping registration review in the hands of humans or making it more automatic.

In principle, some of these possibilities are more realistic than others, mainly because of technical hurdles and the presence of strong vested interests. Moreover, some of them are more applicable to specific property rights and specific rightholders. For instance, due to individuals' bounded rationality, blockchain could more easily support a secondary mortgage market with few professional participants interacting through a permissioned peer-to-peer system than a primary market in real estate with individuals free to trade as sellers, buyers and borrowers.[12]

Moreover, some of these solutions can only be implemented through particular types of blockchain developments, which, in turn, would often require specific legal interventions. Understandably, the more ambitious the application, the more demanding it is in terms of technical constraints and the legal changes required. The least demanding option is that of posting digital identifiers often known as fingerprints and "hashes" of title deeds in an unpermissioned blockchain to enhance record integrity. However, registering actual title records in a blockchain requires a permissioned blockchain to make it viable in terms of mining (validation) costs; a blockchain system of conveyancing or registration based on tokenized titles requires transforming property titles into negotiable instruments; and a blockchain register based on a smart contract would also require a strict, low numerus clausus of rights to make such a contract writable.

2.4 Blockchain in Conveyancing and Registering

The impact of the blockchain on conveyancing and property titling is affected by the basic characteristics of both legal processes, which, in line with the incentives of participants, are mostly private in conveyancing and intrinsically public in registration. In particular, both processes are defined by the fact that in all property systems parties are free to choose their lawyers, conveyancers, and notaries public (Arruñada, 2003, pp. 424–428). Conversely, third-party protection leads the law to universally restrict parties' choice of the office that records their titles or the registrar that preserves and reviews their rights, as well as the judge who presides over a suit of quiet title or any equivalent judicial procedure. Therefore, blockchain should find it easier to expand into notarization and data archiving. It will be more difficult for blockchain to replace the current functions of centralized land registries, especially in jurisdictions such as Australia, England, Germany and Spain that have registers of rights, also often called "land registration" or "title by registration" systems (Arruñada, 2003, pp. 406–423). Replacing them would require at least a low numerus clausus and substantially greater investments in artificial intelligence.

[12] Note, however, that missing the private keys is more irreversible for mortgages and other abstract property rights, as they lack possessory evidence which could be used to restore the right.

To the extent that even in civil law jurisdictions notaries public are freely chosen by parties to private contracts, the blockchain will likely play a bigger role in notarization, even in real estate transactions. The only functions for which notaries used to be superior were for identifying parties and, in civil law countries, for ascertaining their legal capacity and serving as providers of settlement, closing, and escrow services for parties (Arruñada, 2007). These advantages are now substantially affected by blockchain, which has allowed the development of services that prove to other parties that you are who you say (authentication) and that you have the required permissions (authorization). Likewise, with respect to settlement, trade implemented through a blockchain can now provide conditioned simultaneous enforcement by using the principle of "atomicity," which, in essence, ensures that both parties fulfill their promises at the same time (Narayanan et al., 2016, p. 274).

Conversely, the applicability to registries of a truly decentralized blockchain (i.e., without trusted intermediaries) will likely require a greater effort than in notarization because registries have a public legal function, that of protecting the interests of unrepresented third parties, and are therefore much more than mere public databases. Centralization and monopoly in registries are not rooted mainly in economies of scale but in the need to enhance the neutrality (with respect not only to parties to the contract but also to strangers to it) required to reach universal legal effects.

However, blockchain enthusiasts often follow the path of efforts in property titling and administrative simplification, paying scant attention to the legal function of registers. This bias is visible in the diagnoses of existing systems by blockchain entrepreneurs trying to test the technology in the area of property titling, whose policy failures they seem to attribute to incomplete and slow data management, with an engineering perspective that makes no reference to the register's incentives (Kempe, 2017, p. 15). However, in reality, the harder task of property registries is not archiving information, but *producing* reliable information. It is not a problem of *keeping* a record of perfectly "purged" (i.e., non-contradictory) property rights, but purging them and making sure that intended transactions do not collide with preexisting property rights. The tasks of "collecting and recording the data" (Da Costa Cruz, Schröder, & von Wangenheim, 2019, p. 323) are necessary but are not the key element of property systems, for which multiple rights on an asset must be enforced in rem. Despite the fact that purging rights is mainly a legal issue, not a technological one, attempts to apply blockchain in property registration often focus instead on archiving and on keeping the integrity of the information (e.g., Sachs, 2016), disregarding how the information is produced and, especially, the whole process of how property rights are purged of contradictions.

Consequently, if this purging is something for which blockchain is perhaps of little use, grand claims on the potential of the technology in this area should be substantially diluted. This helps to explain why pilot projects often stall. It also explains why analysts focusing on data management fail when pondering the effects of blockchain on Torrens registers' indemnity levels (Graglia & Mellon, 2018, pp. 105–106) and US title insurance premiums (Sachs, 2016), which they seemingly contemplate as independent of the title purging function performed, respectively, by registrars and lawyers (Arruñada, 2002a). Moreover, the question as to how much security is in fact provided by blockchain is an empirical one.

On the positive side, however, blockchain may lower the costs of identifying rights and assets, making new types of registers viable, and enabling finely-tuned solutions for more detailed rights in intellectual property as well as completely new registries for certain high-value assets, as suggested by the Everledger initiative for registering diamonds and other specially valuable assets (Lomas, 2015).

2.5 Blockchain in Recordation of Deeds

It is conceivable that a deed recordation system might be replaceable by an automatic system of dating private contracts and preserving their integrity. In this case, new laws should be enacted to modify the rules of evidence—that is, to set the priority of the blockchain as a source of evidence for in rem adjudication, which in US law would require granting exclusive powers to produce constructive notice to the blockchain. This is because, for a blockchain to produce in rem effects, all parties must be explicitly or implicitly (through priority rules) obliged to express their will through it. Moreover, the priority of blockchain must not only be legally established but also effective. This means that, as with any other source of evidence, judges must in fact trust the blockchain and, therefore, those designing, putting in place, and—to some extent—governing, or at least affecting, the government of the blockchain system. Otherwise, whatever the legally defined priorities, the conventional conflict between alternative sources of evidence would likely arise (Rose, 1988), with judges using any available excuse (often based on implied notice or lack of good faith) to overcome the formal priorities set by statutory law.

Let us take these three dimensions (i.e., register replaceability, priority rules and judicial trust) to examine the first main—if modest—attempts to apply blockchain within recordation systems.

First, while the firm developing the pilot project carried out in Cook County (Chicago, Illinois) seemed optimistic (Lifthrasir, 2017), the official report concluded that relying on an unpermissioned peer-to-peer system would be too costly in terms of energy and would force most owners to rely on third parties. It therefore favored permissioned systems, limiting the use of blockchain to conveyancing and lodging while retaining the existing legal framework according to which "the county government record is the only official record" (Yarbrough, 2017, p. 22). No replacement is in sight and, in the pilot, priority was planned to be established by filing a deed at the public record office. (Apparently, finally it was never recorded.) The plan was for the blockchain transaction to be notarized in a conventional "confirmation deed" (a type of deed mostly used to correct mistakes). In a similarly minimalistic vein, the report considers that the chosen technique of "tokenizing" title (thus transforming real property into negotiable instruments) would pose substantial new legal challenges, and using digital signatures would facilitate secrecy and endanger the identification of participants.

Second, the pilot carried out in Vermont by Propy, an online real estate listing service specialized in cross-border deals and expanding into conveyancing and closing services, also falls short of replacing the register, which in this case would mean replacing the register's software with that of Propy. A legislative decision modifying the rules of evidence made it possible for a couple of paper deeds produced using Propy's smart-contract, Ethereum-based, blockchain platform to eventually be lodged at the record office of the city of South Burlington. In this respect, the pilot was therefore less limited in scope than that of Cook county. However, the paper deeds lodged at the record office included information (the deed smart contract's address) as to where the transaction is located in Propy's blockchain, therefore providing some degree of cross-verification. As with the Cook county pilot, the city's clerk is skeptical even about the complementary use of blockchain, which seems far from Propy's aim of having the statutes changed so that its blockchain would produce constructive notice "regardless of the status of the existing municipal title records" (Voloshyn, 2018). The Secretary of State was also skeptical, arguing that "blockchains do not solve any problems that the State of Vermont and its political subdivisions have.... In fact, more problems might be introduced with having a set of records stored in a blockchain that now, too, must be preserved and have access provided to it" (Vermont Secretary of State, 2019, pp. 37–38). In any case, even if it had been fully developed, the system would not have contemplated peer-to-peer transactions but would have relied on conventional intermediaries intervening via the blockchain-based platform.

Lastly, the application developed by the land register of Georgia also illustrates the importance of titling institutions being trusted by the courts. The starting point is an unreliable register which was legally defined as a register of rights, but in practice lacked proper registration review and worked as a recorder of deeds competing with the Cadaster in the provision of title evidence to judicial decisions. This explains why in 2017 the Constitutional Court removed the presumption of accuracy that the law granted to registry records. In this context, blockchain was implemented to make the register more trustworthy on the eyes of judges by, first, using a private permissioned blockchain for archiving notarized deeds (i.e., a unified version of the notaries' "protocol") and, second, relying on the public unpermissioned Bitcoin blockchain to publish snapshot hashes of the title certificate, in the hope of enhancing integrity and precluding the manipulation of records.

2.6 Blockchain in Company Registration

The case of company registries is similar to that of recordation of deeds, to the extent that most company registries are closer to recordation than to registration systems. However, company registries could also be challenged by initiatives like the Ethereum blockchain, as these allow the creation of virtual decentralized and autonomous organizations that would be defined only by a given set of rules running in the blockchain. In principle, such organizations can be flexibly organized, allocating specialized managerial and contractual functions in different manners (Abramowicz, 2016).

However, a historical perspective throws light on the potential contribution and likely difficulties of this contractual approach to company incorporation. The experience of the English "unincorporated companies" prior to the creation of the English Company Registry in 1844 provides relevant insights (Arruñada, 2010a; Harris, 2000). In general terms, these authors suggest that, even assuming perfect immutability of the blockchain, the explicit backing of the law and judicial rulings seem indispensable for avoiding future conflicts ex post and providing parties with the necessary certainty ex ante.

Understandably, the state of Delaware launched in May 2016 an ambitious "Delaware Blockchain Initiative" in partnership with a software firm, contemplating applications to archiving, secured corporate loan filings and share registration, but it collapsed a few months later, amid a controversy over the real value added and alleged vested interests of registered agents (Baker, 2018). It was soon replaced by a more modest strategy, which led to a pilot on special-purpose corporations and to allowing companies to keep their records and handle their stock ledgers on a blockchain. Other states have been active in using blockchain to compete for the corporate franchise business. For instance, a law enacted in the US state of Vermont allows the incorporation of blockchain-based limited liability companies (BBLLCs), making it possible for blockchain platforms to formalize their governance structures instead of being informal partnerships (Tashea, 2019).

In addition to keeping share registers updated and tracking beneficial ownership more effectively, with potentially serious repercussions for corporate governance and financial transparency, blockchain also has important implications in less glamorous corporate areas. In particular, it has the potential to automate "corporate actions": any announcements made by a public company affecting its securities and which may require a response from either investors or their representatives. Examples include dividends and coupon payments, offers to issue or redeem securities, stock splits, mergers, and spin offs. Most of this data is now communicated to investors through a complex channel involving suppliers of financial data, securities' custodians, and investment fund managers, who then also carry investors' decisions in the opposite direction. In both directions, blockchain aspires to make the whole process automatic and more efficient (Hobson, 2016).

2.7 Blockchain in Registration of Rights

All registers of rights include a record of claims in their lodgment book, which they use to establish priorities before subjecting intended transactions to registration review—i.e., during the registration gap between lodgment and registration, the register of rights acts in fact, for the intended transaction, as a register of deeds. What has already been said about recordation systems therefore applies to the lodgment book of registers of rights.

In comparison with property recordation and company registries, the defining stage of registers of rights is registration review—the essential task to safely upgrade personal claims into real rights—, as keeping a reliable and verifiable register of rights should not be qualitatively different from keeping a reliable record of deeds. Therefore, the specific difficulties are not so much those of combining blockchain with registration review performed by humans, as seemingly suggested by some analysts,[13] but whether it is possible, and at what cost, to perform such a review automatically.

Applying blockchain to registration review means replacing humans with an automatic system. From a theoretical perspective, this replacement would face similar difficulties to those considered above with respect to contractual completion. From an empirical perspective, it would pose similar challenges to the centralized automatic review which has been operating since 2009 in New Zealand, where solicitors were given the power to modify a Torrens register of indefeasible rights. As analyzed elsewhere (Arruñada, 2010b), the effectiveness of such automatic review is open to question and its sustainability, given current difficulties to collocate economic risks and decision rights (Thomas, Low, & Griggs, 2012), is in doubt and has to be judged in the long run.

Blockchain partisans would likely take issue with this analysis arguing that, in a truly peer-to-peer system, no centralized third-party verification is necessary because all rights would be in the blockchain and rightholders themselves would be granting their consent directly to the automatic system. This is true but both requirements are too tight.

First, when creating modern land registries, the standard historical solution to have most in rem rights registered and to simplify registration review has been to reduce the variety of rights enforceable in rem, defining a smaller and closed number of in rem rights (Hansmann & Kraakman, 2002; Merrill & Smith, 2000). This reduction of property rights is worthwhile to the extent that it makes it possible for registers of rights to function or, in general, reduces information asymmetries in markets (Arruñada, 2003). However, it is also costly because a smaller set of rights benefits from the advantages of being enforced in rem. (Note that the effect is not so much to constrain freedom of contract—parties remain free to contract personal rights—as to limit enforcement possibilities.)

Second, in a fully decentralized system of property, all individuals would take care of their rights by themselves. They would need to keep their cryptographic keys and to decide about any transaction that other individuals propose which might

[13] These theoretical analyses reach negative conclusions on different bases and referring to different registries. For instance, Thomas (2017) argues that a blockchain system based on trading "colored" coins through Bitcoin could not support a Torrens register because it would not allow verification by an independent registrar. Also assuming a Torrens register, Griggs, Thomas, Low, and Scheibner (2017) consider that blockchain would not avoid two of the typical forms of title-related fraud. Gallego Fernández (2017) contends that a register of rights based on an unpermissioned blockchain would find it hard to enforce priority and would preclude registrars' review. Moreover, a permissioned blockchain would offer no advantage over conventional technical solutions.

affect their rights. As mentioned previously, many individuals, probably the majority, would prefer to rely, at least partly, on trusted private and institutional intermediaries, including conveyancers, title insurers, banks and registrars.

Proposals to apply blockchain in the registration of real property confirm this analysis as they opt to preserve the review role of registrars. For instance, a Swedish pilot project (Kempe, 2016, 2017) provides a valuable illustration as, in essence, it is limited to reorganizing the in personam contractual process precedent to the in rem property transaction.[14] The changes proposed thus resemble the system of electronic conveyancing and registration implemented in New Zealand, but with a key difference: the Swedish Land Register (the *Lantmäteriet*) would retain all its powers to review and decide on registration (Kempe, 2017, p. 59). The register would also define the assets and, supposedly, the authority to deal (ibid., p. 38). Therefore, the only substantial change is the development of a private permissioned blockchain application for electronic conveyance, which would allow all parties involved to work with the same information, expanding their knowledge and reducing duplications and mistakes (ibid., pp. 43–44). A benefit would be that all parties would also gain instant access to any filing in the register that may affect the legal standing of the rights being traded.

Acknowledgements This work, prepared for the Conference on "Disruptive Technology, Legal Innovation and the Future of Real Estate" at IDC Herzliya, 23–24 June, 2019, is a heavily revised version of Arruñada (2018) that deepens and updates both its theoretical and empirical analyses of blockchain applications in contract and property rights. This new version has greatly benefitted from the written comments of Fátima Antelo, Jesús Remón Peñalver and Rod Thomas to an earlier version. It received support from the Spanish Government through grant ECO2017-85763-R and the Severo Ochoa Program for Centers of Excellence in R&D (SEV-2015-0563). Usual disclaimers apply. An extended version with the same title has been published at the European Property Law Journal (2020, 8(3), 231–59).

References

Abadi, J., & Brunnermeier, M. (2018). Blockchain economics. In *NBER Working Paper* 25407.

Abramowicz, M. (2016). Cryptocurrency-based law. *Arizona Law Review, 58*(2), 359–420.

Andreessen, M. (2014, January 21). Why bitcoin matters. *New York Times*. Retrieved from http://dealbook.nytimes.com/2014/01/21/why-bitcoin-matters, visited April 25, 2019.

Arruñada, B. (2002a). A transaction cost view of title insurance and its role in different legal systems. *The Geneva Papers on Risk and Insurance—Issues and Practice, 27*(4), 582–601.

Arruñada, B. (2002b). The quasi-judicial role of large retailers: An efficiency hypothesis of their relation with suppliers. In E. Brousseau & J.-M. Glachant (Eds.), *The economics of contracts: Theories and applications* (pp. 337–357). Cambridge: Cambridge University Press.

Arruñada, B. (2003). Property enforcement as organized consent. *Journal of Law, Economics, and Organization, 19*(2), 401–444.

Arruñada, B. (2007). Market and institutional determinants in the regulation of conveyancers. *European Journal of Law and Economics, 23*(2), 93–116.

[14] The current proposal for the English Land Register (Tombs, 2019) does something similar.

Arruñada, B. (2010a). Institutional support of the firm: A theory of business registries. *The Journal of Legal Analysis, 2*(2), 525–576.

Arruñada, B. (2010b). Leaky title syndrome? *New Zealand Law Journal*, 115–120.

Arruñada, B. (2012). *Institutional foundations of impersonal exchange: Theory and policy of contractual registries*. Chicago: University of Chicago Press.

Arruñada, B. (2017). Property as sequential exchange: The forgotten limits of private contract. *Journal of Institutional Economics, 13*(4), 753–783.

Arruñada, B. (2018). Blockchain's struggle to deliver impersonal exchange. *Minnesota Journal of Law, Science & Technology, 2018*(19), 55–105.

Arruñada, B., Espinosa, M., & Garicano, L. (2018, April 10). Blockchain: The birth of decentralized governance. In *Economics and Business Working Paper Series*, 1608. Pompeu Fabra University. Retrieved from https://ssrn.com/abstract=3160070, visited April 25, 2019.

Arruñada, B., & Vázquez, X. H. (2006). When your contract manufacturer becomes your competitor. *Harvard Business Review, 84*(9), 135–145.

Baker, K. (2018, February 2). Delaware eases off early blockchain zeal after concerns over disruption to business. *Delaware Online—The News Journal*. Retrieved from https://eu.delawareonline.com/story/news/2018/02/02/delaware-eases-off-early-blockchain-zeal-after-concerns-over-disruption-business/1082536001/, visited April 28, 2018.

Buterin, V. (2017, December 17). Notes on blockchain governance. *Vitalik Buterin's website*. Retrieved from https://vitalik.ca/general/2017/12/17/voting.html, visited June 14, 2019.

Casey, A. J., & Niblett, A. (2017). Self-driving contracts. *Journal of Corporation Law, 42*(1), 101–131.

Catalini, C., & Gans, J. S. (2016). Some simple economics of the blockchain. In *NBER Working Paper* 22952.

Cooter, R., Kornhauser, L., & Lane, D. (1979). Liability rules, limited information, and the role of precedent. *Bell Journal of Economics, 10*(1), 366–373.

Cooter, R., & Ulen, T. (2016). *Law and economics* (6th ed.). Berkeley Law Books. Retrieved from http://scholarship.law.berkeley.edu/books/2, visited April 25, 2019.

Cuomo, J. (2019). Why is Interoperability Important in Blockchain? Quora, May 15. Retrieved from https://www.quora.com/Why-is-interoperabilityimportantin-blockchain/answer/Jerry-Cuomo-1?ch=10&share=153d8f51&srid=tzUlE, visited December 23, 2019.

Da Costa Cruz, J., Schröder, A. S., & von Wangenheim, G. (2019). Chaining property to blocks—On the economic efficiency of blockchain-based property enforcement. In W. Abramowicz & A. Paschke (Eds.), *2018 business information systems workshops* (pp. 313–324). Berlin: Springer.

De Soto, H., Ghersi, E., Ghibellini, M., & Instituto Libertad y Democracia. (1986). *El otro sendero: la revolución informal*. Lima: El Barranco. (English ed.: De Soto, H. (1989). *The other path: The invisible revolution in the third world*. New York: Harper & Row).

Evans, D. S. (2014, April). Economic aspects of bitcoin and other decentralized public-ledger currency platforms. In *Working Paper* 685. University of Chicago, Coase-Sandor Institute Institute for Law & Economics. Retrieved from https://ssrn.com/abstract=2424516, visited April 25, 2019.

Fernández, G., & Antonio, L. (2017). Blockchains and title registration. *IPRA-CINDER International Review, 1*, 26–51.

Gallego Fernández, L. A. (2017). Blockchains and title registration. IPRA-CINDER International Review, 1, 26–51.

Gans, J. S. (2019). The fine print in smart contracts. In *NBER Working Paper* 25443.

Graglia, J. M., & Mellon, C. (2018). Blockchain and property in 2018: At the end of the beginning. *Innovations: Technology, Governance, Globalization, 12*(1–2), 90–116.

Griggs, L., Thomas, R., Low, R., & Scheibner, J. (2017). Blockchains, trust and land administration: The return of historical provenance. *Property Law Review, 6*(3), 179–194.

Hadfield, G. K., & Bozovic, I. (2016). Scaffolding: Using formal contracts to support informal relations in support of innovation. *Wisconsin Law Review, 5*, 981–1032.

Hansmann, H., & Kraakman, R. (2002). Property, contract, and verification: The *Numerus Clausus* problem and the divisibility of rights. *The Journal of Legal Studies, 31*(2), S373–S420.

Harris, R. (2000). *Industrializing English law: entrepreneurship and business organization, 1720-1844*. Cambridge: Cambridge University Press.

Hobson, D. (2016, January). Case study—Corporate actions. In M. Walport (Ed.), *Distributed ledger technology: Beyond block chain* (pp. 58–59). London: Government Office for Science.

Holden, R., & Malani, A. (2018, February). *Can blockchains solve the holdup problem in contracts*. Chicago: Becker-Friedman Institute. *Working Paper* 2018-12. Retrieved from https://bfi.uchicago.edu/wp-content/uploads/WP_No.2018-12.pdf, visited May 4, 2019.

ISDA (International Swaps and Derivatives Association). (2016, September). The future of derivatives processing and market infrastructure. In *ISDA Whitepaper*. Retrieved from https://www2.isda.org/attachment/ODcwMA==/Infrastructure%20white%20paper.pdf, visited April 25, 2019.

Kempe, M. (Ed.). (2016, July). The land registry in the blockchain: A development project with Lantmäteriet (The Swedish Mapping, Cadastre and Land Registration Authority), Telia Company, ChromaWay and Kairos Future. In *White Paper*. Stockholm: Kairos Future.

Kempe, M. (Ed.) (2017, March). The land registry in the blockchain—Testbed: A development project with Lantmäteriet, Landshypothek Bank, SBAB, Telia company, ChromaWay and Kairos Future. Stockholm: Kairos Future.

Klein, B., & Leffler, K. B. (1981). The role of market forces in assuring contractual performance. *Journal of Political Economy, 89*(4), 615–641.

Larimer, D. (2018, June 27). The 'intent of code' is law. *Medium*. Retrieved from https://medium.com/@bytemaster/the-intent-of-code-is-law-c0e0cd318032, visited June 9, 2019.

Lessig, L. (1999). *Code, and other laws of cyberspace*. New York: Basic Books.

Lessig, L. (2006). *Code: Version2.0*. New York: Basic Books.

Levin, J. (2003). Relational incentive contracts. *American Economic Review, 93*(3), 835–857.

Lifthrasir, R. (2017, June 28). Permissionless real estate title transfers on the bitcoin blockchain in the USA!—Cook County Blockchain Pilot Program Report. *Medium*. Retrieved from https://medium.com/@RagnarLifthrasir/permissionless-real-estate-title-transfers-on-the-bitcoin-blockchain-in-the-usa-5d9c39139292, visited April 25, 2019.

Lomas, N. (2015, June 29). Everledger is using blockchain to combat fraud, starting with diamonds. *Tech Crunch*. Retrieved from https://techcrunch.com/2015/06/29/everledger/, visited April 25, 2019.

Merrill, T. W., & Smith, H. E. (2000). Optimal standardization in the law of property: The *Numerus Clausus* principle. *Yale Law Journal, 110*(1), 1–70.

Moore, J. (1992). Implementation, contracts, and renegotiation in environments with complete information. In J.-J. Laffont (Ed.), *Advances in Economic Theory: Invited Papers to the World Congress of the Econometric Society* (Vol. I, pp. 182–281).

Narayanan, A., Bonneau, J., Felten, E., Miller, A., & Goldfeder, S. (2016). *Bitcoin and cryptocurrency technologies: A comprehensive introduction*. Princeton University Press: Princeton.

Ortolani, P. (2016). Self-enforcing online dispute resolution: Lessons from bitcoin. *Oxford Journal of Legal Studies, 36*(3), 595–629.

Ortolani, P. (2019). The impact of blockchain technologies and smart contracts on dispute resolution: Arbitration and court litigation at the crossroads. Uniform Law Review. 16 May. Retrieved from https://doi.org/10.1093/ulr/unz017, visited December 23, 2019.

Posner, R. A. (1973/2007). *The economic analysis of law* (7th ed.). New York, NY: Aspen Publishers.

Rose, C. M. (1988). Crystals and mud in property law. *Stanford Law Review, 40*(3), 577–610.

Sachs, G. (2016, May 24). *Profiles in innovation: Blockchain—Putting theory into practice*. New York: Goldman Sachs Group, Inc. Retrieved from https://pgcoin.tech/wp-content/uploads/2018/06/blockchain-paper.pdf, visited April 25, 2019.

Shapiro, C. (1983). Premiums for high quality products as returns to reputations. *Quarterly Journal of Economics, 98*(4), 659–679.

Shavell, S. (2004). *Foundations of economic analysis of law*. Cambridge, MA: Harvard University Press.
Shea, R. (2016, June 17). Simple contracts are better contracts: What we can learn from the meltdown of the DAO. *Medium*. Retrieved from https://medium.com/@ryanshea/simple-contracts-are-better-contracts-what-we-can-learn-from-the-dao-6293214bad3a, visited April 25, 2019.
Surden, H. (2012). Computable contracts. *University of California Davis Law Review, 46*(2), 629–700.
Szabo, N. (1997). The idea of smart contracts. *Nick Szabo's Papers and Concise Tutorials*. Retrieved from http://www.fon.hum.uva.nl/rob/Courses/InformationInSpeech/CDROM/Literature/LOTwinterschool2006/szabo.best.vwh.net/idea.html, visited April 25, 2019.
Szabo, N. (1998–2005). Secure property titles with owner authority. Retrieved from http://www.fon.hum.uva.nl/rob/Courses/InformationInSpeech/CDROM/Literature/LOTwinterschool2006/szabo.best.vwh.net/securetitle.html, visited April 25, 2019.
Tapscott, D., & Tapscott, A. (2016). *Blockchain revolution: How the technology behind bitcoin is changing money, business, and the world*. New York: Penguin.
Tashea, J. (2019, March 1). Wyoming and vermont hope to attract tech entrepreneurs by passing laws favorable to blockchain. *ABA Journal*. Retrieved from http://www.abajournal.com/magazine/article/blockchain-wyoming-vermont-regulations-laws, visited May 15, 2019.
Taylor, S. (2016, January). Definitions. In M. Walport (Ed.), *Distributed ledger technology: Beyond block chain* (pp. 17–18). London: Government Office for Science.
Thomas, R. (2017). Blockchain's incompatibility for use as a land registry: Issues of definition, feasibility and risk. *European Property Law Journal, 6*(3), 361–390.
Thomas, R., Low, R., & Griggs, L. (2012, 12–13 July). *Land fraud and inappropriate dealings in an electronic environment: An Australian and New Zealand perspective*. Paper presented at the 11th Australasian Property Law Teachers Conference, National University of Singapore. Retrieved from https://eprints.qut.edu.au/51014/2/51014.pdf, visited May 25, 2019.
Tombs, L. (2019, May 24). Could blockchain be the future of the property market? *HM Land Registry Blog*. Retrieved from https://hmlandregistry.blog.gov.uk/2019/05/24/could-blockchain-be-the-future-of-the-property-market/, visited June 4, 2019.
Vermont Secretary of State. (2019, January 15). *Blockchains for public recordkeeping and for recording land records*. A White Paper of the Vermont State Archives and Records Administration.
Voloshyn, A. (2018, March 21). First Government sanctioned blockchain recorded real estate deal in the US. *Medium*. Retrieved from https://medium.com/propy/first-government-sanctioned-blockchain-recorded-real-estate-deal-in-the-us-bb83e8292a7f, visited April 25, 2019.
Williamson, O. E. (1985). *The economic institutions of capitalism*. New York: The Free Press.
Yarbrough, K. A. (2017, May 30). *Blockchain Pilot Program Final Report*. Cook County Recorder of Deeds, Chicago. Retrieved from http://cookrecorder.com/wp-content/uploads/2016/11/Final-Report-CCRD-Blockchain-Pilot-Program-for-web.pdf, visited April 14, 2019.

Part III
Changing Landscapes of Property Rights

The Future of Property Rights: Digital Technology in the Real World

Amnon Lehavi

Abstract Digital technology can open new frontiers in the formation, registration, and enforcement of property rights in land. This chapter explores the prospects—but also the limits—of digital technology in streamlining efficient land use and land markets. In particular, it asks whether the digital production and dissemination of information can enhance a more optimal use of land, such as by the three-dimensional (3D) delineation of real estate into distinct segments and specific rights thereto, including for subsurface infrastructure, or by the digital pooling of non-adjacent assets for purposes such as creating collective security interests in them. This chapter shows that while aligning the digital production of information with a corresponding system of "legal volumes" and 3D zoning regulation can innovate land markets, the growing multiplicity of property rights in multi-layered tracts faces a genuine collective action problem, having both commons and anticommons features. Digital technology should thus be matched with a legal reform on the institutional governance of multiple uses and interests in and across tracts, somewhat like in the case of condominiums.

Keywords Collective action · Condominium · Governance · Land · Property · Strata title · Zoning

---

A. Lehavi (✉)
Dean, Harry Radzyner Law School, Interdisciplinary Center (IDC) Herzliya, Israel

Academic Director, Gazit-Globe Real Estate Institute, IDC, Herzliya, Israel
e-mail: alehavi@idc.ac.il

A. Lehavi, R. Levine-Schnur (eds.), *Disruptive Technology, Legal Innovation, and the Future of Real Estate*, https://doi.org/10.1007/978-3-030-52387-9_4

1 Introduction

The Fourth Industrial Revolution, embedded in the rapid development of digital technology and other technological/scientific advances, purports to transform all walks of life, such that "the real opportunity is to look beyond technology, and find ways to give the greatest number of people the ability to positively impact their families, organisations and communities" (World Economic Forum, 2020). Land use and land markets are definitely instrumental for the future of families and communities. Yet at first glance, land seems to be a less natural candidate for outright revolution, given its finite supply and physical traits, unlike other forms of economic activities.

This chapter looks at how digital technology can be utilized to advance a more extensive and efficient use of land, primarily by the 3D digital slicing or pooling of land, dissemination of this information to all relevant actors, and matching of such geographical and technological data with a more flexible multi-use approach to land-use regulation (and zoning in particular) and a multi-layered allocation of property rights. Such a legal development could extend beyond the current closed list (numerus clausus) of types of property rights to meet this changing landscape.

At the same time, the growing sophistication of digital technology and its application to land-use regulation and to legal aspects of property rights do not inherently solve genuine collective action problems that typify intensive, multi-use, multi-party land developments. In fact, the growing intensity of use and multiplicity of stakeholders enabled by digital technology can also increase potential frictions among such stakeholders: from neighboring (vertical or horizontal) users of land, to multiple financiers holding competing or overlapping security interests in land. Such collective action problems can implicate both issues of commons (Hardin, 1968), in which multiple stakeholders in the same asset will tend to over-exploit and under-invest in it—and ones of anticommons (Contreras, 2018; Heller, 1998), in which over-fragmentation of private property rights in legally separate but practically interdependent assets can lead to inefficient results or outright deadlocks, by preventing coordination or integrative use of such assets. These collective action problems can result from either strategic behavior, such as holdouts or free riding, or from genuine heterogeneity among stakeholders about their preferences and priorities.

While digital technology can provide better information to all parties about the spatial features of land, and a corresponding reform in zoning regulation and the composition of property rights can potentially give them more flexibility in exploiting physical space, such developments do not in themselves offer a mechanism for resolving potential frictions and deadlocks among parties. What is therefore needed is a dynamic decision-making framework that would accompany various types of multi-use, multi-layered land developments, facilitating institutional governance that draws inspiration from the legal design of condominiums and other forms of strata title.

The rest of this chapter is structured as follows. Part 2 discusses the traditional allocation of property rights in land, which is based largely on a two-dimensional identification of a single tract's surface, with certain particular exceptions that still fall short of a flexible spatial approach. Part 3 shows how different forms of common interest developments, including condominiums, have been able to create an institutional and legal framework for the governance of multi-party, multi-layered use of land, mostly in the residential context, despite their reliance on a static, pre-digital delineation. Part 4 demonstrates recent experiments with the digital production of 3D spatial data and a corresponding adaptation of zoning regulation and 3D land registration of "legal volumes." Part 5 suggests that, in addition to innovative 3D slicing, digital technology can also facilitate the pooling of non-adjacent properties for purposes such as cross-asset collective security interests. Part 6 shows that while digital technology can facilitate a more dynamic and intensive use of land, it cannot in itself resolve potential collective action problems that persist or may be even exacerbated by the growing multiplicity of property rights and numbers of stakeholders. Any such innovation must be matched with the legal design of multi-party institutions of governance.

2 Traditional, Suboptimal Slicing of Property Rights in Land

Prior to discussing how current digital technology can transform the spatial allocation of property rights in land, this part briefly identifies the piecemeal development of legal and regulatory doctrine on multi-layered property in the face of previous generations of economic, social, and technological changes. In principle, such exogenous changes may implicate demand and (to a lesser extent) supply of physical space, as well as the relative costs and benefits of following a certain system of property rights, thus leading to potential changes in legal and regulatory policy (Demsetz, 1967). While such changes have indeed occurred for land, especially over the past two centuries, it would be fair to say that longstanding principles of property in land have not been entirely disrupted, but were rather gradually adjusted and fine-tuned. Moreover, this development has often been unsystematic, leaving much room for ambiguity, such that the overall spatial system of allocating property rights in land is presently suboptimal.

The starting point is that of the *ad coelum* rule. Under the Latin maxim, which dates back to the times of Gaius and Justinian: "Cuius est solum eius est esque ad coelom et usque ad inferos" ("Whoever owns the land owns the property all the way to heaven and all the way to the center of the earth"). While exceptions to this rule have already been introduced during Roman times through the *actio de superficie*, allowing for the creation of horizontal surface rights owned by subjects other than the owner of the estate, it has proven resilient over centuries (Parisi, 2002). In the common law system, the *ad coelum* rule became influential after it was cited by

Edward Coke in the seventeenth century and William Blackstone in the eighteenth century (Rule, 2011).

At its core, while referring to a three-dimensional space, the *ad coelum* rule is in fact dominated by the two-dimensional delineation of the land's surface for establishing property rights. The identification of a two-dimensional space and title thereto automatically governs rights over open space above and below the surface. Moreover, such delineation controls rights to other valuable objects: from subterranean minerals and other materials, to above surface human-made structures through the principle of accession, or 'fixtures' in Anglo-American legal terminology, mostly in a landlord-tenant context (van Erp & Akkermans, 2012).

In Continental Europe, nineteenth-century civil codes, including the 1804 Code Napoléon, adhered to the *ad coelum* rule by disallowing the horizontal severance of land into multiple surface and subsurface estates. But property owners occasionally continued to do so. While such agreements on the partition of land into multiple surface and subsurface estates could not formally commit to conveying real title to the various land strata, parties to such transactions sought to bypass this impediment by agreeing not to invoke accession rules for any structures (such as buildings) erected on the land. With time, civil courts developed a more accommodating approach and allowed such atypical forms of property fragmentation to survive in the shadow of the law. Subsequently, twentieth-century civil codes, including the 1900 German BGB, moved away from applying the strict principle of physical unity, allowing in effect for limited forms of fragmentation, involving typically not more than two layers: surface and subsoil (Parisi, 2002).

A more systematic legal challenge to the *ad coelum* rule began in regard to airspace with the start of aviation in the early twentieth century. In the seminal case of United States v. Causby (1946), the US Supreme Court moved away from a strict application of the *ad coelum* rule—reasoning this doctrine "has no place in the modern world" (p. 261). It distinguished between an upper altitude that serves as a "public highway" for air travel, and the lower layer of airspace above the land's surface that may be practically usable, such that the "landowner owns at least as much of the space above the ground as he can occupy or use in connection with the land" (pp. 264–265).

That said, the *ad coelum* rule, and the underlying dominance of the two-dimensional delineation of the land's surface for establishing property rights and legal control, are far from abolished. For both airspace and subsurface, the *ad coelum* rule has been occasionally adjusted to accommodate economic, social, and technological changes, but it otherwise maintains the control of the surface owner over usable spaces or those in which invasions might otherwise impact such use and enjoyment. Thus, regarding unauthorized invasions to the lower airspace and immediate subsurface, courts generally adhere to a strict version of the *ad coelum* rule (Smith, 2015).

The complexity of managing a multiplicity of layers in the face of the *ad coelum* rule, and not less importantly, in a system of property rights and land registries that still generally follows a two-dimensional approach, manifests itself even more vividly in the case of subsurface rights.

Subsurface rights are created most frequently through the voluntary creation of easements on relevant routes across/in the subsurface or materials located in the subsurface. Easements—defined generally as an irrevocable license to enter and use land owned by or in possession of another person—are recognized as property rights in the various legal systems and can be registered accordingly in the land registry. In the case of the right to enter the surface and/or the subsurface in order to remove materials such as timber, minerals, oil, and gas, such an easement is traditionally referred to as a *profit à prendre*, or simply as a profit (Restatement, 2000). In particular, the law governing easements relating to subsurface oil, gas, and minerals has developed into a separate and complex branch of doctrine, with unique rules applying to such subsurface interests (Dukeminier et al., 2018; Kostrub & Christenson II, 2012). The multi-layered structure of a subsurface right of easement is further challenged in light of recent technological developments, such as horizontal drillings or hydraulic fracturing (Wilkerson, 2015).

In addition to transaction-based easements, the need for surface or subsurface public infrastructure, such as roads and railways, electricity lines, water pipes, fiber-optic cables, etc., may require the government to use its power of eminent domain to obtain an easement or right of way in the surface or subsurface (Morriss, Brandys, & Barron, 2014). Some legal systems—including those of many US states—may also grant private entities, such as oil and gas companies, the right to use the power of eminent domain to obtain such easements or rights of way (Klass, 2008; Righetti, 2016). That said, the *ad coelum* rule continues to play a major role, such that any form of permanent physical invasion of the surface or subsurface requires either the consent of the landowner or exercising the power of eminent domain for public use against the payment of due compensation. This may be so even if such a physical invasion is very limited in scope and does not practically deny current use and enjoyment of the land by the owner, as famously articulated by the US Supreme Court in the case of Loretto v. Teleprompter Manhattan CATV Corp. (1982).

Another type of multi-layered fragmentation of property rights in land, which emerged as an exception to the *ad coelum* rule, concerns the ability to separate ownership of a building or another structure from the ownership of the land. In Roman law, it is known as a *superficie*s. While as a general rule, civil law systems adhere to the maxim of *sepreficies solo cedit* (adopting the rule of accession for any such building or another structure), civil codes were amended and other pieces of legislation or regulation were introduced to recognize a self-standing right of superficies. That said, the exact content of the right of superficies (for example, in regard to future construction rights, or the right to enter the land to access the building) is often not set by law, but should be specifically determined between the parties (van Erp & Akkermans, 2012).

The separation of land ownership from property rights in structures or buildings has also been gradually introduced in Anglo-American systems. However, such fragmentation is done in specific contexts, when the practical need for this manifests, often with little or no statutory or regulatory provisions linking such exceptions to the *ad coelum* rule or to the law on fixtures.

One such setting, introduced in the United States, is that of the Community Land Trust (CLT). The CLT is a community-based, non-profit organization that acquires land for the purpose of retaining perpetual ownership in it to facilitate affordable housing. An eligible buyer leases the land for a long period of time (typically 99 years) and becomes owner of the building erected on it. The lease agreement on the land divides the bundle of rights between the individual and the CLT during the tenancy and upon its transfer by inheritance or resale. In the latter case, to keep the land available for affordable housing in perpetuity, the CLT repurchases the property itself or monitors its direct transfer from seller to buyer, while ensuring that the resale price is restricted to a set formula. This is done to allow the exiting homeowner to receive a reasonable return on investment, while granting income-eligible buyers affordable access to the housing unit. Most US states allow for the legal fragmentation of rights between the land and the housing unit, whereas in a couple of states (Ohio and North Carolina) there is a gray area in the law, suggesting that such a separation of title is not permitted. In such cases, the CLT leases out to the buyer both the land and the building (Davis, 2010; Lehavi, 2013; Miller, 2013). The CLT model, with its division of property title, is now becoming familiar also in Britain (Chadwick, 2018).

Finally, another limited and often incomplete feature of multi-layered entitlements in land, which exceeds the paradigm of two-dimensional property rights over a single tract, concerns transferrable development rights (TDRs), also referred to colloquially as "air rights." TDRs are a regulatory mechanism that allows landowners to buy unused development rights from owners of other lots, under specific terms set out in statutory law or local zoning provisions, and to add such development rights to their own lots. The mechanism was originally introduced in New York City, prominently as in-kind compensation for owners of designated landmark buildings restricted from altering the building or building on top of it, by allowing them to sell such unused development rights to owners of other, non-restricted lots in the area (Ellickson et al., 2013).

Gradually, TDRs have come to be employed in a broader fashion, such that in New York City and elsewhere today developers can acquire unused development rights from owners of properties, whenever the two lots share a physical boundary, but the developers can then go on to assemble more development rights from consecutive lots (Wainwright, 2019). While TDRs start to have a substantial impact on land use and land markets, it should be noted, first, that the term "air rights" is misleading in the sense that landowners do not actually acquire the property rights in the physical unbuilt spaces in other lots, and secondly, that unlike property rights, unused development rights are typically not registered as such in land registries. In these and other respects, TDRs are limited in their ability to create a comprehensive and transparent system of efficiently allocating property rights, horizontally or vertically, across different tracts of land.

The large picture that emerges from the current legal landscape of multi-layered property in land is one of piecemeal, often ad-hoc solutions to address the growing complexity and intensity of land use and land markets in light of social, economic, and technological changes. The two-dimensional approach to land ownership, expressed in the *ad coelum* rule, but also pertinent in traditional land registries and land use regulation, continues to serve as the default rule for the allocation and control of property rights in land.

Exceptions are carved out specifically and gradually, looking to solve particular problems with airspace, surface rights of way and subsurface exploitation of oil, gas, and minerals, etc.—but lacking a systematic approach to transform the two-dimensional tradition into a flexible, transparent, and accessible system of multi-layered property. Accordingly, easements (whether voluntary or compulsory), superficies, and other types of limited proprietary rights allowing for the use of—or the taking of profit from—certain subsurface, surface, or above-surface parts of a tract of land are subject to many intricacies and ambiguities, and are often not featured clearly and comprehensively in traditional land registries.

Moreover, to the extent that a certain legal system currently wishes to avoid ambiguities in defining a certain multi-level property right, it must often engage in excessive subdivision of parcels given the features of two-dimensional land registries. Thus, for example, in many countries, in the case of a right of superficies for a building that is constructed under, on, or over a part of a tract of land, the said object would be projected on a two-dimensional parcel map, and the parcel would be further subdivided into smaller parcels, to be able to register such a property right. Such a subdivision would often make little sense for the principal use of the land (Stoter et al., 2017). This means that the division or aggregation of pieces of land and rights thereto might not be driven by efficiency or other normative considerations, but rather by technical constraints, obsolete doctrine, or other varieties of path-dependency (Fennell, 2019).

The traditional system of multi-level allocation of property rights is thus often suboptimal. As the next parts will show, what is required is a systematic transformation into a three-dimensional model, which not only enables efficient spatial allocation of property rights, but also sets up an institutional mechanism for a long-term governance of multi-layered interests and stakeholders. Similar steps should be taken to enable the virtual and legal pooling of non-adjacent assets, such as for creating cross-asset security interests, to promote land markets and real-estate financing.

3 Condominiums (Strata Title) as an Institutional Exception

This part identifies the most important exception to the above-surveyed systematic deficiency in multi-layered property rights. In the context of residential land use, basically all legal systems have introduced over the past few decades common interest developments (CIDs). The term CID refers here to various types of shared-interest residential developments, such as condominiums, planned unit developments, stock cooperatives (co-ops), and community apartment projects. Not all forms exist in all countries, and the organizational and legal structure of each type of CID, as well as the terminology used, somewhat diverge among different legal systems (Lehavi, 2016).

Thus, for example, the vertical (but also horizontal) division of property rights in apartment buildings, which is typically governed by the legal institution of condominiums in the United States, is referred to as strata title in Australia. It is the most prevalent form of CID in the world.

Horizontal subdivisions—under which a real estate development comprises detached homes or housing units, with other areas serving as common facilities—are generally known as "planned unit developments" in the United States and as "community title" in Australia (Sherry, 2017).

This part focuses on condominiums or strata title as legal institutions for multi-layered property rights. It shows how such a volumetric allocation of space—while still relying on paper-based or static techniques for 3D allocation—is effectively intertwined with mechanisms for collective governance of both the common amenities and at least some aspects of the individual units. This part then presents the emergence of the "stratum subdivision" in Australia, which governs mixed-use developments, including structures having diverse types of commercial uses.

The condominium consists of an "undivided interest in common in a portion of real property with a separate interest in [a] space called a unit" (California Civil Code, 2014). The basic legal structure is one by which the housing units are individually owned, whereas the hallways, staircases, elevators, etc. of the structure (or complex of structures), alongside exterior spaces and amenities, such as yards, lawns, inner streets, or sports facilities, are owned in common by the group of unit owners. Condominiums developed at different stages and a diverging pace across the world. In Western Europe, early forms of condominiums have been in existence for a few hundred years, but the major push toward comprehensive legislation came in the aftermath of the world wars, which caused an acute housing shortage alongside growing popular demand for homeownership (van der Merwe, 2015). Emerging economies in Southeast Asia followed mostly Australian legislation during the 1960s and 1970s to meet growing local and foreign demand for condominium-type dense developments (Rabenhorst & Ignatova, 2009). Condominiums were introduced in the United States only during the later 1950s and early 1960s, but have since been burgeoning rapidly (McKenzie, 1994; Schill, Voicu, & Miller, 2007). Transitional economies have more recently seen the need for the legal design of condominiums mostly in their urban cores, as demonstrated in the case of China or that of Russia (Chen & Kielsgard, 2014; Lehavi, 2015).

As suggested above, the key institutional feature allowing condominiums to function effectively over time in governing multi-owned, multi-layered properties is the establishment of decision-making bodies with broad powers. Thus, for example, under the Australian model (introduced in New South Wales in 1961 and essentially followed in all other Australian states), a body corporate, constituted by all owners, is automatically created by the registration of the subdivision plan of the strata title. This body corporate is granted by statute the power to raise levies for maintenance, insurance, and administration, as well as the power to enforce bylaws.

While the statute provides for default bylaws, the body corporate can alter such bylaws (for some provisions unanimously, for others by special majority), and subsequently engage in creating new bylaws, typically by special, non-unanimous resolution. Importantly, such bylaws may govern not only the use and enjoyment of the shared property, but also the physical features and use of the privately owned apartments. Such bespoke bylaws, particularly for large schemes, can include provisions about paint colors, mailbox style, plant type, pet type and weight, etc. There are some limits imposed by statute on the power of the body corporate, such that most Australian states ban bylaws that restrict transferring, leasing, or mortgaging lots (Sherry, 2017).

The organization and scope of power of internal bodies that govern multi-owned properties are similar in other countries, such as in the United States. The core of the collective action among homeowners in condominiums lies in the governing documents, composed of "declarations" containing a set of conditions, covenants, and restrictions (CC&Rs), which are recorded with the land registrar. Though based on contractual provisions, the governing documents and subsequent amendments, rules, and regulations adopted by the association go well beyond the law of contracts, awarding these rules a more credible and reciprocal nature. This is so because under enabling legislation, individually owned lots or units are "burdened by a servitude that imposes an obligation that cannot be avoided by nonuse or withdrawal" (Restatement, 2000).

As the California Supreme Court reasoned in its decision in Pinnacle Museum Tower Association v. Pinnacle Market Development (2012), having a single set of recorded covenants and restrictions that applies to an entire residential association "protects the intent, expectations, and wishes of those buying into the development and the community as a whole by ensuring that promises concerning the character and operation of the development are kept" (p. 524). The fact that such provisions are enforced as servitudes and not merely as contractual provisions—which might otherwise allow an infringing homeowner to avoid specific performance and instead pay compensatory damages—secures the endurance of collective action.

As is the case in Australia, rule-making powers of condominium associations extend beyond the establishment and management of common facilities, and may also control cross-apartment externalities resulting from the use of privately owned units, with such types of private ordering coming in addition to—and not in lieu of—public regulation, such as zoning or nuisance law.

Elected directors and officers of the association have broad authority to "exercise all the powers of the community except those reserved to the members." This authority also regularly includes the power to adopt "reasonable" rules that govern the use of the common property and the use of individually owned property when this is required to protect the common property. In reviewing the board's actions, courts regularly adopt either a "reasonableness rule" or corporate law's "business judgment rule"—both bearing a similar deferential content (Restatement, 2000). As for decisions taken by the general body corporate of homeowners, unless expressly limited by law or the association's declarations, simple majority is effective to amend the declarations or to otherwise adopt rules. Unanimous consent is required for restrictions on individual uses that cannot be grounded in common interest; changes made to the basis for allocating voting rights or assessments among homeowners; or rules that do not apply uniformly to similar units/lots.

In practice, however, US courts tend to broadly construe enabling legislation and declarations so as to settle for simple majority to amend the declaration or to promulgate new rules in nearly all instances. In Villa De Las Palmas Homeowners Association v. Terifaj (2004), the California Supreme Court upheld a majority-approved amendment to the condominium's declarations imposing a no-pet restriction, by viewing such a use restriction as "crucial to the stable, planned environment of any shared ownership arrangement" and holding that all homeowners, including those who purchased their units prior to the amendment, are bound by it. The court read Section 1355(b) of California's Civil Code on declaration amendments as settling for simple majority, reasoning that it is designed to prevent a "small number of holdouts from blocking changes regarded by the majority to be necessary to adapt to changing circumstances and thereby permit the community to retain its vitality over time" (p. 1228). Amendments made by simple majority thus generally enjoy a presumption of reasonableness, shifting the burden to the challenging party, who must show that these restrictions are "wholly arbitrary, violate a fundamental public policy, or impose a burden on the use of affected land that far outweighs any benefit" (p. 1231).

While these broad powers may at times seem controversial, especially when they have a practical effect of singling out certain homeowners, or when they otherwise infringe on what may be considered to be fundamental individual rights, there is no doubt that, generally speaking, the governance mechanism that is attached to the proprietary setup of condominiums or strata title is essential for the effective allocation and control of multi-owner, multi-layered properties. As such, it allows for a more intensive use of urban land in an age of increasing density and demand.

A recent development in Australia, which seeks to offer an institutional solution to multi-owned, multi-layered properties beyond residential buildings, is that of 'stratum' or 'volumetric' subdivisions. Realizing that strata title legislation was not adequate for mixed-use developments with residential and commercial owners, or with diverse commercial owners, such that a single body corporate may find it difficult to make decisions, Australian legislation was amended to allow for the subdivision of a building by a deposited plan into separate stratum lots, limited by height or depth by reference to the Australian Height Datum. Such stratum lots can be further divided by a strata plan, creating a residential or commercial strata scheme within that stratum lot, which becomes a 'stratum parcel.' Each such stratum lot or parcel could be then governed by its own set of bylaws. To address the vertical and lateral interdependencies between the different stratum lots, such stratum subdivisions require the introduction of easements intended to grant separate stratum owners access to shared property, which is partly or entirely located in another stratum owner's lot or parcel. Further, in order to deal with maintenance costs and other issues that require ongoing coordination across the different stratum lots or parcels, owners must register Building Management Statements (BMS) and Strata Management Statements (SMS). Such documents must include provisions on insurance, damages, and disputes, but may also and typically do include many other issues. In addition, the BMS must establish a Building Management Committee, which includes all stratum lot or parcel owners (Sherry, 2017). This committee is discussed further in Part 6, by illustrating how it facilitates collective governance.

4 Digital Production of 3D Spatial Data and Move to "Legal Volumes"

Digital technology and other types of innovations are being increasingly employed by both governmental agencies and private entities across the world in the context of land use and land markets. This includes the use of advanced technologies and professional standards, such as interactive graphic visualization, geographic information systems (GIS), building information modelling (BIM), and the land administration domain model (LADM) (Lemmen, van Oosterom, & Bennett, 2015).

The key challenge for efficiently implementing such new technologies lies to a large extent in the ability to integrate them across different professional and governmental platforms that are relevant to land use and land markets, and particularly in land registries and cadastral systems. Optimally, such geographical, technical, and legal tools should be formalized and accessible to all parties concerned, and governed by a unified system of registration (Yu et al., 2017).

Such techniques are being increasingly used in an attempt to gradually switch cadasters and land registries from two-dimensional systems to three-dimensional ones, with diverging degrees of success in introducing 3D systems and in synchronizing industry and governmental platforms. Accordingly, there is a growing body of literature on the recent experiences with 3D cadasters and/or land registries worldwide (Paasch et al., 2016), with numerous works focusing on case studies in countries such as Australia (Atazadeh et al., 2017), Croatia (Vučić et al., 2017), Korea (Kim & Hoe, 2019), India (Hamid et al., 2016), and Slovenia (Drobež et al., 2017).

In 2016, The Netherlands experimented with the first registration of an interactive 3D visualization of "legal volumes"—i.e., 3D physical spaces identified each as a distinctive unit—in the cadaster and the land registry (Stoter et al., 2017). As shown below, by legally validating and providing access to such a new type of physical identification and registration of rights in regard thereto, this regulatory and legal innovation seeks to serve not only current stakeholders, but even more so future transferees and other stakeholders of these multi-level property rights. As such, the introduction of legal volumes not only facilitates a more flexible approach to the division or aggregation of space over time in the face of social, economic, and technological changes, but may also enable the development of new types of property rights, outside of the current closed list (*numerus clausus*)—thus better serving future organizational and legal design.

The program was run for the Delft Railway Zone Project. The project covers an area of 24 hectares, but the 3D cadaster was introduced for a smaller part, consisting of the combined new Railway Station and City Hall, together with the underground platforms and railway tunnel, several technical installations, and underground bicycle parking (Stoter et al., 2017). This multi-layered construction combined the property rights of three parties: Municipality of Delft, which is the owner of the land and the City Hall; the Dutch railroad company for passenger transportation ("NS Real Estate" or "NS Vastgoed"), which is the owner of the Station Hall, shops, and technical installations; and the Dutch railroad infrastructure company ("ProRail" or "Railinfratrust B.V."), which owns the travelers' area, the tunnel, and the platforms. To address this multi-level setup, six legal volumes and property rights thereto have been established:

1. Residual legal volume, not covered by the other five legal volumes (represented as "Index 1" in Fig. 1 below)—under a right of ownership of the Municipality of Delft.
2. Tunnels ("Index 2" in Fig. 1)—right of superficies, Railinfratrust B.V.
3. Travelers' area ("Index 3" in Fig. 1)—right of superficies, Railinfratrust B.V.
4. Station Hall ("Index 4" in Fig. 1)—right of superficies, NS Vastgoed.
5. Elevators and stairs ("Index 5" in Fig. 1)—right of superficies, NS Vastgoed.
6. Technical installations ("Index 6" in Fig. 1)—right of superficies, NS Vastgoed.

Because of the experimental nature of the 3D registration process, in order to avoid the economic risks of delay in doing so, the property rights were initially recorded in the land registry through traditional 2D registration. In the deed, the six legal volumes were described textually, and were accompanied by 2D maps, illustrating the various cross sections. For this initial registration process, new ground parcels were formed by the cadaster—such that the original parcels were consolidated and subsequently subdivided to specify the different accumulation of rights of the new complex (Stoter et al., 2017).

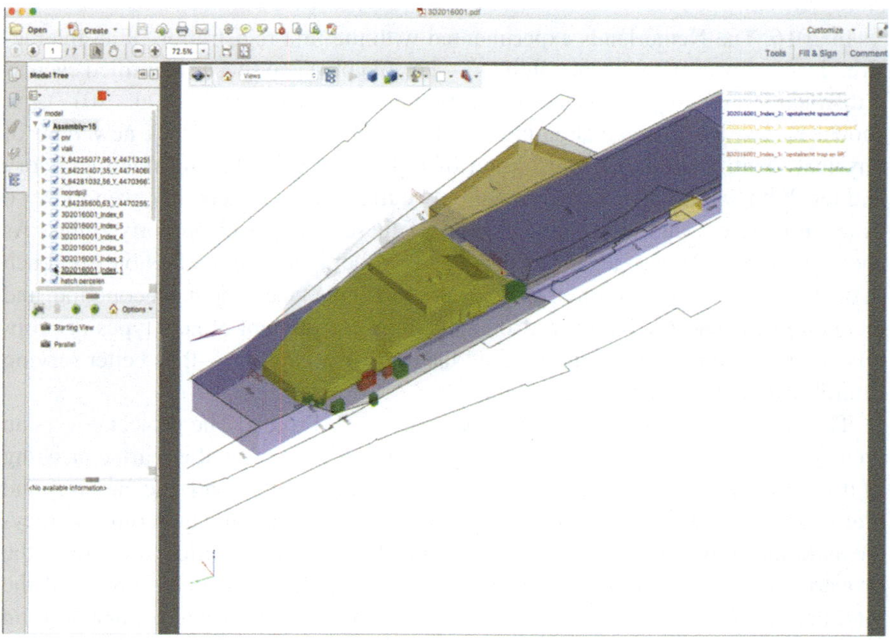

Fig. 1 Frame taken from the interactive 3D PDF of the Delft Railway Zone Project, as deposited in The Netherlands' national cadaster and the land registry (Source: Kadaster, 2016)

Then, for the 3D registration, the architect of the building complex converted the 3D data of the construction itself, using BIM technology, into 3D geometries representing the six legal volumes, based on the design data of the complex, the already registered deed with 2D maps of the complex, and the input of all stakeholders collected via four work sessions. Next, the 3D representations of the property rights were converted into a 3D PDF. This also included a legend of the rights, the 2D cadastral map in which the parcels were identified, and the x, y, and z coordinates of the national reference system. Subsequently, a notary firm issued a certificate for the deposit of the 3D PDF in the land registry as an official deed (Stoter et al., 2017).

In the cadastral registration, a 3D complex ID was generated and the different rights were assigned unique indices (numbered 1 to 6, as shown in Fig. 1). Additionally, a reference was made in the cadastral registration to the interactive 3D visualization of property rights. The 3D data itself was stored by the cadaster to accommodate future needs, which may require the adjustment of the legal situation. The 3D data is stored and maintained by the public registries.

The 3D PDF is publicly viewable not only from the public registries, but also from the cadaster, and can be viewed in any PDF viewer that supports 3D. In the viewer, the 3D setup can be interactively viewed, such that one sees the relationship between the different legal volumes. Each volume is visible for further inspection, such that by clicking on each one of the objects, one sees the 3D indices and identity of the property owner of the legal volume (Kadaster, 2016).

Without going into further technical details and addressing other intricacies that may be the result of the transition from a 2D registration system of property rights to a 3D system, a few comments are in order about the prospects—but also the limits—of this technological and legal innovation.

First, the transition into 3D interactive registration has clear benefits for facilitating more efficient land use and land markets. The inefficiency of relying on 2D maps and accompanying textual descriptions is especially significant in cases of multi-level property rights, wherever boundaries are not exactly on top of each other when projected on a 2D plane (Stoter et al., 2017). Under 2D systems, there is often a need to artificially create tiny parcels to accommodate potential mismatches between the location of 2D cadastral boundaries and the projection of the 3D construction. Moreover, future division or aggregation of current legal volumes may also not conform to purely vertical or horizontal divisions. It may employ geometrically irregular—but economically efficient—3D shapes. A system of 3D surveying of the land for cadastral purposes, followed by a system of 3D land-use regulation and the 3D creation of legal volumes allows for more flexibility for both the initial stage of developing the project and any future redevelopment.

Second, while the benefits are clear, the regulatory and technical challenges in synchronizing the different industry and governmental platforms are still prevalent and not merely the result of conservatism or other path-dependency. Thus, for example, BIM systems and cadastral surveying methods often have a different level of accuracy, which may result in physically small but important implications for questions of property rights, use, and future development of lands. As shown in the case of the Delft Railway Zone Project, this may also call for an active input by all stakeholders in setting up the multi-layered property scheme to resolve any such ambiguities.

Third, and relatedly, the potential for dynamic reconfiguration of legal volumes and property rights thereto, embedded in an interactive 3D system, may require that the relevant stakeholders be involved in any processes of change in real time to mitigate the potential for disputes or ambiguities for any such future reconfigurations. This may strengthen the need for intertwining the development of systems for the 3D planning, allocation, and registration of property rights, with the establishment of institutional governance mechanisms for the various stakeholders that hold multi-layered property rights. This point is discussed further in Part 6 below.

Finally, the switch to a more flexible, transparent, and dynamic system of allocating and reallocating property rights across subsurface, surface, or above-surface spaces may provide an opportunity for creating new types of property rights—ones that may better accommodate up-to-date needs coming from developers, financiers, tenants, and so forth, and that may be supported by digital technology and legal innovation.

As noted, in the case of the Delft Railway Zone Project, the Dutch railroad company for passenger transportation and the Dutch railroad infrastructure company, which together own five out of the six legal volumes, were granted a superficies right—and not an ownership right—in view of traditional legal constraints, whereas the Municipality of Delft retains its ownership of the complex and rights to the residual legal volume. While such a division may make sense, there is no reason to a-priori rule out a different type of allocation of rights, including by setting up a new kind of property right that may be particularly appropriate for complex settings of multi-layered property rights. This could have implications not only for increasing legal certainty, but also for the ability to finance the acquisition and development of a certain legal volume by pledging such a new type of right, in light of current constraints that often apply to limited proprietary rights, such as the superficie. In considering the list of recognized property rights as embedding "optimal standardization" that balances between increasing the efficiency of land use and land markets and the social costs of introducing new types of rights (Merill & Smith, 2001), the innovation of 3D registration and legal volumes might create a new optimal standard in determining the number and variety of property rights in land.

5 Interactive Pooling of Non-adjacent Assets and Portfolio Financing

Digital technology, big data analytics, interactive graphic visualization, and other innovative tools can push forward land use and land markets in various other ways. Thus, alongside the ability to more effectively slice tracts through the integration of three-dimensional visualization, land use, and land registration systems, new technologies can also be utilized to pool together non-adjacent assets. Such interactive pooling, which could also carry legal consequences in bundling property rights to non-adjacent assets, could serve current and future economic needs, especially in the context of real-estate financing and real-estate-backed investment securities.

To understand why current forms of real-estate financing challenge traditional boundaries (literally speaking), consider the observation by which "loans secured on real estate today are amended, redeemed, subjected to both initial and subsequent syndication, assigned, certified, secured by charges against more than one property, divided up and sold in part" (Stöcker, 2012).

What this new reality means is that individuals, business corporations, and financial institutions increasingly engage in practices that move away from the single loan/single asset model for a secured transaction in real estate. These practices include securitization of real-estate-based credit, which includes both pooling of multiple loans and the reslicing of such agglomerated debts into different tranches of bonds, and their consequent trade in stock-exchange markets (Basel Committee on Banking Supervision, 2014). Modern credit instruments may also involve portfolio financing, by which multiple real-estate properties collectively serve as security for large-scale financing schemes. Portfolio financing is currently more prevalent for movable goods and intangible assets, especially in the context of receivables financing, by which a financial institution that extends credit to a business corporation acquires a proprietary interest in the monetary claims (receivables) that the corporation has vis-à-vis its own debtors (Lehavi, 2019).

In fact, the ability to increase the usage of portfolio financing for real estate may hinge to a large extent on improving the ability to consolidate information and to link proprietary rights—and particularly security interests—in non-adjacent assets in a flexible and efficient manner.

In the case of movable goods or intangible assets, the constant replacement of assets that serve as part of the package of the collateralized assets can be generally done in a flexible way. This is so because the financier and/or debtor do not need to register a distinct security interest in each specific movable or intangible asset, but can generally rely on a "floating lien" and related legal instruments to provide general priority to the financier over other, non-secured creditors. The floating lien is thus premised on placing a "charge on assets both present and future," with such assets "expected to change in the normal course of business," thus allowing the corporation to sell such assets—including its commercial inventory—to buyers in the ordinary course of business, while subjecting new/future assets to the floating charge, and so forth (Sheehan, 2017).

Differently, under the current dominant approach across various legal systems, placing a security interest over a tract of land or a standalone unit in a subdivision (such as a condominium unit) requires the registration of a specific security interest on each tract/unit. Accordingly, any change in the security interest or its termination requires a specific process of registration. When security interests are placed on various tracts/units for the purpose of portfolio financing, the different tracts/units are neither visually nor legally interrelated. Current land registries do not agglomerate the different locations of the charged assets in a single map, registration deed, or other instrument. Unlike the floating lien, a legal action taken in regard to one tract/unit does not have direct effect on other assets that are allegedly under the same portfolio- financing scheme. This means that bundling, slicing, or otherwise updating such a scheme requires a relatively cumbersome analogical process, and that the overall picture of the composition and status of the securitized assets is not readily and digitally accessible to right-holders and other stakeholders.

Enabling portfolio financing for real estate thus requires, first, the employment of digital technology that would identify in real time the various assets placed under a security interest—thus pooling visual and textual information on such multiple, non-adjacent properties. In so doing, this technology can rely, at least to some extent, on existing platforms related to security interests, such as information made available for mortgages under the US Home Mortgage Disclosure Act (HMDA) of 1975, which grants access to much of the raw data—modified to protect applicant and borrower privacy—and accordingly enables cross-asset visual and textual analysis (Consumer Financial Protection Bureau, 2019). Thus, in 2016, almost 7000 institutions released over 16 million records, making HMDA an invaluable administrative dataset on housing and homeownership for policymakers, regulators, and researchers, and this data is increasingly used for digital, publicly available cross-asset analysis, such as interactive boom and bust maps (Urban Institute, 2019). Presenting such pooled information on non-adjacent assets could prove essential for land use and land markets in many other contexts. One could think, for example—especially considering the gloomy history of the 2007 subprime crisis—about requiring issuers of real-estate-based securitized bonds to make available to investors real-time cross-asset visual and textual data. This would allow investors to better understand the tranches of securitized loans, including local and regional risks of default, foreclosure, and realization of real-estate assets. The degree of diversification of the bond portfolio could be better understood by the use of digital technology.

In addition to employing digital technology to link together non-adjacent assets through the provision and dissemination of cross-asset information, portfolio financing or real-estate-backed security investments could be further facilitated by legal innovation. One could think about a new type of security interest in land, located somewhere between the traditional fixed mortgage and the floating lien (for movables and intangible assets), which would allow for a swift replacement of real-estate assets that are used as a collective collateral by a certain borrower.

To facilitate a streamlined legal process of replacing charged assets, parties holding a security interest, other creditors, and additional stakeholders would have access to a digital platform, which presents at any given time the current assets placed under security interests and the overall value of the security vis-à-vis the debt—based also on third-party evaluations of the land in question, such as those done for purposes of property taxation. To accommodate potential conflicts in the transition of security interests across different real-estate assets, such a new type of charge should set rules on the date that would apply as the starting date of the charge on a replacement asset (such as the filing date of the charge on the original/previous asset) and any other rules that would establish the priority of such a replacement charge vis-à-vis other rights. While the details of such a legal reform should be tailored more specifically to meet the changing needs of real-estate finance, there is no doubt that such legal innovation would prove effective only if it relies on interactive digital visualization and registration platforms that link non-adjacent lands.

6 Multiplicity of Property Rights: Digital Information and Collective Action

As the previous parts have shown, digital technology and other innovations can provide better information to all parties about the spatial features of tracts of land. A corresponding reform in zoning regulation and the composition of property rights can potentially give them more flexibility in exploiting physical space. That said, the potential for coming up with new or more sophisticated forms of multi-layered property rights or the pooling of non-adjacent assets does not in itself create a mechanism for resolving potential frictions and deadlocks among multiple holders of property rights and other legal interests. In fact, any such type of digital or legal innovation intended to facilitate more intense land use or more sophisticated land markets may also generate new types of collective action problems.

Such coordination challenges can implicate the 'tragic' dynamics of commons (Hardin, 1968), in which multiple stakeholders that simultaneously occupy and use the same physical space might tend to over-exploit it and under-invest in it. Correspondingly, the allocation of a certain physical space among multiple parties can implicate the mirror-image problem of anticommons (Contreras, 2018; Heller, 1998), under which over-fragmentation of private property rights in legally separate but practically interdependent spaces can lead to inefficient results or outright deadlocks, by preventing coordination or integrative use of such assets. These collective action problems can result from either strategic behavior, such as holdouts or free riding, information asymmetries, or genuine heterogeneity among stakeholders about their preferences and priorities.

Examples for collective action problems resulting from multi-layered, multi-party uses of lands abound. One such instance, prevalent in the United States, concerns conflicts among landowners and utility companies, when the latter are granted the power of eminent domain to create involuntary easements in their favor for the construction and the laying-out of power lines, pipelines, communication lines, and other utilities in and across privately owned lands. Unlike cases of eminent domain in which the fee simple estate (ownership) is condemned, such that the utility company becomes the owner of the entire land, the creation of an involuntary easement results in the division of property rights and use of space. Also, unlike the case of a voluntary easement, where parties not only negotiate the initial allocation of rights, but also address future contingencies to alleviate frictions resulting from the existence of simultaneous rights, the parties in the case of such involuntary easements find themselves entangled in long-term governance problems with basically no tools to address them efficiently and fairly (Morriss et al., 2014).

In particular, despite the fact that the creation of multi-layered, multi-party property rights embedded in such infrastructure projects requires repeated interactions on a variety of issues, there is no institutional arrangement that accompanies such projects and practically no default legal rules against which parties would be able to act collaboratively over time. This is a type of problem that no digital technology can solve. As a pure governance problem, it requires a legal solution that sets up a mechanism for long-term institutional governance of such assets.

What is therefore required to facilitate new forms of land uses and land markets, which are otherwise made possible by digital technology and other innovations, is a systematic legal reform that establishes dynamic decision-making frameworks tailored to accommodate such innovations. Just as condominiums and other forms of residential strata title have been able to develop and create real innovation in land use and land markets, so do other new forms of multi-layered, multi-party interests in land depend on the ability of property owners and other stakeholders to engage in long-term institutional governance. To ensure coordination, order, and a reasonable balance between predictability and flexibility in the on-going governance of such new types of land uses and markets, such institutions should be supported by default legal rules that establish the various issues that are relevant for such types of real-estate schemes. Such rules should address issues such as voting rights, required majorities for decisions, mechanisms for assessment of fees, maintenance and improvement, or rights-of-way and other easements.

To illustrate how the future of land use and land markets can and should be complemented by setting up rules and institutions for long-term collective governance, tailored to the specific intricacies of such innovations, consider again 'stratum' or 'volumetric' subdivisions, which seek to offer an institutional solution to multi-owned, multi-layered properties beyond residential buildings, as mentioned in Part 4 above. In order to deal with various issues relating to the vertical and lateral interdependencies between the different stratum lots, such as establishing easements intended to grant separate stratum owners access to shared property that is partly or entirely located in another stratum owner's lot or parcel, or dealing with maintenance costs, lot owners must register Building Management Statements (BMS) and Strata Management Statements (SMS) that address such issues. Beyond the initial rule-setting for the allocation of rights and responsibilities to private and common spaces, the BMS must establish a Building Management Committee, which includes all stratum lot or parcel owners, although owners may be excluded from the Building Management Committee with their consent (Sherry, 2017). The Committee is intended to deal with the ongoing governance of the 'stratum' subdivision, considering also the unique features of each type of stakeholder in such mixed-use projects.

While still underdeveloped legislatively and regulatory, and not often analyzed by Australian courts, stratum subdivisions have a significant potential in furthering new types of developments. As such, they can also serve as a source of inspiration for other kinds of multi-layered, multi-use developments, including those involving large surface or subsurface infrastructure utilities. The same can also hold true for the governance of portfolio financing or other proprietary interests that implicate non-adjacent assets, as discussed in Part 5 above. At its core, every type of intensive, interconnected land-use or land-market novelty calls for such collective governance.

7 Conclusion

Digital technology has enormous—but not unlimited—potential to promote efficient land use and land markets. Thus, three-dimensional surveying, visualization, registration, and planning are increasingly being introduced around the world, fostering legal innovation in the form of "legal volumes" and rights thereto, and opportunities for more intensive, sophisticated land uses. In addition, the interactive pooling of non-adjacent real-estate assets through digital technology can push forward current market practices, such as portfolio financing, and in turn encourage legal innovation in the form of new types of property rights, providing a more flexible approach to security interests as a means to broaden financing opportunities and expand land markets.

That said, while digital technology and other innovations open up new opportunities, and allow for broad dissemination of data in real time, they cannot solve in themselves what are largely interpersonal challenges of governance and decision-making. Collective action problems resulting from strategic behavior or genuine heterogeneity require dynamic institutions of governance and a system of substantive and procedural rules that supports collective action.

On a final note, the analysis in this chapter might echo the voluminous discussion about blockchain as an alternative, decentralized, and verified recording system for transfers of asset ownership—one that allows for validating and registering various transactions by bypassing traditional centralized channels such as banks, while alleviating problems of conflicting transactions or unauthorized transfers of rights (Koch & Pieters, 2017). However, to truly replace current systems of market transfers and registration of property rights in the context of land, the blockchain technology must be supported by legal innovation. Thus, blockchain-based transactions should be broadened in scope to include other types of proprietary rights, such as security interests and easements, alongside the right of ownership. Accordingly, blockchain ledgers and protocols should also be governed by priority rules and governance bodies that settle potential conflicts between different types of property rights in the same asset. It is a challenge that can be met, but it cannot rely merely on digital technology. It requires legal innovation and mechanisms for multi-party governance institutions that are based on human judgment.

References

Atazadeh, B., et al. (2017). Building information modelling for high-rise land administration. *Transactions in GIS, 21*(1), 91.

Basel Committee on Banking Supervision. (2014). *Basel III document: Revisions to the securitisation framework*. Retrieved from https://www.bis.org/bcbs/publ/d303.htm

Chadwick, H. (2018). Community land trust solutions to local housing issues. In *AMPS Conference 10: Cities, Communities and Homes: Is the Urban Future Livable?* (p. 164). University of Derby.

Chen, L., & Kielsgard, M. D. (2014). Evolving property rights in China: Patterns and dynamics in condominium governance. *Chinese Journal of Comparative Law, 2*(1), 21.

Consumer Financial Protection Bureau. (2019). *Mortgage data (HDMA)*. Retrieved from https://www.consumerfinance.gov/data-research/hmda/.

Contreras, J. L. (2018). The anticommons at 20: Concerns for research continue. *Science, 361*, 335.

Davis, J. E. (Ed.). (2010). *The community land trust reader*. Cambridge, MA: Lincoln Institute of Land Policy.

Demsetz, H. (1967). Toward a theory of property rights. *American Economic Review Papers & Proceedings, 57*, 347.

Drobež, P., et al. (2017). Transition from 2D to 3D real property cadaster: The case of the Slovenian cadaster. *Computers, Environment and Urban Systems, 62*, 125.

Dukeminier J., et al. (2018). *Property* (9th ed.). New York: Wolters Kluwer.

Ellickson, R. C., et al. (2013). *Land use controls: Cases and materials* (4th ed.). New York: Wolters Kluwer.

Fennell, L. A. (2019). *Slices and lumps: Division and aggregation in law and life*. Chicago & London: The University of Chicago Press.

Hamid, Q., et al. (2016). Arc GIS and 3D visualization of land records: A case study of urban areas in Punjab. *National Academy of Sciences Letters (India), 39*(4), 277.

Hardin, G. (1968). The tragedy of the commons. *Science, 162*, 1243.

Heller, M. A. (1998). The tragedy of the anticommons: Property in the transition from Marx to markets. *Harvard Law Review, 111*, 621.

Kadaster, The Netherlands. (2016). *3D deeds*. Retrieved from https://3d.bk.tudelft.nl/news/2016/03/21/3DKadaster.html

Kim, S., & Hoe, J. (2019). Registration of 3D underground parcel in Korean cadastral system. *Cities, 89*, 105.

Klass, A. B. (2008). The frontier of eminent domain. *University of Colorado Law Review, 79*, 651.

Koch, C., & Pieters, G. C. (2017). Blockchain technology disrupting records systems. *Financial Insights, (Federal Reserve Bank of Dallas), 6*(2), 1. Retrieved from www.dallasfed.org/outreach/insights/fi1702

Kostrub, D. B., & Christenson, R. S., II. (2012). Canons of construction for the interpretation of mineral conveyances, severances, exceptions, and reservations in producing states. *North Dakota Law Review, 88*, 649.

Lehavi, A. (2013). *The construction of property: Norms, institutions, challenges*. Cambridge: Cambridge University Press.

Lehavi, A. (2015). Law, collective action, and culture: Condominium governance in comparative perspective. *Asia Pacific Law Review, 23*(2), 5.

Lehavi, A. (2016). The culture of private law. *Real Estate Law Journal, 45*(1), 35.

Lehavi, A. (2019). *Property law in a globalizing world*. Cambridge: Cambridge University Press.

Lemmen, C., van Oosterom, P., & Bennett, R. (2015). The land administration domain model. *Land Use Policy, 49*, 535.

McKenzie, E. (1994). *Privatopia: Homeowner association and the rise of the residential private government*. New Haven & London: Yale University Press.

Merill, T. W., & Smith, H. E. (2001). Optimal standardization in the law of property: The numerus clausus principle. *Yale Law Journal, 110*, 1.

Miller, S. (2013). Community land trusts: Why now is the time to integrate this housing activists' tool into local government affordable housing policies. *Zoning and Planning Law Report, 36*(9), 1.

Morriss, A. P., Brandys, R., & Barron, M. M. (2014). Involuntary cotenants: Eminent domain and energy and communications infrastructure growth. *LSU Journal of Energy Law & Resources, 3*, 29.

Paasch, J. M., et al. (2016). Building a modern cadastre: Legal issues in describing real property in 3D. *Geodetski Vestnik, 60*, 256.

Parisi, F. (2002). Entropy in property. *American Journal of Comparative Law, 50*, 595.

Rabenhorst, C. S., & Ignatova, S. I. (2009). *Condominium housing and mortgage lending in emerging markets—Constraints and opportunities*. Urban Institute Center on International Development and Governance. Retrieved from www.urban.org/publications/411921.html

Restatement (Third) of Property (Servitudes). (2000). *American Law Institute*.

Righetti, T. (2016). The private pore space: Condemnation got subsurface ways of necessity. *Wyoming Law Review, 16*, 77.

Rule, T. A. (2011). Airspace in a green economy. *UCLA Law Review, 59*, 270.

Schill, M. H., Voicu, I., & Miller, J. (2007). The condominium versus cooperative puzzle: An empirical analysis of housing in New York City. *The Journal of Legal Studies, 36*, 277.
Sheehan, D. (2017). *The principles of personal property law*. Oxford: Hart Publishing.
Sherry, C. (2017). *Strata title property rights: Private governance of multi-owned properties*. London and New York: Routledge.
Smith, H. E. (2015). The persistence of system in property law. *University of Pennsylvania Law Review, 163*, 2055.
Stöcker, O. (2012). The Eurohypothec. In B. Akkermans, A. F. Salomons, & J. H. M. van Erp (Eds.), *The future of European property law* (pp. 65–77). Munich: Sellier.
Stoter, J., et al. (2017). Registration of multi-level property rights in 3D in The Netherlands: Two cases and next steps in further implementation. *International Journal of Geo-Information, 6*, 158.
Urban Institute. (2019). *Home mortgage disclosure act data*. Retrieved from https://www.urban.org/policy-centers/housing-finance-policy-center/projects/home-mortgage-disclosure-act-data
Van der Merwe, C. G. (2015). Introduction and content. In C. G. van der Merwe (Ed.), *European condominium law* (pp. 1–24). Cambridge: Cambridge University Press.
Van Erp, S., & Akkermans, B. (2012). *Cases, materials and text on property law*. Oxford & Portland, OR: Hart Publishing.
Vučić, N., et al. (2017). Overview of the Croatian land administration system and the possibilities for its upgrade to 3D by existing data. *International Journal of Geo-Information, 6*, 223.
Wainwright, O. (2019, February 5). Super-tall, super-skinny, super-expensive: The 'pencil towers' of New York's Super Rich. The Guardian.
Wilkerson, G. (2015). Rigging rights of passage: Analyzing subsurface easements in horizontal drilling. *Mississippi Law Journal Supra, 84*, 135.
World Economic Forum. (2020). *Fourth industrial revolution*. Retrieved from https://www.weforum.org/focus/fourth-industrial-revolution
Yu, C., et al. (2017). LADM-based modeling of the unified registration of immovable property in China. *Land Use Policy, 64*, 292.

Legislation

California Civil Code (as amended, 2014). West's Annotated California Civil Code, § 4125.

Cases

Pinnacle Museum Tower Association v. Pinnacle Market Development, 145 Cal.Rptr.3d 514 (2012).
United States v. Causby, 328 U.S. 256 (1946).
Villa De Las Palmas Homeowners Association v. Terifaj, 90 P.3d 1223 (Cal. 2004).

Social Innovation as a Disruptor of Tenure: Recognising Land Rights of Slum Dwellers in Odisha, India

Rebecca Leshinsky, Serene Ho, and Pranab Choudhury

Abstract Ownership of much land globally is formally unrecorded. Advances in geospatial and drone technologies are enabling unmapped land to be recorded in ways which do not reflect traditional surveys, and introduce new ways of achieving cadastral data for the purposes of registration. Disruption is challenging established land law, and creating novel opportunities for individual land certification—rattling indefeasibility and tenure. The chapter looks to Odisha, India, as a case study, to raise systemic problems around urbanization and affordable housing, and how social innovation has been a lever for aligning slum owners with land ownership. We explore an understanding of the nature of social innovation, and how it has spurred legal innovation for land rights in Odisha. Given the global proliferation of urban informal settlements, understanding catalysts for disruption into land law/lore offers learnings for comparative jurisdictions as they address their own complex challenges in the formalization of settlements, thus contributing to global progress in achieving the Sustainable Development Goal of 'leaving no one behind'.

Keywords Slum living · Disruptive land rights · Social and legal innovation India

R. Leshinsky (✉) · S. Ho
RMIT University, VIC, Melbourne, Australia
e-mail: rebecca.leshinsky@rmit.edu.au

P. Choudhury
NRMC Center for Land Governance, Bhubaneswar, Odisha, India

A. Lehavi, R. Levine-Schnur (eds.), *Disruptive Technology, Legal Innovation, and the Future of Real Estate*, https://doi.org/10.1007/978-3-030-52387-9_5

1 Introduction

Land rights and the provision of tenure security has long been underpinned by a neoliberal approach to policy and implementation. In the land sector, this agenda was notably given form in De Soto's (2000) writings on the significance of private property rights in well-functioning national economies, but it has largely been perpetuated by western governments and the neoliberal policies of global non-state actors like international aid and lending organisations. Of these, the influence of the World Bank on developing countries has been singular: it has been a proponent of privatisation, liberalisation, deregulation and market-led growth. Most significantly, the Bank saw investment in land tenure privatisation to produce secure, indefeasible titles as a key platform for both generating lending markets and stimulating global growth (Independent Evaluation Group, 2016). It is now the largest financier of public investment in land administration projects including land policies, land titling, land registration and the establishment of relevant information systems (Muñoz & Bourguignon, 2015).

Achieving tenure security for all is now acknowledged as critical to sustainable development (Sustainable Development Goal 1.4.2). In reality, both markets and states have failed to deliver land tenure security in many countries. Experts estimate that less than 50% of countries (and only 13% in Africa) have mapped or registered private land in capital cities, and less than 30% of countries maintain digital land data for effective urban decision-making (Deininger, 2018).

As technologies have rapidly advanced and become more accessible, technological innovation has become a focal point of enabling change since formalisation of tenure relies on traditional surveying methodologies. These methodologies are now recognised as too expensive, elitist and exclusive (by being completely reliant on professional expertise, of which there is limited capacity in developing countries) and hence, unrealistic as the path for achieving sustainable development (Enemark, Bell, Lemmen, & McLaren, 2014). A 'third-generation' of land tools are now emerging to make the technical aspects of titling and registration cheaper, easier and more responsible (Bennett et al., 2017). These include, for example, point cadastres, digital pens, unmanned aerial systems and machine learning for boundary recognition (Koeva et al., 2017; Stöcker et al., 2019; Zevenbergen, De Vries, & Bennett, 2015).

There is no question that these technological innovations are sorely needed. But no matter how good, they are only part of the solution since tenure—essentially the relationship between people and land—relies on a legal doctrine that legitimises exclusion, thereby creating winners and losers (Boone, 2019). With *haves* and *have nots*, land administration chronically rates amongst the most corrupt of public institutions (Transparency International, 2013). There are of course many other contributing factors, including poorly capacitated local governments (Asean Studies Centre and Centre for Liveable Cities, 2010) and weak compliance and enforcement institutions and processes (Hutter, 1997; Leshinsky, 2012; Leshinsky & Schatz, 2018). Altogether, this leads to dissonance between public expectations and government performance, creating immense risk for current and future urban populations especially women and other vulnerable groups.

The role of social innovation to achieve tenure security has been growing in importance. For many state and non-state actors, social innovation is seen as a way to tackle those seemingly intractable social problems that defy the traditional logics of both market and state administration models (Murray, Caulier-Grice, & Mulgan, 2010). This turn towards social innovation in land administration can be inferred from international initiatives, such as the joint International Federation of Surveyors and World Bank's advocacy for 'Fit-for-Purpose' (FFP) approach to land administration, which strives for building and sustaining land administration systems that respond to particular national culture, contexts and capacities over 'blindly complying with top-end technological solutions and rigid regulations for accuracy' (Enemark et al., 2014, p. 5). Each jurisdiction is therefore encouraged to adopt its own way of 'allocating' and 'recording' land interests. However, taken from the lens of a more formal land tenure system such as the Torrens title system found in Australia and New Zealand, these approaches may appear (comparatively) to be an affront to established tenure models and thereby challenge indefeasibility of title.

To better understand how social innovation drives disruptive change to produce more secure and just outcomes in land administration, we present a case study from Odisha, India, where social innovation has produced a new form of land rights and tenure security. The *Odisha Land Rights to Slum Dwellers Act* of 2017 ('the Odisha Act') strives for slum dwellers to be allocated special land rights to former slum land and offers great hope for the future eradication of slums. Underpinning this, is a constellation of new collaborations enrolling the state, philanthropic organisations, the private sector, civil society organisations, and communities themselves, to participate in the initiative, striving for more equitable land use and access opportunities.

This chapter begins by raising social innovation as a change agent. Then, we present the case study focusing on three key elements of social innovation and their potential impact on tenure: (1) the novel legislation, (2) the new types of relationships that formed, and (3) the potential for nurturing social and cultural capital amongst informal settlement communities to participate in change. We critically introduce how the 2017 Odisha Act is being implemented, and end on an understanding that more research is required in this field of enquiry, as it is still early in the implementation process.

2 Background

Many development challenges today are complex and intersectional, requiring responses that are cross-disciplinary and often cross-jurisdictional. Land and its sustainable planning, use and development, is one such challenge. Innovation in this space has been difficult and has been mostly led by a market-driven approach, including from the World Bank, where formal titling (or land regularisation) is underpinned by a drive for economic emancipation (i.e. pro-poor) and legal empowerment (i.e. pro-rights) (Boone, 2019).

However, the success of such an approach has been questioned with strong evidence that such reforms do not always deliver intended outcomes (Independent Evaluation Group, 2016). Putzel, Kelly, Cerutti, and Artati (2015) further argue that the formalisation-as-development approach, which is often implemented as top-down structural adjustment of land administration systems based on prevailing standards of 'best practice', often result in negative externalities that worsen outcomes, often for those very marginalised groups these reforms aim to assist.

This recognition of the limits of markets, especially in the production of goods and services that are public goods or have public value, has stimulated the rise of the concept of social innovation as a non-market based concept that promotes inclusion and participation (Moulaert & Ailenei, 2005). It has driven the desire to adopt a different type of analysis that not only takes into consideration the types of practices and relationships involved, but in response to the limitations of an economic paradigm, incorporates theories of empowerment to provide new insights into what just and sustainable economies could look like (MacCallum, Moulaert, Haddock, & Vicari, 2016). This has seen social innovation become mainstreamed in public policies, providing a value framework for governments and non-profit programs, but has tended to be more prolific in practices in western and post-industrialist countries like Europe, the United States, Canada, Australia, the United Kingdom and New Zealand.

Social innovation is less about the traditional technology-focused notion of 'innovation' and more about the 'social', i.e. leveraging and building on the social and cultural capital of communities instead. Inherent in such a broad conceptualisation is the difficulty in reaching agreement as to what is social innovation (Pol & Ville, 2009). Therefore, while myriad definitions of social innovation exist (and multiple instances of literature reviews on this topic), these nonetheless tend to have several things in common (e.g. Bason, 2010; Bureau of European Policy Advisors, 2010; Goldenburg, Kamoji, Orton, & Williamson, 2009; Howaldt, Kaletka, & Schröder, 2016; MacCallum et al., 2016; Murray et al., 2010):

- **objective/output of the innovation is socially oriented**, a new idea, model, service or product targeting specific social needs and problems that remain poorly addressed by existing institutions or practices, or are entirely unaddressed by existing markets;
- **consequence of the innovation as new social relations,** creation of new types of collaborations between primarily citizens and non-state actors (i.e. bottom-up) that cultivate greater agency and participation; and
- **outcome of the innovation,** the creation of social or public value, and maybe a public good, which contributes to social and/or societal transformation.

The European Commission categorises social innovations into three types, broadly determined by the level at which they manifest, which reflects the types of issues addressed, outcomes produced, and actors involved (Bureau of European Policy Advisors, 2011, p. 10):

- Grassroots level: social innovations that respond to pressing social demands not addressed by the market and are directed towards specific groups;
- Societal level: social innovations that respond to societal challenges where the boundary between 'social' and 'economic' blurs, and activities are aimed at broader society; and
- Systems level: social innovations that target fundamental changes (e.g. in attitudes and values, strategies and policies, organisational structures and processes, delivery systems and services) and are commonly initiated by institutions. These types of innovations play a part in reshaping society to become more participative.

While the ideology of social innovation (i.e. inclusion, democracy, participation, novelty, etc.) appeals to many, Nicholls and Murdock (2012) argue that such innovation is not value neutral and is, in fact, almost always socially (and politically) constructed. Critics of the concept of social innovation argue that, despite the use of the term 'social' and a discourse framed around empowerment, policy positions around social innovation appear to be ultimately predicated on neoliberal ideals (Montgomery, 2016; Moulaert, MacCallum, & Hillier, 2013), especially reflected in references to the relationship between the state, new markets and citizens, competition, and emphasis on public sector efficiencies (e.g. see Bureau of European Policy Advisors, 2011; Mulgan, 2006; Murray et al., 2010). It therefore becomes important to discern what *social and political values* infuse the concept of social innovation. Montgomery (2016) observes that where a neoliberal ideology on social innovation dominates versus a more democratic one, this can result in the 'creative destruction' instead of 'creative transformation' of social relations, which directly impacts how marginalised groups participate and therefore what types of social outcomes can be achieved and diffused (p. 1992).

Of importance to this chapter is the application of social innovation in territorial development, and the setting of boundaries, which has mainly been written and researched about in the context of Europe, where it has focused on local and regional territorial development (Moulaert et al., 2007). In this chapter, we centre this consideration on new, and disruptive, law and policy, from the state of Odisha, India, which strives for slum eradication.

3 Case Study

3.1 Informal Settlements ('Slums') in India

In Odisha, which has a population of 42 million people (eleventh highest in the country), 17% of households qualify as slum households. The fact that more than 10% of scheduled castes and scheduled tribal households live in slums also make slums an inclusion concern in terms of social categories along with economic poverty (Chopra, 2017). The policies and schemes being implemented by the

Government have focused more on people living in identified slum areas and less on slum-like households living outside slum areas.

3.1.1 Policy Approaches to Address Tenure Security of Slum Dwellers in Odisha

Since the 1980s, Odisha had been trying to address slum challenges through varied policy measures ranging from rehabilitation, integrated development, and slum free missions—all with a component to provide land tenure. In the capital, Bhubaneswar, three clusters of government rehabilitation sites were identified in the 1980s, where slum dwellers were resettled. Households living in these sites were given plot sizes of approximately 600 sq.ft (about 183 sq.m) along with some financial assistance (e.g. loan or grant) and a 90-year lease agreement.

The Jawaharlal Nehru National Urban Renewal Mission (JNNURM), the Basic Services for Urban Poor (BSUP) initiative, was launched in December 2005. Its sub-mission, together with the Integrated Housing and Slum Development Programme (IHSDP), consists of a scheme for provision of basic amenities and services to the urban poor including security of tenure in Bhubaneswar. An additional 355 dwelling units planned for the town of Puri, a coastal town 70 km from Bhubaneswar on the Bay of Bengal (see Fig. 1). By 2012, 31% of dwellings were completed in Bhubaneswar, with individual houses under the BSUP scheme, on single plots with 90-year lease agreements.

The program, 'Rajiv Awas Yojana' (RAY), or 'Slum-free India' (running from 2011 to 2023), was administered by the state Ministry for Housing and Urban Affairs, and was targeted at slum dwellers and the urban poor. It envisaged a 'Slum-free India' through encouraging States and Union Territories (UTs) in India, to tackle the problem of slums in a definitive manner. Central Assistance under RAY was predicated on the condition that States/UTs would assign legal title to slum dwellers/urban poor over their dwelling space through suitable legislation for property rights as a first step in the State's Slum Free Plan of Action (Government of India, 2011). In contrast to BSUP, under which nearly 40% of slum households were relocated, RAY prescribed a 10% limit on slum relocation and focused more on in-situ development.

As part of a new policy framework, the State government also introduced the Slum Rehabilitation and Development Policy (SRDP), "Housing for all", and the Odisha Property Rights to Slum Dwellers and Prevention of New Slums Bill (GOO, 2011; GOO, 2012). Under this bill, every landless person living in a slum area in any urban area as, on a date, was entitled to a dwelling space at an affordable cost provided they held an Economically Weakened Section Certificate. This 'title' document was to be in the name of the female head of the household or in the joint name of the male head of the household and his wife. The housing provision was both for in-situ redevelopment and ex-situ rehabilitation as per tenability of the site following applicable planning and building regulations. This policy was approved by the state cabinet on 25 September 2012 with objective to benefit 25% of the

Fig. 1 Map of Odisha, showing locations of the capital city of Bhubaneswar and the coastal city of Puri

urban population (1.75 million). According to the then Secretary of Housing and Urban Development, Odisha would be the second state in the country after Jammu and Kashmir to introduce and implement such legislation (India Times, 2019).

3.2 *Odisha Land Rights to Slum Dwellers Act 2017*

On 16 October 2017, the government of Odisha approved the enactment of two ordinances with a view to assign land rights to eligible slum dwellers for redevelopment, rehabilitation and up-gradation of slums. The *Odisha Land Rights to Slum Dwellers Act 2017* (the Odisha Act) assured land rights to the urban poor households to smaller urban local bodies (in municipalities and Notified Area Councils) while the slum dwellers in bigger Urban Local Bodies (ULBs, i.e. municipal corporations) would be granted property rights under the *Odisha Municipal Corporation (amendment) Act 2017*.

These statutes are important as they extend to urban areas in the whole of the state of Odisha covering all the 116 ULBs in Odisha and seeks to grant land rights to slum dwellers in 200,000 slum households. The broader objective of the law was disruptive, as it would turn titled slums into liveable habitats, enabling them access to better sanitation and credit, better healthcare, education and housing services. Some may argue that the new law was drafted and passed hastily, and this has been to date challenging for implementation strategies which rely on multi-stakeholder platforms and use of technological advances to scale rapid success. However, with innovative processes, including drone mapping of slum plots, there has been a successful grant of land rights to more than 50,000 households.

The new law was consciously designed to be simpler and smaller: the Act is in fact nine pages, whereas the bill was 19 pages. The focus of the Act has been on conferring land rights (versus dwelling space) as far as practicable in-situ[1] and on an as-is, where-is basis in a time bound manner using geospatial technology. This is implemented through specifically constituted institutions at ULB and slum levels supported by multi-stakeholders at different levels.

3.3 *New Relationships*

The implementation of the Odisha Act adopted a multi-stakeholder effort which reflected a strong collaborative approach (Memon & Pandey, 2018). The array of stakeholders and their roles are depicted in Table 1. The state government's department of housing and urban development, in partnership with Tata Trusts, led the implementation process. While Tata Trusts have been the implementing partner coordinating the project across stakeholders and facilitating at the ground, different partners have been responsible for activities within the realm of their expertise. Technical partners such as, the Spatial Planning and Analysis Research Centre, Transerve and Surbana Jurong, have been involved in deploying drone surveys to map land and create slum settlement and household boundaries. The technology companies received strategic direction and guidance from Omidyar Network, which had previously recommended, funded and assisted drone mapping as an effective tool in the Philippines.

Local government stakeholders facilitated the convening of community members and added method and protocol to the process. They also facilitated access to physical maps from revenue departments for determination of land eligibility. Importantly, the Act advocated for the community as the most critical stakeholder and all partners worked in tandem to uphold that tenet. Community awareness, buy-in and participation were the focus for all through the process (Memon & Pandey, 2018).

NGOs were engaged through DUDA, conducted digital household (Urban Slum Household Area Survey) and spatial survey, assisted revenue authorities and ULB with measurement of land, formed Slum Dwellers' Association and assisted them with preparation of slum dwellers rehabilitation and resettlement plans and assisted

[1] In-situ settlement is allowed for a household to the extent of 45 sq.m (484 sq.ft) within a Municipality and 60 sq.m (646 sq.ft) within a Notified Area Council (NAC), while in case of relocation, 30 sq.m (323 sq.ft) for both Municipality and NAC.

Table 1 Stakeholders and activities around Land Rights to Slum Dwellers (adapted from Bridgespan, 2018)

Stakeholders	Identify partners and slums	Mobilize community and conduct drone survey	Collect information through HH survey	Create draft proposal map for slum	Apply for land rights	Validate and approve settlement
HUDA	Identify and partner with TA Onboard and train TA, NGO, ULB	Constitute UASRCC in each ULB	USHA survey questionnaire and household sticker			
DUDA	Identify NGO					Approve settlement and issue Land Rights Certificate
District Administration	Conduct inception meeting	Provide permission for Drone Survey				
Urban Local Bodies/ UASRRC	Identify and list slums					Validate HH list and publish eligible list, invite objection, settle dispute, prepare final HH list
Revenue Department and Cell				Provide cadastral map and RoR, identify areas and change land classification		Update RoR

(continued)

Table 1 (continued)

Stakeholders	Identify partners and slums	Mobilize community and conduct drone survey	Collect information through HH survey	Create draft proposal map for slum	Apply for land rights	Validate and approve settlement
Technical Assistance (GIS Firms)		Identify slum boundary, conduct drone survey, create ortho image		Integrate ortho image, cadastral map and RoR, Area statement and map tracing, incorporate update and create draft proposal map		Update Land information system
NGO		Identify key influencer, Form SDA	Sticker household and conduct USHA survey, digitize response, mark HH and public areas on ortho map, collect document proofs			
Slum Dwellers' Association					Validation and consensus building on proposal and apply for settlement of LR	

Learning	Fast tracking can affect consensus building, level playing field and bid completeness, need of Communication and its uniformity, Capacity building require more strategic and continuous approach, more so for ULB, training of trainers need more investment	Clarity on community mobilization, limited to brief duration in the beginning, uniformity of message, role of ULB, permission for drone survey, tight timeline; limited role of NGO; quality of drone maps	Questionnaire design and accommodating common exceptions, manual-digital collection issues, preparing community before survey, capacity of NGO around digital survey and marking boundaries/polygons on orthomap	Accurate geo-referencing of cadastral maps critical for small parcels, limited availability of trained surveyors, lack of updating of land classification in old cadastral maps, capacity of revenue staff to change land classification and area, involvement of urban planner	Focused capacity building of SDA	Capacity of scrutiny committee, addressing disputes, and exceptions, limited role of SDA and NGOs, RoR updating

ULB in the issue of LRC within a period of six months. The payment was as per number of slum households at the rate of about less than 2 USD. 24 local (NGO) partners were engaged by the DUDA, either from the district or outside. It is important to note that the NGO marked the households and public areas in the slum on the map during the USHA survey, and returned it to the technical agency as an input to calculate the area to be settled for each household and plan the layout for the slum for settlement. Whilst NGOs have been known more for their role around social mobilization and institution building, here they were used as service providers around household and spatial survey.

The area for the Land Rights certificate was calculated by a geospatial technology firm based on the polygons drawn by NGOs over ortho-corrected images of the drone survey, usually looking at the roof area of households, during USHA survey.

The scope of work of technical partnerships included description on mapping of slum households and generation of outputs (in form of standard soft and hard versions) through use of high-resolution aerial image acquired by small UAVs. The base maps generated had to be represented through GIS, linked to the household enumeration data as well as overlaid with the official ROR information of land type and ownership, as well as overlaid with the maps of non-household areas of the slums. There was also a requirement to set up a fully functional Land Information System (LIS) to capture the data and visualization being generated for each slum. Out of ten agencies approached to submit a bid in 10 days, five submitted, with one submitting only for LIS. Input provided by the agencies and the results of the test bed demonstrations were evaluated by the same consortium of input givers who had helped create the RFP. The state, constituting of 30 districts was divided among the three technical agencies, with SPARC responsible for 14 districts, Transerve for 11 districts and Surbana Jurong for the remaining five districts. The agencies were expected to cover 46 ULBs covering about ~100,000 households in a span of six months. The drone survey took about 15 min per slum. Pre and post work on the survey added up to an hour of work for every slum. The draft proposal map created on a 1:500 scale, while cadastral maps of the state have been in 1:4000 scale.

4 Discussion

In this section, we critically consider the case study in the context of the impact of social innovation as an alternative to traditional approaches to land rights.

4.1 Social Innovation in Terms of Novel Legislation

For the state of Odisha to pass law to grant rights to slum dwellers was a significant disruption to the social, political and economic order of Odisha, and to India itself. Although it is early days for implementation, the allocation of certificate of land rights to hundreds of thousands of households, as quickly as possible, has been a significant challenge (Memon & Pandey, 2018).

The Land Rights Certificate (LRC) issued under the Odisha Act were a new legal instrument, conferring limited land tenure rights. This new tool lacked precedence, and connection to existing land rights regime in the state, as compared to the older (traditional) Record of Rights. Unlike other such land rights granted/recognized under other laws including the *Odisha Land Reforms Act* of 1960, the *Odisha Government Land Settlement Act* of 1962 or the *Forest Rights Act* of 2005, there is no provision in the current Act or Rules to integrate this right into the Record of Rights. The new LRCs lacked any reference map and a sub-divided unique parcel number. Hence, there are incomplete land records which have been created.

It should be noted that land tenure security is not a basic pre-requisite for access to public services and entitlement for a slum dweller. Pursuant to the Odisha Act, a land rights certificate will be issued jointly for married couples and will be acceptable as a valid address proof. Listing of slums and households are equally important, even on untenable or government lands. Listing of persons residing in under serviced settlements qualifies them to obtain identity cards and basic urban services as per the Orissa Municipal Corporation Act 2003, irrespective of their land tenure status and ownership. Slum listing has been argued as an "organic practice" which opens up channels of negotiation with power (Raman, 2015; Richter & Georgiadou, 2016). Formal recognition as a "slum" is regarded as the ticket for poor communities to negotiate not only access to basic services and other state resources, but also their presence in the city (Arabindoo, 2011). Whether it is for assigning property rights to the urban poor or for listing of slums, negotiations around urban citizenship are governed by external factors including, urban environment, urban environmental practices and politics as observed by Hagn (2016) in Puri, Odisha.

A drone survey was conducted in 2017 with geo-referencing to calculate land area, but was not used to generate the map. Unlike the Record of Rights, the area in the LRC is given in square feet and is signed by the District Collector as the authorized officer under the Act and Rules. While a copy of such certificate is shared with the Revenue Department, it is not clear if the Digital Land Registry (textual and spatial) is updated. The adds a further layer of uncertainty for the new land rights system.

Additionally, many households commonly use areas adjacent to their house (with roof) for cooking, bathing and other works regularly without having a permanent roof. These areas have been mostly excluded from their individual rights and have been added to public spaces. Shapes of smaller houses, not always confirming to straight lines, add error and biases to measurements. Poorer households with smaller houses as well temporary roofs also lose out on area limit. While such technology and legal limitations (including that of date) challenges inclusion, the requirement of voluntary surrender of occupied land more than the permissible limit and relocation of households for public amenities or to avoid disaster risk, often warranting contestations and conflict.

4.2 Social Innovation in Terms of New Relationships

Allocating land rights to eligible households is a complex process. It involves identifying eligible slums and slum boundaries, mapping land, checking the tenability of land for granting individual rights, validating demographic details, addressing conflicts and finally granting titles. Further, the Act by design, elevates the voice of the community by stipulating the formation of slum dweller associations (SDAs) in each slum. This comprises of community members who actively participate in the process and compile the final list of eligible slum households. The state government has recognized that executing such a task will require support from external stakeholders and use of modern technology ie. drones, though they were not reflected in the Act and Rules.

The Omidyar Network champions mapping technologies, specifically drones, as the most cost-effective surveying solution to scale the delivery and believe that their support leads to capturing detailed, accurate, high-resolution images for mapping in less than a week, compared to the months and resources expended on mapping boundaries through manual surveys. While use of drones has definitely aroused curiosity and community involvement in the slum mapping process, there are challenges in terms of appreciation of technology and underlying interpretation process in absence of targeted and deliberate communication through appropriate channels. The impact of drone use on mapping and inclusion of stakeholders requires further research and policy considerations for land rights, as does the integration of drone image in the Record of Rights. There may also be other simpler and community participatory technology options, which have been attempted elsewhere, under similar contexts, which could be considered, but to date, have not been raised in the mapping of the land for LRCs in the Odisha slums.

4.3 Social Innovation as Nurturing Social and Cultural Capital in Communities

Not all people in slums lack land tenure security. In Bhubaneswar, the largest municipal corporation in Odisha, where the implementation of the Act is yet to start, 116 of 436 recognized slums are on lands with some form of tenurial rights (Anand & Deb, 2017). The accepted slum definition, based on which census and estimates are made, does not take tenure into consideration. Targeting scales based on these numbers, can be unrealistic while putting overwhelming pressure on implementers. Moreover, addressing complexities and disputes of past and present tenure can be often tedious, requiring more capacity and consensus.

Under the Odisha Act, land can only be used for residential purposes. However, about 17% of slum houses are used for non-residential purposes as per 2011 Census. A "landless person" means a person who is a citizen of India and does not own either in his own name or in the name of any member of his family any house or land, or land rights granted or inherited under this Act, in the urban area as per this Act. In absence of updated land record, which continue to clog India's civil courts with disputes and haunt India's flagship DILRMP, it is very difficult to conclusively identify a landless person. Even thought the Act has the provision of cancellation of LTC in case of false information, it may be difficult to do so. Similar requirement of evidence in terms of government documents, may deny inclusion for the poor who may lack them due to different reasons.

A significant factor for the new approach, has been a strong and continued leadership by the Secretary of HUDD with a complete buy-in and unflinching support by the state political leadership. This has been promoted as an important project for the Chief Minister with the highlighting of its achievement and impacts through his presence, branding and numerous awards that it has received so far. This has also raised the expectations from the project in terms of impacts and numbers, often channelizing expediency and urgency through a top-bottom flow, affecting time and efforts required to ensure process, consolidate learnings and address disputes. While a clear command and supportive power structure has enabled quicker decisions, timely adaptations resulting in impacts at speed and scale it has also weakened sporadic innovations, local participations and at times inclusion, largely owing to tenure complexities and limited local capacities.

Memon and Pandey (2018) note further, that such a collaborative approach has brought together unique strengths and, the implementation has been able to embody best practices from some of the most sophisticated land titling programmes globally. There are also challenges, and the authors report that learnings from the ground have reasserted the importance of three critical mechanisms. First, strong accountability frameworks. The legislation is unique in its determination to stick to a time frame. Accountability lies at the core of such commitments and establishing these frameworks that outline accountability and chain of command will ensure that issues can be resolved efficiently. Accountability frameworks also incorporate decision-making roles and empower stakeholders to effectively deal with crises.

Second, a critical need to invest upfront on alignment and on creating tighter management protocols. Given the novelty of the programme, there is no existing template to ensure success. However, clarity in laying out roles, management structures, and creating standard operating processes in parallel will not only ensure a smoother process but also serve as a credible public good to other states or programmes with similar aspirations. We have been witness to many successful multi-stakeholder programmes and absorbing the best practices that emerge here can help in creating a stronger guide. Third, a mechanism to course correct and define change management protocols along the way. There is a need to both capture and utilize learnings that will arise from this exercise to further fine-tune the implementation process. By defining in-process measurement metrics, capturing progress, distilling learnings and adopting a strong feedback loop, the Act will be able to create a template that other states can learn from.

Land administration processes are costly to establish, and enforce, and the creation of a new system is a significant step which many jurisdictions cannot afford. The fit-for-purpose approach offers opportunity for quicker mapping via drone and other GPS technology. The data collected must still be post-processed and validated with communities, and there continues to be a high margin for real error.

The rationale here is not too dissimilar to enforcement of law. Implementation, compliance and enforcement of existing laws is in itself highly challenging. Many local governments openly admit that they simply do not have the resources to police illegal municipal breaches and they only enforce the rules against the "worst offenders", who often come to their attention through reporting of neighbour behaviours (Hutter, 1997; Leshinsky, 2012; Leshinsky & Schatz, 2018). New processes, especially those which seek to create or consolidate existing land rights, can be difficult for all stakeholders to accept.

It is at this point where social innovation can play a vital role in normalising new forms of tenure. Social innovation has a place to play, in the context of the fit-for-purpose approach to educate all stakeholders of the benefits for new approaches such as the granting of land rights to slum dwellers.

Whilst established and effective land administration systems are not likely to change, important for new adopters, is the support and encouragement for those in need of change, and assistance to reach this objective is necessary. Such change in those jurisdictions wanting to empower their citizens must come at the level of the public sector and may involve institutional and organisational reforms, including legal framework, processes and procedures, and awareness in terms of incentives and accountability. FIG/World Bank note that to drive this change process there must be effective knowledge-sharing to ensure the lessons learnt and good practices are widely implemented.

5 Conclusion: Can Social Innovation Facilitate Greater Equity for Land Tenure?

Granting land rights not in the fashion undertaken by more formal and established tenure systems is disruptive, yet, also empowering. This is particularly important to patch inequalities. The pathway to land rights, which provide security of tenure, requires a system based on accountability, transparency, ethics but also strong compliance and enforcement, which is costly. For many jurisdictions, however, these criteria ask too much where citizens struggle with daily life.

The Odisha government can potentially stimulate a revolution to not only better the lives of one million slum dwellers. Further, they have the ability to set an example for other governments, both in India and in elsewhere, who believe that access to land and access to dignity are not that far apart.

In Odisha, change is truly underway stemming from social and political will to change the lives of slum dwellers, who have been marginalized groups for decades.

Social innovation can act as a facilitator for more equitable law for slum dwellers. To understand the real impact of its operation, this must be observed long term, as it offers lessons for law making which can disrupt tenure. The Odisha slum law was enacted in 2017, and whilst there has been innovation in its implementation, with new technologies, and community participation processes, it is still early to measure effectiveness. With more research, and analysis, Odisha is set to be an important case study for social innovation as a catalyst for more equitable land rights.

References

Anand, G., & Deb, A. (2017). *Planning, 'violations', and urban inclusion: A study of Bhubaneswar*. New Delhi: YUVA and IIHS.

Arabindoo, P. (2011). Rhetoric of the 'slum'. *City, 15*(6), 636–646.

Asean Studies Centre and Centre for Liveable Cities. (2010). *Urbanisation in Southeast Asian Countries*. Retrieved from https://www.iseas.edu.sg/images/centres/asc/pdf/UrbanSEAsia-prelimasof13Jul10.pdf

Bason, C. (2010). *Leading public sector innovation: Co-creating for a better society*. Briston: The Policy Press.

Bennett, R., Gerke, M., Crompvoets, J., Ho, S., Schwering, A., Chipofya, M., … Stöcker, C. (2017). *Building third generation land tools: Its4land, smart sketchmaps, UAVs, automatic feature extraction, and the geocloud*. Annual World Bank Conference on Land and Poverty. Retrieved from https://www.conftool.com/landandpoverty2017/index.php/11-07-Bennett-288_paper.pdf

Boone, C. (2019). Legal empowerment of the poor through property rights reform: Tensions and trade-offs of land registration and titling in sub-Saharan Africa. *The Journal of Development Studies, 55*(3), 384–400. https://doi.org/10.1080/00220388.2018.1451633

Bridgespan. (2018). *Odisha: Land Rights to Slum Dwellers: Observations on detailed work flow process maps*. Jaga Mission, Housing & Urban Development Department, Government of Odisha. Retrieved from http://www.jagamission.org/pdf/Compendium%20Land%20Rights.pdf

Bureau of European Policy Advisors. (2010). *Empowering people, driving change: Social innovation in the European Union*. Retrieved from http://ec.europa.eu/DocsRoom/documents/13402/attachments/1/translations/en/renditions/native

Bureau of European Policy Advisors. (2011). Empowering people, driving change: Social innovaiton in the European Union. https://doi.org/10.2796/13155

Chopra, H. S. (2017). Estimating "Slum-like Households" in India, SARVEKSHANA, Journal of National Sample Survey Office, Government of India, Ministry of Statistics and Programme Implementation National Sample Survey Office, New Delhi, www.mospi.gov.in, Vol. 103, pp. 1–12. Retrieved from http://mospi.nic.in/sites/default/files/publication_reports/sarvekshana_103.pdf

De Soto, H. (2000). *The mystery of capital: Why capitalism triumphs in the west and fails everywhere else*. New York, NY: Basic Books.

Deininger, K. (2018). *For billions without formal land rights, the tech revolution offers new grounds for hope | Let's Talk Development*. Retrieved August 9, 2018, from World Bank Blog website: http://blogs.worldbank.org/developmenttalk/billions-without-formal-land-rights-tech-revolution-offers-new-grounds-hope

Enemark, S., Bell, K. C., Lemmen, C., & McLaren, R. (2014). *Fit-for-purpose land administration*. Retrieved from https://doi.org/https://www.fig.net/resources/publications/figpub/pub60/Figpub60.pdf

Goldenburg, M., Kamoji, W., Orton, L. and Williamson, M. (2009). Social Innovation in Canada: An Update. CPRN Research Report (Sept 2009). Canadian Policy Research Networks Inc. Retrieved from: http://citeseerx.ist.psu.edu/viewdoc/download?doi=10.1.1.567.5844&rep=rep1&type=pdf.

Government of India. (2011). Draft: Guidelines for Preparation of a Slum Free City Plan of Action Under the Rajiv Awas Yojana. New Delhi: Ministry of Housing & Urban Poverty Alleviation, Government of India. Retrieved October 9, 2013 (http://mhupa.gov.in/ray/planning_guidelines.pdf).

Government of Odisha. (2012). *The Odisha property rights to slum dwellers and prevention of new slums bill, 2012*. Retrieved January 25, 2020, from http://www.urbanodisha.gov.in/(S(mmsysc45j1g52d55er0ffn45))/pdf/ODISHA_PROPERTY_RIGHTS_TO_SLUM_DWELLERS_BILL_2012

Government of Odisha, Housing & Urban Development Department. (2011). *Slum rehabilitation & development policy*. Government of Odisha.

Hagn, A. (2016). Of slums and politics in Puri, Odisha: The localisation of the slum-free cities mission in the temple city. *South Asia Multidisciplinary Academic Journal* [Online], 14 | 2016, Online since, connection on 24 January 2020. Retrieved from http://journals.openedition.org/samaj/4226; https://doi.org/10.4000/samaj.4226

Harris, H. (2010). "Discretion and Expediency in the Enforcement of Planning Controls" 81 Town Planning Review 675.

Howaldt, J., Kaletka, C., & Schröder, A. (2016). Social entrepreneurs: Important actors within an ecosystem of social innovation. *European Public & Social Innovation Review, 1*(2), 95–110.

Hutter, B. M. (1997). *Compliance: Regulation and environment*. Oxford: Clarendon Press.

Independent Evaluation Group. (2016). Lessons from Land Administration Projects: A Review of Project Performance Assessments. Washington DC: The World Bank Group. Retrieved from: https://ieg.worldbankgroup.org/evaluations/lessons-land-administration-projects-review-project-performance-assessments.

India Times. (2019). Retrieved January 23, 2020, from https://economictimes.indiatimes.com/news/politics-and-nation/slum-dwellers-to-get-property-rights-in-poll-bound-odisha/articleshow/16557594.cms?from=mdr

Koeva, M., Bennett, R., Gerke, M., Crommelinck, S., Stöcker, C., Crompvoets, J., & Kundert, K. (2017). Towards innovative geospatial tools for fit-for-purpose land rights mapping. *International Archives of the Photogrammetry, Remote Sensing and Spatial Information Sciences—ISPRS Archives, 42*(2W7). Retrieved from https://doi.org/10.5194/isprs-archives-XLII-2-W7-37-2017

Leshinsky, R. (2012). Use of planning agreements to support sustainability and environmental preservation: A case study from Victoria, Australia. *International Journal of Law in the Built Environment, 42*, 157.

Leshinsky, R., & Schatz, L. (2018). "I don't think my landlord will find out:" Airbnb and the challenges of enforcement. *Urban Policy and Research, 36*(4), 417–428. https://doi.org/10.1080/08111146.2018.1429260

MacCallum, D., Moulaert, F., Haddock, J. H., & Vicari, S. (2016). Introduction. In D. MacCallum, F. Moulaert, J. H. Haddock, & S. Vicari (Eds.), *Social innovation and territorial development*. Oxon and New York: Routledge.

Memon, N., & Pandey, S. (2018). *What the Odisha Land Rights Act can teach us*. Live Mint. Retrieved February 8, 2019, from https://www.livemint.com/Opinion/ztenupgTJBSxIhrtElzYeL/Opinion%2D%2DWhat-the-Odisha-Land-Rights-Act-can-teach-us.html

Montgomery, T. (2016). Are social innovation paradigms incommensurable? *Voluntas: International Journal of Voluntary and Nonprofit Organizations, 27*(4), 1979–2000. https://doi.org/10.1007/s11266-016-9688-1

Moulaert, F., & Ailenei, O. (2005). Social economy, third sector and solidarity relations: A conceptual synthesis from history to present. *Urban Studies, 42*(11), 2037–2053. https://doi.org/10.1080/00420980500279794

Moulaert, F., Martinelli, F., Gonzalez, S., & Swyngedouw, E. (2007). Introduction: Social innovation and governance in European cities. Urban development between path-dependency and radical innovation. *European Urban and Regional Studies 14*(3), 195–209.

Moulaert, F., MacCallum, D., & Hillier, J. (2013). Social innovation: Intuition, precept, concept, theory and practice. In F. Moulaert, D. MacCallum, A. Mehmood, & A. Hamdouch (Eds.), *The international handbook on social innovation: Collective action, social learning and transdisciplinary research* (pp. 13–24). Cheltenham: Edward Elgar.

Mulgan, G. (2006). The process of social innovation. *Innovations: Technology, Governance, Globalization, 1*(2), 145–162. https://doi.org/10.1162/itgg.2006.1.2.145

Muñoz, J. A., & Bourguignon, C. (2015, March 23–27). Fifty years of World Bank engagement on land tenure issues. In *Annual World Bank Conference on Land and Poverty*. Washington, DC: The World Bank.

Murray, R., Caulier-Grice, J., & Mulgan, G. (2010). *The open book of social innovaiotn*. Retrieved from https://www.nesta.org.uk/sites/default/files/the_open_book_of_social_innovation.pdf

Nicholls, A., & Murdock, A. (2012). The nature of social innovation. In A. Nicholls & A. Murdock (Eds.), *Social innovation: Blurring boundaries to reconfigure markets* (pp. 1–30). Basingstoke and New York: Palgrave Macmillan.

Pol, E., & Ville, S. (2009). Social innovation: Buzz word or enduring term? *The Journal of Socio-Economics, 38*(6), 878–885. https://doi.org/10.1016/j.socec.2009.02.011

Putzel, L., Kelly, A. B., Cerutti, P. O., & Artati, Y. (2015). Formalization as development in land and natural resource policy. *Society & Natural Resources, 28*(5), 453–472. https://doi.org/10.1080/08941920.2015.1014608

Raman, Bhuvaneswari. 2015. The Politics of Property in Land: New Planning Instruments, Law and Popular Groups in Delhi. *Journal of South Asian Development 10*(3), 369–395. https://doi.org/10.1177/0973174115610186.

Richter, C., & Georgiadou, Y. (2016) Practices of legibility making in Indian cities: Property Mapping through Geographic Information Systems and slum listing in government schemes. *Information Technology for Development, 22*(1), 75–93.

Stöcker, C., Ho, S., Nkerabigwi, P., Schmidt, C., Koeva, M., Bennett, R., & Zevenbergen, J. (2019). Unmanned aerial system imagery, land data and user needs: A socio-technical assessment in Rwanda. *Remote Sensing, 11*(9), 1035. https://doi.org/10.3390/rs11091035

Transparency International. (2013). *Global Corruption Barometer 2013*. Retrieved from https://www.transparency.org/gcb2013/report

UN-Habitat. (2006). *Enabling shelter strategies: Review of experience from two decades of implementation*. Nairobi: UN-HABITAT.

Zevenbergen, J., De Vries, W., & Bennett, R. (Eds.). (2015). *Advances in responsible land administration*. CRC Press.

Web Sites

Retrieved from https://medium.com/@Un_Common_Law/odisha-land-rights-to-slum-dwellers-act-a-brief-analysis-28e8e83dce41

Retrieved from https://www.livemint.com/Opinion/ztenupgTJBSxIhrtElzYeL/Opinion%2D%2DWhat-the-Odisha-Land-Rights-Act-can-teach-us.html

Part IV
Land Registration and Blockchain

Blockchain-Based Land Registers: A Law-and-Economics Perspective

Georg von Wangenheim

Abstract Both land registration and blockchains pursue the production of immutable information. Land registration is hence among the most often suggested use cases of the blockchain technology. However, only a very small number of successful large-scale applications exist in the wild. This chapter aims at explaining why this number is so low despite blockchain's *prima facie* suitability for land registration. After laying technical and legal foundations, we argue that trading shares of real estate investment funds on a blockchain has little to do with land registration. This allows us to concentrate on the benefits that the blockchain technology may provide for land registration in a proper sense. We show that "anchoring" land registers in public blockchains by regularly writing hash values of their content in one or several of those blockchains can overcome lack of trust in the immutability of digitized land registers without affecting the latter's rules and organization. In contrast, implementing the entire land registration system on a blockchain and change rules and governance accordingly may result in high efficiency and effectiveness. This may be a big leap forward for many jurisdictions. In jurisdictions with already well-functioning land registration systems, the gain from a transition to the blockchain technology tends to be small for both deeds recordation and title registration systems, in fact often too small to justify the costs of transition. The major reason is that many inevitable links between real-estate reality to its blockchain representation require human decisions to balance the diverging interests of affected parties.

Keywords Blockchain · Land registration · Real estate investment · International comparison · Cost-benefit analysis

---

G. von Wangenheim (✉)
Faculty of Economics, University of Kassel, Kassel, Germany
e-mail: g.wangenheim@uni-kassel.de

A. Lehavi, R. Levine-Schnur (eds.), *Disruptive Technology, Legal Innovation, and the Future of Real Estate*, https://doi.org/10.1007/978-3-030-52387-9_6

1 Introduction

Despite the hype about blockchain technology in late 2017 and early 2018, successful use cases for the technology are still rare. Land registration and, more general, exchange of real property is one of the few cases, for which a small number of, at least seemingly, successful examples exist and for which many advocates of the technology expect more successful examples to arise. They believe that blockchains and the underlying distributed ledger technology will be able to substantially accelerate and facilitate the procedure of transferring property in real estate, reduce fixed costs of these procedures and thus open real estate for divided and small scale investments and crowd funding, obsolesce notaries for transferring real property and at the same time increase the reliability of land registration.

In fact, several administrations like those of Sweden and Georgia have endeavored to implement land registration or parts of the underlying procedure on a blockchain (Benbunan-Fich & Castellanos, 2018; Kaczorowska, 2019). Some US American counties (Teton County, Wyoming, and South Burlington, Vermont) are collaborating with Blockchain firms to move their deeds registers to blockchain applications (Hamilton, 2019). Attempts of other jurisdictions, like e.g. Honduras, have failed (Benbunan-Fich & Castellanos, 2018)–probably not the least due to the threat of secure registration that was unwelcomed by land-grabbing politicians. In countries where land registration is feeble and developing slowly, private organizations have been and still are striving for a blockchain-based registration system to complement and, eventually, substitute the official government system (e.g. Kenya's *Land Layby Listing*, see LandLayBy, 2018) and development aid organizations like the German *GIZ* suggest to rely on the blockchain technology to implement workable land registration systems.

However, none of the attempts to bring land registers to a blockchain has been completed yet. Many proposals to establish blockchain-based land registration appear to neglect many of the intricacies of land registration. This chapter aims at clarifying why moving land registration to a blockchain is so difficult or not worthwhile at all. At the same time, the chapter also attempts to look at the problem from a positive angle by asking how blockchains and the underlying distributed ledger technology can improve land registration.

To answer these questions, I will clearly distinguish between four different modes of connecting real estate to a blockchain: blockchain-based real estate funds, anchoring digitized land registers in blockchains, digitizing deeds registers in a blockchain including the Swedish case of pre-registration of deeds, and, finally, tokenization of rights in real estate. Only the latter two are moving land registration to a distributed ledger *sensu stricto* and can be applied only to deeds registration systems and, respectively, title registration systems. Hence these two approaches deserve more detailed discussion than the former two. Before diving into this discussion, I will provide some technological background of the blockchain and distributed ledger technology, the understanding of which is prerequisite for a sound discussion of land registers on a blockchain. Similarly, I will briefly recall some features and distinctions of land registration law.

Other authors like Arruñada (2018), Kaczorowska (2019) or—most pessimistic—Barbieri and Gassen (2017) have also discussed the prospects of using the blockchain technology to improve land registration. What this chapter adds to the literature is that it carefully distinguishes modes of combining blockchain and land registration and at the same time considers the variations of land registration in many dimensions.

2 Technical Background

Assessing the merits of various approaches to connect land registration to blockchains requires some central elements of the underlying technology. This is not the place to review blockchain and distributed ledger technology in general (see Biais, Bisière, Bouvard, & Casamatta, 2019; Chen, Cong, & Xiao, 2019; Zheng, Xie, Dai, Chen, & Wang, 2018 for concise overviews). I will rather concentrate on the elements of the technology that are indispensable for discussing the pros and cons of registering land on blockchains. As the Bitcoin blockchain is prototypical for all blockchains on distributed ledgers and relatively simple to understand, I will use this blockchain to introduce the technology.

In the Bitcoin system we must distinguish two chains. One is the chain of blocks of information, which produces immutability, and the other is the chain of transactions, which secures correctness of ownership of bitcoins or shares thereof (*Satoshis*). Blocks of information are chained to each other by the hash value of the previous block. As the hash value is like a fingerprint and extremely hard to reproduce by an alternative block of information, it is impossible to alter any information in a past block of a blockchain without altering all subsequent blocks as well. To make such a reproduction of an alternative chain difficult, Satoshi Nakamoto, the unknown inventor of Bitcoin, stipulated requirements for the validity of a block which can only be fulfilled if the worldwide computing power used to work (honestly) on the Bitcoin blockchain is busy for about 10 min (Nakamoto, 2008). Inventing an alternative chain then requires at least half of this hashing power—whence the label "51-percent attack"—or chances to catch up with the ongoing calculations of new blocks in the correct chain are extremely low. Garay, Kiayias, & Leonardos (2015) suggest that other types of attacks also require a majority of the computing power used for mining in the relevant blockchain.

All (full) nodes of the system—during the last 2 years about ten thousand—store this chain of blocks of information and compare their information to the chain of others. As storing and working on the production of valid new blocks is only valuable if one stores the same chain that most others accept, every owner of a node (a "miner") aims at working with the version of the chain that he expects others to work with. On first sight, this seems to be what economists call a beauty contest (first introduced by John M. Keynes, 1936, p. 156). However, there is a strong empirical signal of what chain other miners will work with if there are more than one branches: the longer a branch, the harder it is to change ex post and thus the better it is to work with this branch. As a consequence, if the blockchain forks (which it does from time to time), very quickly the miners re-coordinate on one of the branches, namely the one that grew longer the fastest. This "consensus mechanism" is called "proof of work" because a branch grows faster if more work (i.e. hardware and energy to run it) is invested in it. The consensus mechanism has been strong enough to forestall any ex-post mutations of the Bitcoin blockchain since its start some 11 years ago.

The chain of transactions secures a proof of ownership of Bitcoins and Satoshis, where the word "ownership" is loosely used and not in a strict legal sense.[1] This chain allows to trace back the transfers of the currency from owner to previous owner to the original producer of the Bitcoins—again a miner. In that respect, the Bitcoin blockchain resembles the very idea of land registers, the more so, if they record deeds rather than register titles.

This combination of (1) a chain of information blocks, (2) a distributed ledger with a self-enforcing consensus mechanism, and (3) a chain of ownership transfers implies a number of desirable properties of the Bitcoin blockchain. These properties induce many to seek solutions to numerous problems, in particular to problems of land registration, in the blockchain technology.

Foremost among these properties is immutability. To change the information that is stored in a block which is older than an hour or so, one would need command of more than half of the total worldwide computing power to calculate hash values or a tremendous amount of luck. As this computing power does not only have to be under one's command but also needs to be fueled by an amount of electricity which is similar to half of the average consumption of Denmark, attacking the Bitcoin blockchain is extremely expensive–which usually turns working for the security of the Bitcoin blockchain far more profitable in expectation than working against it. Hence only very few have attempted to alter information in the Bitcoin blockchain, and no one has ever succeeded during the 11 years that the Bitcoin blockchain exists when this book will be printed.

One should be aware though, that this security of the Bitcoin Blockchain is a consequence of its underlying characteristics. A successful attack is so costly because it requires command of a large proportion of the worldwide computing power—and the corresponding electricity. If the Bitcoin blockchain consumed less computing power—and less electricity—an attack would be far cheaper. Thus, immutability results from Bitcoin's proof-of-work consensus mechanism only because Bitcoin collects a large proportion of the worldwide computing power to calculate hash values and consumes a lot of energy. The number of immutable blockchains based on proof of work hence cannot be large, at most three or four in the world.[2]

A second property of the Bitcoin Blockchain, that makes it so attractive, is its resilience. As the information is stored by about ten thousand nodes all over the

[1] In some jurisdictions Bitcoins as virtual commodities cannot be owned as property nor can they be object of any other legal right.

[2] With five competing blockchains, the smallest one would use less than 20% of the computing power. Redirecting computing power from other blockchains would make a 51-percent attack relatively easy.

world, even a worldwide power outage cannot destroy the immutable ledger. As soon as power is back, the nodes will restart to use, exchange and compare the information and only unaltered chains will become generally accepted.

The third property of the chain is its accessibility for both reading and writing new information to it. The latter, writing accessibility, requires a fee large enough to induce miners to include the new information in the block they are working on. As storage space and the number of transactions that the Bitcoin blockchain can perform is scarce, nobody claims that entire land registration systems could be brought to the Bitcoin blockchain.

Proponents of other blockchains do not simply replicate the Bitcoin blockchain. They rather claim to improve on the technology by altering some of Bitcoin's features. Obviously, that may affect the properties that make Bitcoin so immutable, resilient and accessible. To distinguish between different blockchains, one should look at the following characteristics carefully.

Blockchains may be public ("permissionless") or private ("permissioned"). One should note that a blockchain run by a single firm or a single government body—or consortia thereof—is by definition a private blockchain.

Proof of work as the mechanism making an instance of a chain reliable, may be replaced by other "consensus mechanisms", provided these mechanisms are as hard to circumvent as proof of work. Proof of stake has often been discussed as a candidate because ownership of a chain's currency or other values enshrined in the chain are stakes that will deter any fiddling around with the reliability of the chain. However, proof of stake has not yet been implemented in any large public blockchain until today.

What many people seem to accept as an alternative to proof of work is proof of authority, where endorsement of the chain by one or several authorities secures immutability. These authorities may be powerful firms, like IBM's blockchain based on hyperledger, or a trustworthy government. Proof of authority obviously becomes more reliable if more than one institution runs a blockchain and their consensus (or majority) is required for including the next block into the blockchain. The more these institutions distrust each other, the less likely they collude and thus the safer a consortium-run blockchain becomes. Of course, proof of authority contradicts the idea of a permissionless blockchain and excludes unrestricted access at least to writing to the blockchain.

Scalability is a feature of blockchains that Bitcoin is lacking. However, when talking about land registration on a blockchain, then scalability is of utmost importance.

Finally, blockchains (other than Bitcoin) need not be restricted to storing static information but may also be able to execute programs. While these programs are misleadingly called "smart contracts" (the name "chaincode" used by hyperledger fabric seems to be more appropriate), they are most relevant for registering rights in land, because they allow for conditional transfer of rights which are inevitably executed once the conditions are met.

With this basic understanding of the most relevant properties of the Bitcoin blockchain and of other blockchains, it makes sense to take a brief look at the vast variation of land registration systems we observe in the world before we turn to alternative approaches to bring land registration to a blockchain.

3 Legal Background of Land Registration

The idea of land registration is obvious and simple. Transfer of property as a right *in rem* requires some sort of evidence for the public because *in-rem* rights are valid against all persons (see Baird & Jackson, 1984). Two sources of evidence are traditional to produce publicity of the transfer of property: possession and chain of title (e.g. Arruñada, 2003). While possession and transfer thereof is sufficient information for most movables, possession in land is much harder to observe and to uphold. Hence, land registration either in the form of recordation of deeds of transfer or as registration of titles in land replaces possession for the transfer of ownership (and other rights) on land in most jurisdictions. Land registration in both its variants is similar to blockchains inasmuch as both are append-only ledgers. Land registration therefore suggests itself as a use case for blockchains and corresponding projects are abundant.

However, such projects and suggestions have to survive in, and adapt to, specific legal environments. Few legal concepts aiming at one common objective, though, differ so much in their details across jurisdictions as does land registration. At least a dozen dimensions in which such differences prevail should be considered relevant (see for example Zevenbergen, 2002, pp. 47–82, for an overview on many of these dimensions). Not all are completely independent of each other, but none of them determines the specification of another without any degree of freedom.

First and foremost is of course the distinction between deeds recordation and title registration. While countries like France and most counties in the US record deeds and rely on a long enough chain of recorded deeds for proof of ownership, countries like Germany and Australia register titles and allow ownership to be proven by reference to the title registered. Other countries rely on a combination of both systems (e.g. Sweden) or are in the course of a transition from deeds recordation to title registration (e.g. England and Wales as well as Israel have completed the transition for the vast majority of their territory). Closely related to this dimension is the distinction between what interests in land are registered. On the one hand, England and Wales register all rights including temporary transfer to tenants. On the other hand, most counties in the US only register transfer of property and contractual mortgages while other interests like easements or usufructs in the same real estate may be registered elsewhere or not at all (see Spielman, 2016, pp. 17–19, for an interesting report of the typical procedure), which is the main reason for the existence of the industry of title searchers and title insurance. Most jurisdictions lack registration of administrative-law interests.

Further dimensions are

- the power of the information the register contains: this information may provide conclusive evidence, it may be indefeasible, it may produce good faith or it may be merely informative;
- whether the register provides only positive or also negative evidence: in the former case, the aforementioned power of the information refers to what is actually registered, i.e. anyone can rely on the information included in the register being correct; in the latter case, it also refers to what is not registered, i.e. anyone can rely on the information included in the register being also complete;
- the legal quality of entries into the register: they may be constitutive for the transfer of rights or only declaratory;
- the accessibility of the register: it may be open to anyone, to anyone who is willing to pay a fee (typically per real estate on which he or she seeks information), to anyone who claims or can prove a legitimate interest in the information, or only to notaries;
- the degree of digitization: the register may be based on paper, may be a mere digitization of a paper version, may be a publicly accessible databank, or it may be a platform on which outsiders (like sellers or buyers of real estate, possibly only if represented by a notary or so) can directly alter the content of the databank;
- whether the land register contains a cadaster or refers to a cadaster or is independent of any cadaster;
- the existence of priority notices (warning notes, caution remark, *caveats*, *Vormerkung*), which guarantee that a certain future transfer of rights legally precedes all transfers of rights which are performed after such a notice;
- the role of notaries;
- the reliability of the list of pending registration applications, if such a list exists;
- the share of the land of a jurisdiction that is covered by the register: in particular in countries like England and Wales that have introduced the register only in the recent past (which includes some one hundred years in the case of England and Wales) not all land is already registered.

Given this wide range of possible legal differentiation, writing about, or even doing business in, bringing real estate to the blockchain requires careful consideration of the exact project and how it fares in specific legal environments. While such considerations have to remain far from complete in a mere book chapter, the first two subsections of the next section aim at drawing the reader's attention to the most severe inaccuracies that one should avoid in a discussion of real estate on the blockchain.

4 Different Ways of Moving Land Registers to a Blockchain

Based on the technical and legal background of land registration on blockchains, we study the four different approaches very briefly alluded to in the introduction. We start with a closer look at real estate investment funds or trusts. As this approach does not change land registration but only alters the market for shares of these funds or trusts, the idea will only be briefly discussed. The second approach we look at is what we observe in Georgia, where a digital title register has been newly implemented and connected ("anchored") to blockchains to "borrow" the latter's immutability. This approach may constitute a disruptive change of land registration in jurisdictions currently lacking trust in the immutability of its registers. However, using a blockchain in this way does not interfere with the essence of land registration. Consequential legal questions remain minor.

This is different for a complete transfer of land registration to a distributed ledger. As legal consequences of such "blockchainization" of land registration depend crucially on the type of land registration, this chapter first considers how systems of deeds recordation could be implemented on a blockchain. We can again refer to a prominent example, this time from Sweden. However, the example seems to be less of a success than the Georgian one. Finally, the chapter turns to systems of title registration which imply far more legal problems which seem to require interference with the very idea of a blockchain, its immutability. The difference between the systems becomes most important, if it goes along with the registration being constitutive for the transfer of rights and not only declaratory.

4.1 Reals Estate Funds

Real estate funds organized on a blockchain are by far the most prominent example of business endeavors bringing together real estate and the blockchain technology. From a legal perspective, however, such ideas have hardly anything to do with moving land registration to the blockchain. If they would, severe incentive problems would quickly trim down any profits of the fund and eventually destroy it.

Advertisements of such firms, most often start-ups with little real business, claim that property of real estate can be tokenized in their blockchain application and then splitting property into small shares and trading them is claimed to become as easy as using a smart phone for transferring money. Imagine this were actually so and whoever had a token representing property in a real estate were co-owner of it. Then any decision on the property would require some form of consent of all owners. Unless otherwise agreed upon, unanimity of all co-owners would be required in many jurisdictions, at least when decisions concern transfer of property of the real estate. This would result in severe anti-commons problems as each and every co-owner would be tempted to extract as much as possible from any profitable decisions requiring his consent. If decisions only required majority votes, administering the real estate would still be far too inflexible. Or owners would have to transfer major decision rights to a manager, which would diametrically contradict the very idea of ownership. It is thus no surprise that tokenization of real estate hardly ever takes this legal route.

What the proponents of the approach actually think of, is tokens representing indirect ownership, i.e. ownership of shares of a fund or a company which then in turn is the *sole* owner of the real estate. It is only these shares of a fund or a company that are traded on a blockchain, not ownership of real estate. While this solves the problems associated with multiple ownership in resources, the idea has nothing to do with land registration on a blockchain. Only company or fund shares are traded on the blockchain. Doing so may of course be advantageous on the one hand and raise intricate corporate law questions on the other, but these questions are far beyond the scope of this chapter on blockchain base land registers.

4.2 Digitizing Registers and Anchoring Them in Blockchains

A second approach to linking the blockchain technology and land registration which has actually been applied in the real world is anchoring an existing or newly created digitized land register to an existing blockchain. The idea of the approach is simple: The state of the register (or parts thereof) are fixed and stored from time to time. Hash values of the states are saved in one or several blockchains which are generally accepted as being immutable—like for example the Bitcoin Blockchain or the Ethereum blockchain. As a consequence, anybody who can compare the hash of the state of the register with the hash value stored in the blockchain easily detects every ex post alteration of the content of the register. By anchoring the register to one or several blockchains in this way, the register "borrows" the immutability of blockchains to prove its own reliability.

The most prominent example for this approach is Georgia, where the government collaborated with Bitfury, originally a Bitcoin mining company but later a general blockchain technology firm, to anchor an already digitized, but until then notoriously unreliably title register in the Bitcoin blockchain (for a detailed overview see Shang & Price, 2018).

This approach combines the obvious advantages of digitization on a central register with the immutability of blockchains. The advantages of digitization on a central register are manyfold. On the legal side, the approach does not restrict the details of the land registration system in any way. Legislators need not alter a well-functioning system of land registration in any way or may import or newly design whatever they think to be an ideal system of land registration.

Digital land registers are much more easily accessible than paper-based registers for collecting information on transfers or the state of rights for systems of deeds and, respectively, title registration. Accessibility can easily be restricted or opened up to any desired degree. For example in Germany, no one has access to the information contained in the land register, unless he or she has a legitimate interest, while countries like Austria or Israel grants access to anybody willing to pay the fee. If such access is restricted to information on parcels of land—as is the case in Austria–the fee becomes prohibitive for searching what real estate an individual person owns—a restriction that may be imperative for data protection rights.

Central ledgers allow for far more efficient storage of data while at the same time back-up files can easily be stored with the central authority. In particular for title registration systems, old data on transfer of rights may be deleted without loss of conclusiveness of the information contained in the register.

The approach hinges, of course, on how resistant the blockchains to which one anchors the land register is against attacks and for how long this can be guaranteed. For the time being, only blockchains based on proof of work or proof of authority seem to be sufficiently immutable. Proof of stake has been proffered frequently as an alternative, but no big blockchain is based on this consensus mechanism to date. The reason seems to be that only proof of work is self-enforcing. For any other consensus mechanism large amounts of computing power may be abused to forge the criteria on which the allocation of mining rights is based. Proof of work guarantees at least, that large amounts of computing power can only be used according to the idea of the consensus mechanism. Hence, attacks against the immutability of a blockchain require more than half of the worldwide computing power used for the respective blockchain.

Obviously, this is a severe obstacle for potential attackers only if this computing power covers a large proportion of the overall worldwide computing power. Hence only those three or four proof-of-work blockchains which accumulate the largest share of the worldwide hashing power are relevant candidates for anchoring. In fact, Georgia has chosen Bitcoin as anchor.

Blockchains based on proof of authority derive their trustworthiness and immutability from the promises of the providers that they will keep the blockchain unaltered and that they will control each other. If the individual providers are themselves sufficiently trustworthy and the entire group of providers is sufficiently averse to collude with each other, proof of authority constitutes a valid alternative to proof-of-work blockchains. Capturing a sufficiently large proportion of the nodes to alter the content of the blockchain ex post becomes equally difficult as accumulating more than half of the hashing power of the largest proof-of-work blockchains.

Chromia, the blockchain on which the Swedish approach to connect real-estate property transfers to a blockchain (for details see below) is based, aims at taking this route at least in the long run (ChromaWay, 2019).[3] To further add to the immutability of their blockchain, they reinforce the power of proof of authority by anchoring several such blockchains to each other and combine proof of authority with anchoring their blockchains to the Bitcoin and the Ethereum blockchains.

4.3 Deeds Recordation in Blockchains

Instead of anchoring an existing or newly developed electronic land register to one or several blockchains one may consider implementing the entire land registration on a blockchain in order to fully benefit from the advantages and potentials of the

[3] Outside the area of land registration, proof of authority underlies several major blockchain projects, such as the academic blockchain-based repository "bloxberg" or facebook's "libra" currency.

blockchain technology. In this section we consider the most relevant legal questions and problems that entail for such blockchain-based deeds recordation systems. Title registration systems will follow in the subsequent section.

First and foremost the blockchain underlying the register has to be carefully selected. Public blockchains such as the Bitcoin blockchain may currently look very stable, but for land registration life expectancy of the selected blockchain must be extremely long. Time horizons that appear close to eternal in computer science are far too short when it comes to the durability of land registration. As a consequence, public blockchains that appear and evolve on a voluntary basis of private individuals exhibit too large a chance of being replaced by an even better alternative. To avoid expensive migrations of a blockchain-based land register from one blockchain to another and to avoid phases of unsecure registration when an "old" blockchain is at the edge of being abandoned by most of its users, government-backed private blockchains appear to be the superior choice.

As mentioned earlier, such blockchains tend to use proof of authority as consensus mechanism. However, if there is only one authority running the land registration blockchain, there is little reason to rely on the blockchain technology at all. Either authority is trustworthy enough to make everyone believe in the authorities' restraint from any temptation to change the content of the blockchain retrospectively and thus to believe in the immutability of the register. But then this trustworthiness will not be increased by using the blockchain technology and it will in itself be sufficient to create a high degree of trust in land registration. Using a blockchain in this case is superfluous.

Or the authority is not trustworthy enough to implement a land registration system. But then it is also not trustworthy enough to guarantee the immutability of the blockchain underlying the land registration system. If this is the case, building the blockchain on proof of authority of the members of a larger consortium of authorities is likely to solve the problem. As mentioned earlier, such a consortium of authorities may provide a sufficient degree of trustworthiness if each of the authorities are sufficiently trustworthy and if they mutually mistrust each other. Such consortia for setting up blockchains across several local, regional or even national authorities are likely to be beneficial in other fields than land registration as well.

Whatever the choice of blockchains is, a deeds recordation system requires linking the chain of deeds inside the blockchain to the chain preceding it. As any other electronic register, blockchains may render title searching unnecessary, or a very simple task, if at least registration numbers of deeds are searchable. Obviously, this can only apply to deeds registered in the blockchain system. As they eventually have to refer to the previously existing chain, the latter becomes irrelevant only after a very long time. One could of course consider registering ownership and other rights in land whenever such rights are transferred for the first time by making use of the blockchain-based register. Any person claiming rights in that property would then have to produce a chain of title only lasting to this initial legal status—which would be an easy endeavor given appropriate search functions of the blockchain-based register. However, such a registration of rights would be tantamount to changing the entire system to a title registration system. We abstract from this possibility in this section and refer to the discussion of title registration in the next subsection. Without such a substantial change in the nature of the land registration system benefits from using the blockchain technology for digitizing the deeds records are small and become relevant only after a large number of years or decades.

Further questions, which are not really specific to blockchain-based deeds records but have to be decided for every change of the land registration system, are the interests to be covered by the register, whether the register will have negative or only positive publicity, and—closely related—whether registration is compulsory. In particular if many interests are to be registered, if publicity of the register is both positive and negative, and if registration is compulsory, technicalities of the underlying blockchain become relevant again.

All in all, benefits from implementing a deeds recordation system on a blockchain seem to be too small in countries with a well-functioning system (Arruñada, 2018). Jurisdictions newly introducing land registration cannot and need not refer to pre-blockchain chains of registered deeds. To make the new land registration system reliable, titles thus have to be registered. We will come back to this solution in the next section.

Before, we take a closer look at the example of Sweden with its well-developed land registration system. In the public land-registration-and-blockchain discussion, this country provides an oft-cited example for a realistic and actually to be realized use case of the distributed ledger technology for the purpose of improving public administration. We use this example to show that in countries with a well-developed land registration system, the benefits from blockchaining parts of the registration system are too small to make the transition worthwhile.

In fact, Sweden, like many other countries, has a hybrid land registration system based on declaratory but compulsory registration of deeds that works smoothly. The only problem that many complained about is the delay of several days, weeks or even months between the signing of the deed and its actual registration. As registration is not constitutive for the transfer of property (or other rights), the true legal situation and the legal situation expressed in the register fall apart during the time between signing of the deed and its registration. Since registration is compulsory only within 3 months of signing the deed and the process of registration takes additional time—historically up to 4 months, currently about a week according to the registration authority's homepage (Lantmäteriet, 2020)—and lack of registration fails to interfere with the effectiveness of a land transfer, property is often unregistered when consecutive transfers of the same real estate follow each other within a short time span.

The Swedish authority for land registration—Lantmäteriet—together with ChromaWay, a blockchain startup aiming at developing blockchain technology for public administration, and Kairos Future, a consultancy, have explored how blockchain-based technologies may overcome these problems (Snäll et al., 2018). The consortium saw the solution in electronic deeds to be completed in an app on smartphones and automatically registered in a private blockchain set up by the Swedish land registration authority (to be complemented by other authorities) and anchored in the Bitcoin and Ethereum blockchains. To secure reliable information about the ownership of the concerned land, the app was designed to draw information directly from the land register and the blockchain containing information on deeds yet to be recorded in the register.

The consortium took first steps successfully up to a completed exemplary transfer of property in real estate in the summer of 2018 (Snäll et al., 2018). Since then, news about the project seem to wither. A major obstacle to further realization of the project allegedly is the lack of a reliable system of electronic identification, which is somewhat surprising as Sweden does have a working e-identification system. From an economic perspective, the problem apparently is more grounded in a sound comparison of costs and benefits. Given the well-functioning Swedish system of (hybrid) deeds recordation and the substantial acceleration of the registration process the benefits of the blockchain registration for deeds before inclusion of the deed in the conventional register seem to be minute. Cases where a registration process requiring only a week lasts too long for smoothly transferring property for the next time are too rare for drawing any relevant economic benefits from prepending the conventional records by a blockchain register (Arruñada, 2018, p. 90).

4.4 Tokenization of Property in Real Estate

The most radical way to move land registration to a blockchain-based system is tokenization of property in real estate. The basic idea parallels title registration and is thus most easily implemented with this form of land registration: All rights in real estate are represented by a so-called token the ownership of which is registered and transferred in the blockchain very much like ownership of Bitcoins. Since the initial owner of a Bitcoin is clearly defined as its miner, i.e. the first miner who produced a valid block at a certain stage of the blockchain, immutable registration of all transfers of a Bitcoin allows everyone to unambiguously identify the current owner. Hence registration of transfers is enough to identify the current owner even without explicit registration of the identity of the owner. In the words of land registration, one could say that deeds recordation and title registration are thus equivalent inside the Bitcoin blockchain.

For tokens representing rights in real estate this is not true, because the identification of the initial owner of the token is not implied by the setup of blockchain. On the contrary, the initial owner either has to be deduced from the land registration system preceding the blockchain system or someone—typically the land registration authority—has to deliberately enter the information on the identity of the initial owner into the blockchain. The former alternative would transfer the idea of deeds registration into the blockchain-based land register. The latter, however, is much closer to title registration. To make a blockchain-based land registration ledger resemble title registration, the blockchain could also include information on the current owner of the rights in real estate. Different from current title registers, inconsistencies between transfer chains and registered titles would technically be excluded.

In the remainder of this section, we will concentrate on this replication of title registration on the blockchain.

In order to determine whether tokenizing real estate on a blockchain is economically beneficial, we will first discuss what rights in land can economically be tokenized. This will lead us to the question to what degree the blockchain technology does, or fails to, render land registration authorities redundant. After answering this question to the negative, we will study whether the unavoidable role of land registration authorities implies restrictions to the immutability of the land registration blockchain. The answers to these questions will help us to identify the economic advantages of tokenizing land registration.

The most extensive right in real estate, ownership, and direct derivatives thereof are obvious candidates for tokenization. In fact, mortgages and rights of preemption suggest themselves for tokenization, because they are neither more nor less than a conditional transfer of ownership. As such they can be perfectly represented by smart contracts, i.e. computer code embedded in a blockchain, that transfer ownership on the condition that some event occurs or does not occur. Such conditional transfer of property may be completely automatic or they may require a third party's consent, for example a judge's or an arbitrator's consent. Even the recipient need not be stipulated in person by the smart contract. The latter could also initiate an automated auction of the property, which would closely resemble the current legal situation in, for example, Germany's law on real estates and mortgages.

Rights in real estate that go beyond conditional transfer of the entire property as they exist and are included in land registration in most jurisdictions are harder to replicate in blockchain-based land registers. In principle, covenants, easements and servitudes can be tokenized like ownership. Once defined, transfer of their representing token apparently is a simple way of exchanging such rights. However, their initial definition goes beyond the technical possibilities of a blockchain system. As the amount of variation of such rights is effectively infinite, it is impossible to arrange for all potential covenants, easements and servitudes when designing the blockchain. Humans will be needed to include these rights into the blockchain-based land register long after its setup. We will come back to this problem when we discuss the role of government in a blockchain-based land registration system.

However, once the problem of initial definition of covenants, easements and servitudes is solved, blockchain-based land registration systems can deal with these rights at least as well as any paper-based or electronic register. Just as the existence of such rights is today registered with the information on the encumbered estate, tokenized encumbrances will include reference to the token representing ownership of the real estate. Their existence then becomes obvious to any interested party by an appropriate search in the blockchain. As long as the blockchain-based land register provides both positive and negative publicity, registration of covenants, easements and servitudes in such registers implies perfect definition of property rights in the Coasean sense. Whether free tradability of tokens representing these rights or fixing the tokens to the ownership token of a benefitting estate then maximizes economic efficiency depends on the specificities of the situation. Both are possible and simple in a blockchain-based register (Graglia & Mellon, 2018, develop a similar list of criteria).

Similar arguments extend to lease or rental contracts, which many jurisdictions also include in the set of rights in real estate that can or have to be registered. The stronger tenants are protected in case of transfer of ownership of the real estate the more important becomes reliable information on the existence of lease or rent contracts for an efficient real estate market. Nevertheless, by far not all jurisdictions allow these contracts to be registered. Germany and Austria are prominent examples despite their sophisticated land registration systems and their strong protection of tenants. One reason for the reluctance of these jurisdictions to include lease and rent contracts into land registration is that sophistication of land registration system implies high costs of registration. Since in the end it is the tenants who bear these costs, opening land registration for lease and rent contracts would countervail these countries' objective to protect tenants.

Many of the advocates of bringing land registration to blockchain-based systems claim that administrative costs and the role of government as registration authority could dramatically decline. Whether this is true depends on the blockchain-based land register's ability to function without or with little support by such authorities. We therefore take a closer look to the necessary and desirable roles of government in a blockchain-based land registration system.

In countries where land registration is provided by government authorities, the first aspect where government is indispensable is the legal basis for transferring land registration to a blockchain-based system. Due to its obvious network economies land registration will not turn into a competitive market after moving to a blockchain but will remain a natural monopoly. Hence government will have to decide who runs the blockchain and which blockchain will underlie land registration (Arruñada, 2017a, 2018, pp. 96–97). The most important criteria will be the expectation of long-term existence of the blockchain, its immutability, its scalability and its ability to handle at least a small number of smart contracts.

Long-term existence is an immediate consequence of the time horizon of land registration. Land ownership and registration is probably the legal field with the longest time horizon. The perspective is decades and centuries. This stands in stark contrast to the 11 years that the Bitcoin blockchain—hitherto the most stable and longest existing blockchain—counts since its invention. Since moving a land-registration system from one blockchain to another may be expected to be extremely costly both in terms of administrative burdens and in terms of deteriorating trust in the system, the blockchain to be chosen cannot be based on a proof-of-work consensus mechanism. If it were, immutability would only be guaranteed as long as the blockchain is among the big three or four in the market of blockchains. Smaller blockchains are far too susceptible to 51-percent attacks, which become cheaper the less resources are employed in the mining of the blockchain. Taking market capitalization as a proxy for the resources used to operate the blockchain and thus for the resources needed to run a 51-percent attack, currently only Bitcoin with its 120 billion US$ market capitalization (i.e. 65 percent of the entire market of cryptocurrencies) can be treated as a safe bet. But even Bitcoin is far from immune against better alternatives occurring within the next decades and thus losing its immutability.

To avoid having to switch the land register from one blockchain to another every decade or so, immutability should be supported by another consensus mechanism. At least for the time being, proof of stake has not been implemented successfully and thus proof of authority is without viable alternatives. If authority only stems from the institution operating the blockchain, use of the blockchain technology itself is hard to justify. However, if many institutions form a consortium to operate the blockchain and to control each other in operating it correctly, then their individual trustworthiness will add up and become reinforced by mutual distrust between them. Proof-of-work blockchains may still serve as a safe ground for anchoring proof-of-authority blockchains and thereby further increasing trust in their immutability (see Chromia blockchain as an example).

Beyond operating the blockchain underlying the land register or at least contributing to its operation, and beyond mutually reinforcing trustworthiness, public land registration authorities will have two more indispensable tasks in a blockchain-based land registration system: initiating and guaranteeing the connection between rights in real estate with the tokens representing them and enforcing the law against the blockchain, if necessary (see Arruñada, 2017a, b, for a similar argument).

Establishing and perpetuating the connection between reality and entries in the blockchain is one of the central challenges in most blockchain applications beyond cryptocurrencies. To have ownership in real estate represented by a token in blockchain, a cadastre—be it separate from or included in the land register—is required to define parcels of land that can be owned. With well-defined parcels of land, ownership may be represented by a token if uniqueness of the token is guaranteed. Both the uniqueness and the legally correct identity of the original owner of the token cannot be guaranteed by any programming code structuring a blockchain. What is needed here is the institutional guarantee by the land registration authority.

Once this guarantee exists, transferring the token from one owner to another inside the blockchain and thus transferring ownership in land is simple and may follow the same rules as the transfer of ownership of cryptocurrencies. Conditionality of such transfers can easily be backed by smart contracts and thus mortgages and rights of preemption are relatively simple to implement in a blockchain underlying the land register. No action of authorities is required here unless the parties to a contract so stipulate in their smart contract. The blockchain can take over all tasks that are restricted to control whether the conditions of a transfer of property are met. If the parties define conditions outside the blockchain, they will transform these conditions into actions inside the blockchain. For example, if the mortgage payments are performed outside the blockchain, the parties will define conditions such as "if three out of four clearly named arbitrators sign with their private key inside the blockchain that the debtor failed, then the smart contract triggers an automatic auction of the mortgaged land, the proceeds of which go to the lender".

Other rights in real estate, i.e. rights that cannot be characterized as conditional transfers of ownership, however require actions of the land registration authority as much as ownership itself. Such rights, covenants, easements and servitudes, need to be clearly defined and carefully and exactly added to the database contained in the blockchain. Not only these steps of creating new rights in real estate require human action from the authority's side. Consistency of all encumbrances of any specific parcel of land also has to be guaranteed—a task that cannot be performed by a machine, not even if it possesses artificial intelligence, since controlling for consistency of different encumbrances requires understanding their meaning. Even humans sometimes err here.

These and other possible errors bring us to the last, but not least missions of the registration authority, possibly in collaboration with the courts. Mistakes in registers, be they blockchain-based or not, do occur; the content of the register may deviate from the legal situation. The cause may run the full gamut from simple errors in transposing legal code into computer code via cases of illegal or unjust enrichment or eminent domain to unnoticed legal incapacity to sign a deed. In many of these cases a legal duty of the wrongful owner of a token representing an alleged right *in rem* to transfer the token to the legal owner of the right is insufficient to restitute the law. Transfer of a wrongfully owned token must also be possible without or even against the will of the current owner.[4]

This is not to say that the blockchain has to be corrected retrospectively and thus immutability to be destroyed. What is needed is the power of the registration authority or the courts to induce a transfer of tokens as if they were the owner. The protocol of the blockchain underlying the land register thus has to allows transfers of tokens either by signing the transaction by the private key of the owner or by the signature of the authority or the court. Such alternative signatures are not entirely new. The most relevant blockchains do already allow smart contracts that require *n* out of *m* signatures or even more complex combinations of signatures. This is what is needed here. On the first level, it must be possible to trigger token transfers by either of the two signatures of the owner or the authority or a court. To reduce the risk of abuse of this ability of the authority or the courts and to increase trust in the system the signature of the authority or the courts may again be subject to a so-called multisig requirement, for example allowing to supersede the lack of the owner's signature only by the simultaneous signature of, say, 14 of the 20 authorities forming the consortium to operate the land registration blockchain.

With these conditions—underlying blockchain proof-of-authority as consensus mechanism operated by several authorities; coverage of (almost) all legal rights in real estate; clear definition and guarantee of token-represented property rights by the competent authority; restricted (joint) power of authorities to induce transfer of tokens against the will of the token owner—satisfied, a blockchain-based title register is a legally and technically viable alternative to the existing title registers based on paper or a central database. But is it economically viable too? Proponents of tokenization of land registers proffer acceleration of transactions, increased

[4]The same is true for tokens that are assigned to a blockchain address for which the owner lost his private key. To keep these tokens and the assets the ownership of which they represent tradable, the land registration authority must be able to transfer them to an address that the legal owner controls.

trustworthiness of the land registration system and less red tape as most important economic advantages. While these advantages may be substantial in countries with less developed title registers, in countries with well-functioning title registers low speed, lacking trust and red tape are of only minor relevance, if at all. To admit, completing transactions of real estate may take weeks and months even in Austria, but hardly ever there exists any ambiguity on who has what rights in a parcel of land. And high frequencies of subsequent transactions of rights in real estate are too rare to produce a relevant problem.

Sometimes redundancy of title searches is added as an economic advantage, but this is more a difference between deed recordation and title registration and not so much between blockchain and standard ledger technologies.

In summary, bringing title registers to the blockchain by tokenizing rights in real estate produces economic advantages that justify the transition costs and the risk of failures in setting up a well-functioning system only in countries which so far lack a reliable title register. In countries that already benefit from efficient title registers, blockchain is not a technology that may bring about substantial improvements in real estate.

5 Conclusions

The central and most general insight of this chapter is that one should be very clear about what is meant by calls for moving land registers to a blockchain. Both the existing forms of land registration and the modes of representing them on a blockchain exhibit far too many different variations to measure all of them by the same yardstick. Such care is often lacking in the popular literature stemming from blockchain enthusiasts. The confusion becomes even larger when trading shares of a real estate investment trust on a blockchain is labeled as putting real estate ownership to the blockchain. We clearly separate the two approaches.

We also stress that one should distinguish between the digitizing land registers, anchoring a digitized land register to a blockchain, and implementing land registers on a blockchain. All three have their own virtues and some become relevant only if one combines two of these approaches. Digitizing registers has *per se* nothing to do with blockchains but is of course a prerequisite for anchoring a register to a blockchain. In addition, anchoring the digital register in a blockchain may be a precondition for making digitization worthwhile because it makes the digital register immutable, while pure digitization may even entail an increased risk of posterior mutations of the content of the register. Effective safeguard against ex-post alterations of the register is a relevant argument only in jurisdictions where such alterations are a relevant threat—or where they may become a relevant threat after digitization.

The main thrust of the chapter has been on recordation of deeds in a blockchain and on tokenization of rights in real estate. They are the two approaches to really get land registration on blockchains and thereby extract economic benefits.

The former may substantially facilitate title search in the very long run, but here exactly lies the problem: which blockchain has a long enough life expectancy? If the answer is: private blockchains run by government, then immutability becomes at least debatable and it becomes thus hard to argue why such a private blockchains should have any advantages over any other digitized register run by the same authority. Only if the blockchain is run by a *consortium* of registration authorities, trust in the register will increase by blockchaining the register.

Tokenization of rights in real estate may be a viable alternative to existing paper-based or digitized title registers. That requires proof of authority as the consensus mechanism of the underlying blockchain. In addition, nearly all possible legal rights in real estate should be covered by tokenization. Still, tokenization requires an active role of registration authorities and the court system, and it requires their benevolence, however to a lesser degree than registers without tokenization. Two functions of the registration authorities and the courts are essential. On the one hand, only they can clearly define token-represented property rights and guarantee their enforcement outside the blockchain. On the other hand, immutability of blockchain-based registers necessitates the possibility to transfer tokens without or against the will of the token owner to correct legally false information in the blockchain. Only a carefully selected combination of the registration authorities and the courts, probably of several jurisdictions combined, should be able to perform this task.

Even if all these conditions for making tokenization a viable alternative are met, the use of blockchains in land registration seems to be of very limited merit in jurisdictions with an efficient system. However, there are less efficient systems. And blockchainization of land registers may go beyond the mere transition of an existing system to a blockchain. Once this transition is underway, substantive changes to the system itself may become possible, as was the case in Georgia where a completely ineffective land registration system was at least partly turned into a functioning system under the disguise of blockchainization.

Acknowledgements Thanks for helpful comments go to the participants of the Conference on *Disruptive Technology, Legal Innovation and the Future of Real Estate* at IDC Herzliya and of the Law and Economics Research Seminars at the Universities of Kassel and of Vienna. All remaining errors are mine, of course. This work received support by a generous grant of Metamorphoses GmbH, Baunatal.

References

Arruñada, B. (2003). Property enforcement as organized consent. *Journal of Law, Economics, & Organization, 19*, 401–444.

Arruñada, B. (2017a). Property as sequential exchange: The forgotten limits of private contract. *Journal of Institutional Economics, 13*, 753–783.

Arruñada, B. (2017b). How should we model property? Thinking with my critics. *Journal of Institutional Economics, 13*, 815–827.

Arruñada, B. (2018). Blockchain's struggle to deliver impersonal exchange. *Minnesota Journal of Law Science & Technology, 19*, 55–105.

Baird, D., & Jackson, T. (1984). Information, uncertainty, and the transfer of property. *The Journal of Legal Studies, 13*, 299–320.

Barbieri, M., & Gassen, D. (2017, March 20–24). *Blockchain—Can this new technology really revolutionize the land registry system?* Paper prepared for presentation at the "2017 World Bank Conference on Land and Poverty". Washington DC: The World Bank. Retrieved from https://www.notariato.it/sites/default/files/Land_Poverty_Conference_Blockchain.pdf, last visited April 1st, 2020.

Benbunan-Fich, R., & Castellanos, A. (2018). Digitalization of land records: From paper to blockchain. In *39th International Conference on Information Systems (ICIS 2018) San Francisco, California, USA 13–16 December 2018* (Vol. 2, pp. 1024–1032).

Biais, B., Bisière, C., Bouvard, M., & Casamatta, C. (2019). The blockchain folk theorem. *The Review of Financial Studies, 32*, 1662–1715.

Chen, L., Cong, L., & Xiao, Y. (2019). *A brief introduction to blockchain economics* (August 10, 2019). Available at SSRN: https://ssrn.com/abstract=3442691

ChromaWay. (2019). *Chromia Platform Whitepaper, Version 0.11*. Retrieved from https://chromia.com/whitepaper-english.html, last visited April 1st, 2020.

Garay, J. A., Kiayias, A., & Leonardos, N. (2015). The Bitcoin backbone protocol: Analysis and applications. In E. Oswald & M. Fischlin (Eds.), *Advances in cryptology, EUROCRYPT 2015, Lecture notes in computer science 9057* (pp. 281–310). Berlin: Springer.

Graglia, J. M., & Mellon, C. (2018). Blockchain and property in 2018—At the end of the beginning. *Innovations, 12*, 90–116.

Hamilton, D. (2019, January 11). Blockchain land registry: The new kid on the block. *CoinCentral*. https://coincentral.com/blockchain-land-registry/, last visited April 1st, 2020.

Kaczorowska, M. (2019). Blockchain-based land registration: Possibilities and challenges. *Masaryk University Journal of Law and Technology, 13*, 339–360.

Keynes, J. M. (1936). *The general theory of employment, interest, and money*. London: Macmillan.

LandLayBy. (2018). *Land Layby Listing (LLL) Platform, Harambee Token [Hrbe], White Paper*. Retrieved from https://hrbe.io/images/WHITEPAPER_HRBE06022.pdf, last visited April 1st, 2020.

Lantmäteriet. (2020). *Handläggningstid för inskrivningsärenden*. Retrieved from https://www.lantmateriet.se/en/real-property/change-owner/Handlaggningstid-for-Inskrivningsarenden/, last visited April 1st, 2020.

Nakamoto, S. (2008). Bitcoin. *A peer-to-peer electronic cash system*. Retrieved from https://bitcoin.org/bitcoin.pdf.

Shang, Q., & Price, A. (2018). A blockchain-based land titling project in the Republic of Georgia. *Innovations, 12*, 72–78.

Snäll, M., Suomalainen, D., & Kempe, M. (2018). *Fastighetsköp och lagfart genom en blockkedja—governance och juridik*. Report of Kairos Future and the Swedish land registration authority (Lantmäteriet). Retrieved from https://www.lantmateriet.se/contentassets/8d2b5d7647634c02a329b01e46e61071/publikation-swe-fastighetskop-och-lagfart-genom-en-blockkedja%2D%2Dgovernance-och-juridik-2018.pdf

Spielman, A. (2016). *Blockchain: digitally rebuilding the real estate industry*. MS dissertation Massachusetts Institute of Technology. Retrieved from https://dci.mit.edu/s/spielman_thesis.pdf, last visited on April 1st, 2020.

Zevenbergen, J. (2002). *Systems of land registration–Aspects and effects* (PhD Thesis, Technical University Delft). Delft: Netherlands Geodetic Commission.

Zheng, Z., Xie, S., Dai, H.-N., Chen, X., & Wang, H. (2018). Blockchain challenges and opportunities: A survey. *International Journal of Web and Grid Services, 14*, 2018.

Land Registration in the Twenty-First Century: Blockchain Land Registers from a Civil Law Perspective

Benjamin Verheye

Abstract Few things seem so opposite to each other as the highly innovative blockchain technology and the ancient land registration sector, in which one traditionally feels thrown back into the pre-digital era. However, for some believers this unlikely pair might be on its way to form one of the world's new power couples. This contribution aims at analyzing blockchain technology in land registration matters from a material legal point of view. First, some blockchain land registration initiatives are discussed. Second, the possibilities of blockchain technology for land registration are evaluated on the basis of two variables: the lacunar or complete nature of a land register and its negative or positive nature. In doing so, Belgian, French and German law will be taken into account, offering a thorough civil law perspective on the matter.

Keywords Land registration · Blockchain technology · Complete *v.* lacunar land registers · Negative *v.* positive land registers · Trusted third party

---

This paper is the abbreviated and updated version of an earlier paper on this topic: Verheye (2017, pp. 441–477). See also in Dutch on related topics: Verheye, Verslype, and Danneels (2018, 109 p); Verheye (2018, pp. 212–238). See also, for instance, the special issue of the European Property Law Journal on this topic that appeared in 2017.

B. Verheye (✉)
Institute for Property Law, KU Leuven, Leuven, Belgium
e-mail: benjamin.verheye@kuleuven.be

A. Lehavi, R. Levine-Schnur (eds.), *Disruptive Technology, Legal Innovation, and the Future of Real Estate*, https://doi.org/10.1007/978-3-030-52387-9_7

1 Introduction: Blockchain and Land Registration, Opposites Attract

Few things seem so opposite to each other as the highly innovative blockchain technology—speaking in terms like blocks, hashes, mining, bitcoin and ethereum—and the ancient land registration sector, in which one traditionally feels thrown back into the pre-digital era. However, for some believers this unlikely pair might be on its way to form one of the world's new power couples, given the fact that blockchain technology is, at its heart, a registration technology. This idea first emerged a couple of years ago and in the meantime countries ranging from the Netherlands over Sweden to Georgia have been experimenting with blockchain technology in land registration.

This contribution aims at analyzing blockchain technology in land registration matters from a material legal point of view. First, some blockchain land registration initiatives are discussed. Second, the possibilities of blockchain technology for land registration are evaluated on the basis of two variables: the lacunar or complete nature of a land register and its negative or positive nature. In doing so, Belgian, French and German law will be taken into account, offering a thorough civil law perspective on the matter.

Various issues remain outside the scope of application of this paper. Firstly, I will only focus on existing well-functioning and trustworthy land registers and the possible meaning of blockchain technology for these systems. The meaning of the blockchain for land registration in developing countries thus falls outside the scope of this paper. Secondly, the technical aspects of blockchain technology are discussed in other contributions in this book. I will therefore not repeat them in this contribution.

2 Blockchain Technology and Land Registration

2.1 Blockchain Land Registration: Some Initiatives

A lot has been going on in the land registration world as far as blockchain technology is concerned. A wide range of countries all over the world have been experimenting with blockchain applications for land registration purposes. The objective of this part is to briefly discuss (some of) these initiatives and highlight the particularities of each project.

One of the general motives for the authorities to introduce blockchain land registers is the fact that a blockchain land register increases the speed of registration: whereas in a classical system, days may pass between the agreement itself and the registration thereof. Blockchain registers make it possible to proceed quasi-immediately to registration. However, this speed could also be generated through other measures of digitalization (*cf. infra*). Other motives are: connecting various registers to each other, lower transaction costs—although the blockchain technology must be paid, of course—, e-government objectives, a lower threshold for parties to participate in the market, etc. Again, however, one must wonder whether these advantages cannot also be achieved by means of other technologies than blockchain technology. This question will be touched upon again below (*cf. infra*).

A first interesting project is the Chromaway pilot project in Sweden (https://chromaway.com). The Swedish land register (Landmäteriet) considered its own system too slow, incomplete and outdated. The Landmäteriet has therefore engaged a couple of IT firms (ChromaWay, Telia and Kairos Future) to further enhance the digitalisation of the land register, on the basis of blockchain technology. Landhypothek Bank and SBAB! joined the project in August 2016. As the report on the project clarifies: "Blockchain technology provides the opportunity to solve many of these issues with a modern IT infrastructure that Landmäteriet wants to investigate."

The IT firms have created a blockchain that makes it possible for private parties to transfer real estate to each other through digital applications (apps). In fact, the entire sale process, including the obtaining of a credit, is made digital. However, Landmäteriet will still play an important role, as it is the authority guaranteeing that a digital code in the blockchain truly represents real estate in the physical world and managing the apps and the blockchain. The current register of Landmäteriet will also be maintained connected to the blockchain. A nice demo of the new system can be tried on the Chromaway website.

Nowadays, however, this project seems to have been interrupted. No further information on its development is available.

A second project I wish to talk of here is the Bitfury project in Georgia (the Republic, not the American state) (http://bitfury.com/). Georgia has engaged Bitfury, a blockchain and IT company, to create a blockchain land register for Georgia, in which land titles need to be registered. This register is privately administrated by the Georgian National Agency of Public Registry (NAPR) and integrated in its own registers. Nowadays, it functions well in practice.

The Republic of Georgia is so pleased by the result that it has in the meantime signed a Memorandum of Understanding with Bitfury to apply blockchain technology in other parts of its administration, too. In general, Bitfury is very positive and optimistic about its technology to be used in other land registry issues as well.

Thirdly, the Bitland project that is going on in Ghana should be mentioned (www.bitland.world). Bitland is a non-profit organization that is trying to establish a land register in Ghana—where government land registers are not at all up-to-date and corruption is a major problem—that is entirely based on blockchain technology and is accessible through mobile devices. This happens in cooperation with the Ghana Land Commission. The objective is not only to enhance the land management, land circulation and real credit market and help solving land disputes, but also to avoid corrupt government interventions, fraud and real estate bubbles. In 2016, it had its test project running in 28 communities in Ghana and the first results are positive. At the same time, Bitland develops educational initiatives that enable people to get involved in the digitalizing society. In the future, Bitland hopes to expand its project to other Ghanese communities and even to the entire African continent, with eight 'ambassadors' conducting scouting missions in other countries in 2016.

Other countries, such as Estonia, the United Kingdom, India and Honduras, are also working on blockchain technology in land registration matters, but it is impossible to cover them all in this contribution (Lemieux, 2017, pp. 392–393, 397 ff.; Nogueroles Peiró & Martinez García, 2017, pp. 317–318).

2.2 *Blockchain Technology in Land Registration Matters: An Evaluation*

2.2.1 Introduction

Having all the above-mentioned initiatives in mind, one is enclined to hold for true that the future of land registration lies in the blockchain technology. This might very well be true, but it should not be taken for granted without any further research. The quintessential question is if and, if yes, how blockchain technology can contribute to land registration. This forms the topic of the remainder of this paper.

The possibilities of blockchain technology for land registration will be evaluated on the basis of two variables. I have therefore selected two essential pairs of characteristics of existing land registration systems and will analyse the impact of blockchain technology on each of these characteristics. The two pairs are the complete or lacunar nature of a register and its positive or negative nature.

2.2.2 Complete *v.* Lacunar Land Registration Systems

A first characteristic of land registers' is their ambition as to the information they want to provide: is it their aim to provide all relevant information on land (complete) or do they limit their information to certain aspects, *i.e.* rights and transactions, that are deemed more important than others (lacunar)?

The standard example of a complete register is the German *Grundbuch*: *Vollständigkeit* is an important goal of this register (Bauer & von Oefele, 2013, p. 2, see also pp. 8–24). The *Grundbuch* really has the aspiration of containing all legal information on real estate that it considers important to publish. The Belgian land register, by contrast, is more lacunar: it does not pretend that it contains all relevant transactions concerning real estates (De Page, 1957b, nr. 960 ff., pp. 723–728). As such, to name the most famous lacuna, only transfers of rights *intra vivos* need to be published: transfers *causa mortis* need no publication in the land register (art. 1 of the Belgian Mortgage Act, *a contrario*). This flaw in particular has been heavily criticised in the Belgian legal doctrine ever since the establishment of the land register in 1851. Various attempts have been made in the last few decades alone to remedy this flaw, one in 1994–1985 and one in 1991–1992, but both failed (Jacobs, Michiels, & Van der Meersch, 1997, p. 21). In France, however, an attempt to make the land register more complete has succeeded partially in 1935[1] and definitively and integrally in 1955[2]: since 1955, all transfers *causa mortis* of real estates must be ascertained by a notarial certificate and need to be published in the land register.

Nevertheless, it must be kept in mind that even a complete land register like the German *Grundbuch* is not entirely complete in the literal meaning of the word. Even in Germany, not all encumbrances of real estate need publicity in the land register. To give an example: the *Grundbuch* only concerns private legal information and no public legal information; *öffentrechtliche Lasten* are not mentioned in the *Grundbuch* (see also § 54 *Grundbuchordnung* (*GBO*)). Thus, one may not interpret '*vollständig*' too literally.

The lacunar or complete nature of an existing land register has some important consequences for the possibility of blockchain land registration. These are discussed in the following paragraphs.

Firstly, it is practically impossible or at least very hard to turn an existing lacunar register into a blockchain register. This is related with the question how to create the so-called 'Genesis block'. The Genesis block is the very first block in the blockchain that contains all the information up to that point. For a land registration blockchain, this means that if one wants to turn an existing land register into a blockchain, the Genesis block needs to contain all information from that land register (Vos, 2016, pp. 20–21). In a lacunar land register, however, it is never sure that the land register mirrors the reality at the moment the Genesis block is created: due to the lacunar nature, it is possible that transactions and/or events have occurred—and changed reality—that have not been registered in the land register. This disparity makes it practically impossible to turn an existing lacunar land register into a blockchain register (Vos, 2016, p. 14, 23).

One possible solution for this problem could be to turn other registers, such as the Belgian cadaster, also in a blockchain and combine the various blockchain registers with each other. Nevertheless, it is clear that lacunar land registers create an additional problem to proceed to a blockchain land register.

Secondly, it must be questioned how a blockchain system without a trusted third party, *i.e.* the state authorities, could replace existing land registers in which state authorities have such an important role to play. Let me clarify this with an example. Person X has a public key in the blockchain land register and according to the blockchain, an apartment in Brussels is connected to that key. Sadly, person X dies and his heir is his only son Y. Son Y now becomes the owner of the apartment and he wishes to sell it. Of course, this transfer will need to be put in the blockchain in order to be effective (German law) or to be opposable to certain third parties (Belgium and France). A big problem arises then: son Y does not have access to the public key of his father, because he cannot use his father's private key. Nevertheless, he needs that access to sign the transfer in the blockchain. Unfortunately, the block-

[1] Decree of 30 October 1935 modifying the publicity regime.

[2] Decree nr. 55-22 of 4 Januari 1995 holding the reform of the immovable publicity, *Journal Officiel de la République Française* 7-1-1955.

chain will not allow that and the transfer will be impossible. One way or another, son Y needs access to the key of father X.

This is a problem for both lacunar and complete land registers, although the problem will be more apparent in lacunar registers. If a person acquires real estate on the basis of the law and not on the basis of a transaction, e.g. on the basis of succession, a mismatch arises between the reality and the blockchain land register. One way or another, the blockchain land register needs to be corrected, but this requires the cooperation of the person to whose public key the real estate is connected. Various solutions for this practical problem in case of blockchain registers can be imagined.

One thing is clear: someone will need to have access to the public key of father X, in order to make a transfer of the connected real estate possible. It would be easy if son Y would simply have access to this key: we could imagine him inheriting it. In order to prevent fraud, however, for instance in case other heirs exist, it seems a bad idea to simply grant access to the public key to another person, albeit an heir. This access would need to be carefully checked by a competent authority: this competent authority could subsequently connect the identity of son Y to the public key of his father X. Another solution is that when a person dies, his public key becomes administered by a competent official authority who subsequently transfers the real estate package to the public key of the heir. In both cases, official intervention is needed, which I elaborate upon below (*cf. infra*). Another solution could be the creation of a special kind of injunction, that complies the person to whose public key the real estate is connected to transfer it. Nevertheless, this solution requires that that person is alive and can be reached, which is not guaranteed. It is therefore better to stick to the previous solution.

Thus, it is clear that one must have considerable reserve towards turning existing well-functioning and trustworthy land registers into blockchain registers. First, I have demonstrated how this is very hard for existing lacunar land registers. Second, in both a lacunar and complete blockchain land register, in some cases someone will need to grant access to the public key of the predecessor in title to the successor in title. One thing has become clear in this respect: we need a central authority capable of giving access of the public key of one person to another person, in case that first person is not capable anymore of transferring the real estate package in the blockchain to the new person who is entitled to it, for instance on the basis of inheritance law. Because in a lacunar register more disparities can arise between the real life titular and the registered titular of real estate, all this is even more troublesome in lacunar registers.

2.2.3 Positive *v.* Negative Land Registration Systems

The notions 'positive nature' and 'negative nature' of land registers have everything to do with the presumption concerning the correctness of the published information that a land registration system creates and the subsequent protection of third parties *de bona fide*. Essentially, negative publicity does not guarantee that the information is correct, whereas positive publicity does create this presumption. A negative system only guarantees that all information that is not published, despite an obligation thereto, does not exist/is not opposable to third parties *de bona fide* (Grziwotz, Keukenschrijver, & Ring, 2016, § 892, nr. 2; Storme, 1997–1998, pp. 1175–1176; von Staudinger, Gursky, Gutzeit, Kutter, & Seiler, 2012, § 892, nr. 4). However, no guarantee about the validity of the provided information is given and a third party may by no means trust that an act is valid, because it is published. Thus, the Belgian and—in principle—French land registration systems are both negative systems: publicity of a particular act means nothing as to the validity of that act in respect of third parties. "*La publicité ne purge pas l'acte de ses vices*" (De Page, 1957a, n° 1055; Sagaert, 2014, 728 ff.). If that act is annulled on a later moment in time, even after a third party has acquired rights on the real estate, then that act is also null towards that third party—at least, in principle—, who suddenly appears to have acquired a good from someone who was not the owner—which is necessary for a valid transfer of ownership, we call this the 'chain of owners'—and thus loses the real estate due to the *nemo plus iuris*-principle ("*Nemo plus juris transferre potest, quam ipse habet*") (Byttebier, 2005, nr. 639 ff.; De Page, 1957b, pp. 395–396; Sagaert, 2014, p. 707, 729; Stranart & Alter, 2002, p. 493).

A positive publicity system, by contrast, goes further than only this negative guarantee—which it also gives (!)—: a positive system also guarantees the validity of an act—*i.e.* a previous act—on the moment the register is consulted, it creates *öffentliche Glaube*. A positive system, for instance the German *Grundbuch*, creates the presumption that a published act concerning a real right—*i.e.* the *Eintragung* of a *Einigung*—is valid and that the *Grundbuch* is correct (§ 891 *BGB*, *Vermutungswirkung*) and when a third party *de bona fide* acquires that real right, the validity of the previous act cannot be discussed anymore (§§ 892–893 *BGB*). "*Der Inhalt des Grundbuchs gilt als richtig*." (Wilhelm, 2016, p. 321) Thus, the German publicity system creates more than a mere negative guarantee, it also creates a positive guarantee. Thus it is more protective towards third parties *de bona fide* (*Vertrauensschutz*) and thus towards the free circulation of real estate, which was its explicit aim (*Verkehrsschutz*) (Hager, 1990, pp. 2–3; Lutter, 1964, p. 124; von Staudinger et al., 2012, § 892, nr. 7; Wiegand, 1978, p. 145). This absolutely does not mean that the *Grundbuch* is always correct—hence the possibilities of *Berichtigung* and *Widerspruch*—, but it does mean that it provides third parties *de bona fide* with protection against mistakes in the *Grundbuch*, *i.e.* situations in which the true state of affairs is not mirrored by the *Grundbuch*.

It is important to see how positive publicity in principle implies negative publicity: the validity of acts and the correctness of a register can only be logically guaranteed (positive), if that register also guarantees that all information that is not published, despite an obligation to do so, cannot harm third parties (negative).

Nevertheless, some exceptions must be mentioned in respect to positive systems. Firstly, even in German law, some exceptions exist in which the publicity in the *Grundbuch* has *only* negative effect, for instance as far as *relative Verfügungsbeschränkungen* are concerned: these can only harm third parties if published, but publicity has no effect whatsoever as to their validity (Fehrenbacher,

2004, p. 251, 260; Grziwotz et al., 2016, § 892, nr. 3; Medicus, 2001, p. 295; Wiegand, 1975, p. 207; Wilhelm, 2016, p. 321, 339, 342). Secondly, third parties *de bona fide* cannot rely on *all* information in the *Grundbuch*: the *öffentliche Glaube* is not extended towards mere facts, e.g. the exact surface of a plot of land, and, more importantly, it only concerns the rights of parties on a certain good and *not*, for instance, their capacity to conclude contracts (*Geschäftsfähigkeit*), for this is not a part of the information in the *Grundbuch* (von Staudinger et al., 2012, § 892, nr. 67; Westermann, 1963, p. 2; Wiegand, 1975, p. 207). So even in German law, with its extensive third party protection rules, it remains possible that a third party *de bona fides* acquires real estate from the person who is marked as *Berechtigter* in the *Grundbuch*, but subsequently loses that real estate again, for that *Berechtigter* afterwards appears to have been incapable of concluding contracts. After all, the *Grundbuch* does not guarantee the validity of the *own* legal act. Thirdly, *öffentliche Glaube* in the *Grundbuch* neither protects a third party who has acquired real estate in a different way than through a contract, e.g. through inheritance (von Staudinger et al., 2012, § 892, nr. 81–86 (*Erwerb kraft Gesetzes*); Westermann, Westermann, Gursky, & Eickmann, 2011, p. 713; Wieling, 1992, p. 269; Wilhelm, 2016, pp. 343–344). Fourthly, only third parties *de bona fide* can invoke the protection in German law: third parties *de mala fide* are not protected (von Staudinger et al., 2012, § 892, nr. 140 ff.; Westermann et al., 2011, 711 ff.; Wieling, 1992, p. 272; Wilhelm, 2016, 349 ff).

A final remark concerning French law must be made here. In principle, the French land register is also an example of a negative system. However, French case law and doctrine have developed the theory of the *propriété apparente*, in which publicity in the land register receives a more positive effect towards third parties *de bona fide* (Algiu, 1912, 67 ff.; Boudot, 2003, pp. 13–14; Danis-Fatôme, 2004, pp. 36–124; Leroux RTDC) integral; (Loniewski, 1905, p. 37; Milliet, 1901) integraal; (Rabagny, 2001, pp. 963–983, 993 ff.; Vouin, 1939, pp. 401–404). This interesting evolution falls, however, outside the scope of this contribution.

The distinction between negative and positive land registers is also relevant for blockchain land registration, because it teaches us that one of the key features of traditional blockchain technology, namely that the information in the blockchain is at all times correct and that third parties can trust on that feature, cannot be applied in blockchain land registration. In fact, a blockchain land register is full-fledged positive: it protects third acquirers of real estate in the most absolute way by guaranteeing them that the information in the blockchain is at all times correct. Most land registers, by contrast, are not fully positive.

After all, one of the essential characteristics of a traditional blockchain is its non-reversibility. If a transaction in the blockchain is non-reversible, the acquirer of the real estate will always be protected by the blockchain in his position towards the real estate. This feature is, however, hardly reconcilable with the needs of a negative and even a positive land register. In both a negative and positive land register, it is possible that a certain transaction that was registered in the register is reversed. In fact, this means that the blockchain becomes wrong, in the sense that it does no correctly reflect reality, despite its aim to be correct at all times (Lemieux, 2017,

p. 418). However, solutions to this problem exist, although some creativity is required. Some examples will clarify this solution.

First, let us look at an example where no third party is involved. A sells his house to B and this is registered in the blockchain. Afterwards, however, the sale is annulled and B is obliged to give the house back to A. Thus the first transaction must be reversed. Vos argues that this might be done by adjusting the blockchain: he suggests that a land register blockchain could be a privately administered one—privately in the sense of overseen by an authority—in which reversing transactions is a possibility (Vos, 2016, p. 17). Another solution could be publishing the court decision reversing a real estate transaction in the blockchain (Vos, 2016, p. 17, footnote 53). A third solution could be the following: the required change in the blockchain register could be operated through a court injunction obliging B himself to retransfer the real estate to A. Instead of reversing the transaction, a new transaction takes place which functionally reverses the previous one.

The same solution could be operated in the second example. A sells his house to B, B sells it on to C and afterwards, the sale agreement between A and B is declared null and void. Depending on the substantial law of the legal system, C is protected or not by the fact that he trusted the blockchain register. In a negative system, he is not protected, whereas in a positive system, he is protected. If, however, the problem would occur between B and C—B appears to be incapable of concluding a sales contract, for instance—a positive system will not protect C, either. In both cases, the latest transaction between B and C could need to be reversed and in a negative system, the transaction between A and B could also need to be reversed. All these changes could be operated in the same way as mentioned above, *i.e.* by issuing an injunction to C and/or B to retransfer the real estate to A.

Nevertheless, this last solution requires the cooperation of the counterparty. This cooperation could, despite legal means forcing people to perform an action, be very hard to acquire. What if, for instance, the counterparty has died in the meantime? Or what if he has moved to a country with which hardly any bilateral international agreements exist (Thomas, 2017, p. 383)?

It is therefore better to apply the same solution that was suggested above with regard to the lacunar nature of the land register: the introduction of a central authority that has the power to adjust the blockchain land register. This party would have the power to correct the blockchain by transferring real estate back to an original titular of a right on it, for instance in case of a court injunction as mentioned in the previous paragraph. The party obtaining such injunction could take it then to that central authority, who has the power to adjust the blockchain accordingly.

2.2.4 The Reintroduction of a Central Authority

We will now take a closer look at the central authority that is mentioned in the previous paragraphs. This need for a central authority to exist is, indeed, at odds with one very important characteristic of blockchain technology: the classical public blockchain is a decentralized system in which no central authority has a role to play.

However, this is not necessarily a problem for the application of the blockchain technology: it is technologically perfectly possible to establish a blockchain that is governed by a central authority: this is precisely what is called a private or hybrid blockchains. As far as I am concerned, this is even the only way that blockchain technology could practically be applied in land registration.

Moreover, this central authority could be the 'manager' of the blockchain, *i.e.* the party who sets up the blockchain and governs it. In this respect, this central governing authority can decide who is granted membership of the blockchain—*i.e.* transfer real estate—, who can read the information in the blockchain, under which conditions this happens—e.g. connection of the public key with an e-ID—, who can add blocks to the blockchain, how the blockchain will be technologically managed, etc. Finally, such central authority could also play a role in the correction of blockchain registers, in case these do not correspond anymore with reality. One thing is clear: a blockchain land register must take the form of a private or hybrid blockchain, with the state authorities maintaining an overriding power.

A very practical idea in this respect could be to set up a blockchain that is governed by the existing land register, that possesses a node, but in which all civil law notaries also possess a node and thus mine information. Such blockchain would constitute a hybrid blockchain, with only a limited number of managing members, but with the possibility for all citizens to become 'ordinary members'. The mining could be rewarded by a small retribution that must be paid by all people wishing to put information in the blockchain.

Every private party that wants to transfer a package through his public key to another private party could have direct access to the blockchain, either with or without assistance of a notary—in the demo of the Swedish blockchain register, this is called 'inviting a party to the transaction'—, but without having his computer as a node. In addition, a particular authority maintains an 'overriding' access, which makes it possible to grant access to a public key of, for instance, a deceased person to his rightful heir. Of course, this would mean that all members of the blockchain need to trust the central authority.

However, all this is just one idea. As the technologic possibilities for setting up a blockchain register are countless, many more practical models could be thought of.

2.2.5 Is Blockchain Technology Really Required?

The fact that traditional blockchain technology needs to be adapted by reintroducing a central authority in order to fit land registration needs leads to a further question. This question is whether blockchain technology is really the best suited technology to make important efficiency gains in land registration matters.

After all, blockchain technology does not only offer advantages. It also comes with some important disadvantages: it is new, so people do not exactly know how to operate it yet, which renders it risky from a technological point of view, it is highly energy-consuming, which renders it costly, it is, like other technologies, vulnerable to hacking and bugs, etc. (Lemieux, 2017, 435 ff.; Verheye et al., 2018, pp. 21–22).

Given the fact that one of its main advantages, its decentralized nature, gets lost in a land registration application, one must wonder whether other technologies, *i.e.* centralized, are technologies not better suited for land registration. The Belgian land register, for instance, could benefit more on the short to medium-long run from further digitalization of its historic records and centralization of the various registers than from an application of blockchain technology. Undoubtedly, this is true for other national land registration systems as well.

Blockchain technology must never be a goal in itself for land registration. It is my firm conviction that it should only be used when we are absolutely sure that (1) it leads better results than the existing land registration system and (2) the same better results cannot be achieved by other technologies that are cheaper, better established or safer. These issues need to be thoroughly studied for all blockchain land registration projects in the future.

3 Conclusion: Blockchain Land Registration

Blockchain technology appears to be capable of playing an important role for land registration. Nevertheless, land registration shows some particularities that need to be fully taken into account in order for blockchain technology to be apt to play a useful role in this respect. Therefore, a land registration blockchain should be developed in a particular way.

A completely decentralized blockchain land register—a blockchain in the strict sense of the word—seems neither possible nor desirable for land registration purposes. It must be possible for a central authority to grant access to a public key to another party, in order to avoid situations in which a public key is inaccessible due to the incapability of the titular of that public key to transfer real estate, for instance because that titular is deceased. Furthermore, this central authority can also play a role in adjusting the blockchain land register when it does not correctly represent legal reality anymore. Additionally, this central authority could also be the 'manager' of the blockchain.

Admittedly, this central authority is at odds with the decentralized nature of the blockchain. This is, however, to my opinion, the only option to develop a blockchain register that functions as well as the classic land registers. Some blockchain proponents could very well object that the reintroduction of a central authority denaturates blockchain technology. For these proponents, the essence of a blockchain is precisely that no central authority is involved anymore or that as many nodes are constructed as possible or that anybody can perform the mining. To my opinion, however, it is neither possible nor desirable to construct such 'true' blockchain for land registration matters.

All factors taken into account, I believe that blockchain technology is not as disruptive for land registration as some people want us to believe (Barbieri & Gassen, 2017, p. 12; Lemieux, 2017, pp. 439–440; Nogueroles Peiró & Martinez García, 2017, pp. 318–320; Thomas, 2017, pp. 389–391; Vos, 2016, p. 23). I like to compare this to the modernization of the land register in Belgium in 2001: from that year onwards, it was not required anymore that all deeds were copied by hand, for a scanning system and digital register were established. Nobody, however, described these changes as disruptive. They were merely considered as a modernization of the existing register, but by no means a revolution.

Blockchain technology could very well be the next step in the modernization of land registration systems. It is, however, only a specific form of blockchain technology that could do so, a form in which a central authority still plays an important role and in which all particular sensitivities of land registration and property law are taken into account.

Given this limited impact of blockchain technology on land registration, one must absolutely dare to ask one very important question: is blockchain technology really necessary to achieve the above-mentioned modernization? Other technological solutions might very well be able to achieve the same or even a better result with less costs, risks, or disadvantages. Only if this last question is answered affirmatively for a national land registration system, it becomes useful to consider blockchain technology as a valuable means of modernization of that particular system.

References

Algiu, A.-C. (1912). *Etude sur la règle Error communis facit jius*. Parijs: Marchal & Godde.

Barbieri, M., & Gassen, D. (2017). Blockchain—Can this new technology really revolutionize the land registry systems. In World Bank (Ed.), *Responsible Land Governance: Towards an Evidence Based Approach. Annual World Bank Conference on Land and Poverty* (Vol. 1). Washington: World Bank.

Bauer, H.-J., & von Oefele, F. (2013). *Grundbuchordnung. Kommentar*. München: Verlag Franz Vahlen.

Boudot, M. (2003). Apparence. In *Rép.civ. Dalloz*. Parijs: Dalloz.

Byttebier, K. (2005). *Voorrechten en hypotheken*. Antwerpen: Maklu.

Danis-Fatôme, A. (2004). *Apparence et contrat, Bibliothèque de droit privé*. Parijs: L.G.D.J.

De Page, H. (1957a). *Traité élémentaire de droit civil belge, V*. Brussel: Bruylant.

De Page, H. (1957b). *Traité élémentaire de droit civil belge, VII*. Brussel: Bruylant.

Fehrenbacher, O. (2004). *Registerpublizität und Haftung im Zivilrecht, Deutsches, Europäisches und Vergleichendes Wirtschaftsrecht*. Baden-Baden: Nomos Verlagsgesellschaft.

Grziwotz, H., Keukenschrijver, A., & Ring, G. (2016). *NomosKommentar BGB. III. Sachenrecht*. Baden-Baden: DeutscherAnwaltVerein.

Hager, J. (1990). *Verkehrsschutz durch redlichen Erwerb*. München: C.H. Beck'sche Verlagsbuchhandlung.

Jacobs, H., Michiels, D., & Van der Meersch, B. (1997). Nieuwe bevoegdheden voor de notaris? In *Dossier associatie van notarissen. Bijzonder nummer T.Not.*, 5. Brugge: Die Keure.

Lemieux, V. L. (2017). Evaluating the use of blockchain in land transactions: An archival science perspective. *EPLJ*, 392–440.

Loniewski, A. (1905). *Essai sur le rôle actuel de la maxime Error communis facit Jus*. Aix: J. Nicot.

Lutter, M. (1964). Die Grenzen des sogenannten Gutglaubensschutzes im Grundbuch. *AcP*, 122–182.

Medicus, D. (2001). Besitz, Grundbuch und Erbschein als Rechtsscheinträger. *Jura*, 294–299.

Milliet, G. (1901). *Des effets de la propriété apparente en droit civil*. Parijs: Librairie de jurisprudence ancienne et moderne Edouard Duchemin.

Nogueroles Peiró, N., & Martinez García, E. J. (2017). Blockchain and land registration systems. *EPLJ*, 296–320.

Rabagny, A. (2001). *Théorie générale de l'apparence en droit privé, t. II*. Parijs: Atelier national de reproduction des thèses.

Sagaert, V. (2014). *Goederenrecht, Beginselen van Belgisch Privaatrecht*. Mechelen: Kluwer.

Storme, M. E. (1997–1998). Het grondboek: de vereiste hervorming van de regels betreffende de verkrijging van onroerende zakelijke rechten. *RW*, 1173–1187.

Stranart, A.-C., & Alter, C. (2002). Quel est le sort de l'hypothèque consentie par un acquéreur dont le droit est ultérieurement annulé? In *Liber amicorum Lucien Simont* (p. 493). Brussel: Bruylant.

Thomas, R. (2017). Blockchain's incompatibility for use as a land registry: Issues of definition, feasibility and risk. *EPLJ*, 361–391.

Verheye, B. (2017). Real estate publicity in a blockchain world: A critical assessment. *EPLJ*, 441–477.

Verheye, B. (2018). Blockchaintechnologie en het notariaat bij vastgoedtransacties: Damocles' zwaard of opportuniteit? *T.Not.*, 212–238.

Verheye, B., Verslype, K., & Danneels, P. (2018). *Blockchain en smart contracts. Impact op de notaris als vertrouwde tussenpersoon?* Brussel: Larcier.

von Staudinger, J., Gursky, K.-H., Gutzeit, M., Kutter, H.-D., & Seiler, H. H. (2012). *Kommentar zum BGB. III. Sachenrecht—Einleitung zum Sachenrecht; §§ 854–882 (Allgemeines Liegenschaftsrecht 1)*. Berlijn: Sellier—de Gruyter.

Vos, J. (2016). *Blockchain-based land registry: Panacea, illusion or something in between?* Retrieved from https://www.elra.eu/wp-content/uploads/2017/02/10.-Jacques-Vos-Blockchain-based-Land-Registry.pdf:1-26

Vouin, R. (1939). *La bonne foi. Notion et rôleactuels en droit privé français*. Parijs: Librairie Générale de Droit & de Jurisprudence.

Westermann, H. (1963). Die Grundlagen des Gutglaubensschutzes. *JuS*, 1–8.

Westermann, H., Westermann, H. P., Gursky, K.-H., & Eickmann, D. (2011). *Sachenrecht*. Heidelberg: C.F. Müller.

Wiegand, W. (1975). Der öffentliche Glaube des Grundbuchs. *JuS*, 205–214.

Wiegand, W. (1978). Rechtsableiting vom Nichtberechtigten. Rechtsschein und Vertrauensschutz bei Verfügungsgeschäften. *JuS*, 145–150.

Wieling, H. J. (1992). *Sachenrecht*. Berlijn: Springer.

Wilhelm, J. (2016). *Sachenrecht*. Berlijn: De Gruyter.

Part V
New Technological Applications

Selling LAND in Decentraland: The Regime of Non-fungible Tokens on the Ethereum Blockchain Under the Digital Content Directive

Catalina Goanta

Abstract Rewind to the early 1990s: an infant World Wide Web recently created by Tim Berners-Lee was starting to redefine the way people were connected globally. First came communication services (e.g. e-mail) and a shift from physical to digital marketplaces (e.g. ecommerce). Then came the rise of Internet platforms, in what is now deemed to be Web 2.0. The critics of Web 2.0 claim it is a spoiled version of early Internet promises: freedom from surveillance, online safety (even through anonymity)—in a nutshell, more control and power for the user. The answer to the problems of Web 2.0 is thought to be the third era of the Internet, namely the Decentralized Internet, based on (among others) blockchain technology. While a lot of literature has focused on the legal implications of blockchain assets such as cryptocurrencies from a banking perspective, not the same can be said about the consumer protection angle necessary in tackling the hype that has affected users who spent valuable financial resources on investing, playing on or using blockchain-based platforms. This chapter aims to make a contribution to fill this research gap, and focus on Decentraland, a virtual world where LAND, a non-fungible token is traded in order to allow users to build their own spaces on these plots. In doing so, the chapter elaborates on the notion of Internet of Value, and looks at the inner workins of Decentraland from the perspective of European law, more specifically the Digital Content Directive.

Keywords Decentraland · Blockchain · Digital Content Directive · Consumer protection · Tokens · Internet of value

C. Goanta (✉)
Maastricht Law & Tech Lab, Faculty of Law, Maastricht University, Maastricht, Netherlands
e-mail: catalina.goanta@maastrichtuniversity.nl

A. Lehavi, R. Levine-Schnur (eds.), *Disruptive Technology, Legal Innovation, and the Future of Real Estate*, https://doi.org/10.1007/978-3-030-52387-9_8

1 Introduction

Rewind to the early 1990s: an infant World Wide Web recently created by Tim Berners-Lee was starting to redefine the way people were connected globally. First came communication services (e.g. e-mail) and a shift from physical to digital marketplaces (e.g. ecommerce). Then came the rise of Internet platforms, in what is now deemed to be Web 2.0—prosumers generate content on social media platforms such as Youtube, Facebook, Instagram (e.g. social media), or offer their individual services on peer-to-peer or gig platforms such as Uber, AirBnB or Taskrabbit. These developments have been both lauded and criticized. On the one hand, the Internet as we know it dissolved geographic distances, created new industries, facilitated the distribution of goods of services and empowered individual employment. On the other hand, it gave rise to new questions about what is real and what is fake: what to do if someone posts fake reviews; who to hold accountable for fake news; how to prevent a new wave of labour exploitation, etc. The critics of Web 2.0 claim it is a spoiled version of early Internet promises: freedom from surveillance, online safety (even through anonymity)—in a nutshell, more control and power for the user. Painful public scandals like the sort of Equifax or Cambridge Analytica make it easy to argue that with the rise of data as a commodity, Internet users have indeed lost a lot of this control to data brokers, surveillance agencies and hackers.

The answer to the problems of Web 2.0 is thought to be the third era of the Internet, namely the Decentralized Internet. Blockchain platforms like Steem are used to make decentralized equivalents of a lot of apps we have grown accustomed to: DTube instead of Youtube (DTube, n.d.), Graphite Docs instead of Google Docs (Graphite, n.d.), or Storj instead of iCloud (Decentralized Cloud Storage—Storj, n.d.). The main benefit of decentralization—beyond privacy—is said to be the freedom from monopolies held by centralized platforms that now determine, through their own intransparent algorithms, who gets to see what information on the web. In addition, decentralization proposes a new, trustless constellation of behavioural incentives (e.g. Smart Media Tokens, etc.) and communication infrastructure devoid of intermediaries.

However, while there might be strong market opportunities to embrace in a new Internet era, the law does not move into new ages with the same speed. Decentralization has already been occurring, not in terms of communication infrastructure, but human infrastructures, in the form of individual accessibility: citizen reporters are disrupting press, entertainment and advertising services, and gig drivers are replacing taxis. Emerging practical issues are under-regulated, and challenge legal systems to determine if their classical paradigms are still fitting: is posting fake negative reviews a crime? Are Youtubers professionals or individuals? Do Internet platforms have a duty of care towards their users? Moreover, not just public institutions, but platforms themselves face a problem of scale, and struggle with enforcing legal standards. These are problems that have yet to be solved, which a new Internet version might very well inherit. In spite of such concerns, increased attention is paid to the technology conjured as the game-changer of Internet architecture: blockchain. Expected to hit over $12 billion in investment by 2022 (Mearian, 2019), the blockchain-based array of products has significantly expanded in the past decade. Since Satoshi Nakamoto's famous white paper on Bitcoin back in 2008 (Nakamoto, 2009), blockchain has matured into an ideology that currently fuels more than cryptocurrencies. Or does it?

This chapter focuses on Decentraland as a virtual world where LAND, a non-fungible token is traded in order to allow users to build their own spaces on these plots. This inquiry into Decentraland classifies LAND as digital content, and thus asks the question of what compliance issues may arise out of the application of Directive 2019/770 (the Digital Content Directive) to Decentraland in general, and LAND in particular. While a lot of literature has focused on the legal implications of cryptocurrencies from a banking perspective, not the same can be said about the consumer protection angle necessary in tackling the hype that has affected users who spent valuable financial resources on investing, playing on or using blockchain-based platforms. This chapter aims to make a contribution to fill this research gap, and shed light on some of the considerations which platforms such as Decentraland ought to pay close attention to when creating consumer content or services. To this end, the chapter is structured as follows. Section 2 addresses the development of blockchain products beyond cryptocurrencies and as digital content, under the moniker of Internet of Value. Section 3 describes Decentraland in detail, and explains the role of LAND in the platform's constellation of tools and content. Lastly, Section 4 explores some of the core tenets of the Digital Content Directive and applies specific articles to Decentraland's architecture. Section 5 concludes.

2 The Internet of Value

The Internet facilitated the creation of virtual communities (Abrahams, 2007; Chesney, Chuah, & Hoffmann, 2009; Decentraland, a Virtual World on Open Standards, n.d.; Manning, 2019; Sundquist, 2012), from message boards (Hansen, Shneiderman, & Smith, 2011b; Lidsky, 2009; Wein, 2001) to gaming (Berger, Jucker, & Locher, 2016; Boellstorff, 2015; Karniell & Bates, 2010; Klastrup, 2009; Krzywinska, 2006; Malaby, 2011; Pearce, 2011; Taylor, 2009) and social media (Garofalo, 2013; Hansen, Shneiderman, & Smith, 2011a, c). The appeal of virtual worlds is said to draw on a so-called property of 'worldness', which according to Klastrup emerges out of 'the complex interplay between (a) the aesthetics of the gameworld as both an actualised explorable and mentally imagined universe; (b) the experiences and means of expression the world as a game system and tool allows and affords; (c) the social interaction in and about the world' (Klastrup, 2009). A lot of these communities evolved in plain sight, albeit in designated spaces, such as game worlds. However, a lot of other communities chose to be more protective of their identity and activities, due to a plethora of reasons, such as engaging in illegal trade (e.g. the Silk Road marketplace), (Chen, 2011) or supporting social movements against surveillance (e.g. Riseup.net). Cryptography facilitated the veiling of online activities, and communities deploying it for various functions (e.g. identity; communication), while building an ideology around the importance of cryptography are referred to as cryptocommunities.[1]

Early on, during the rise of personal computing in the 1980s, when cypherpunks like Tim May became public proponents of cryptolibertarianism (Hughes, 1993; Popper, 2018), cryptocommunities were mainly using digital technologies for communication purposes. It was during this period that David Chaum tried, albeit unsuccessfully, to create digital cash which would allow secure and private currency transfers to take place without surveillance from state or commercial entities such as banks (Khan, 2016; McCullagh, 2001; Mowbray, 2006). This changed for the second generation cryptocommunities, as dark marketplaces such as the Silk Road had already started using cryptocurrencies (e.g. Bitcoin) as of early 2011. While the Bitcoin White Paper acknowledged the role of the original cryptocurrency as 'online cash' (Nakamoto, 2009), labelling cryptocurrencies as money is no easy task (Adimi, 2018; Alvarez, 2018; Gikay, 2018; Liedel, 2018). For instance, in 2014, the Dutch Court of Overijssel analysed the nature of the Bitcoin cryptocurrency, to determine whether it may be categorized as 'money' under Article 6:112 of the Dutch Civil Code.[2] The court found that even though in principle this article allowed for payment in currencies not originating directly from the state, to be considered 'money', the currency in question must be a legal tender, which was not the case for Bitcoin.[3]

In more recent iterations, cryptocommunities are becoming even more sophisticated in their use of cryptography. With over 1200 types of cryptocurrencies listed on Coinmarketcap in 2019, the concept of digital currencies as tech alternatives to national currencies designed to eliminate financial intermediation gradually morphed into a more general expression of value. This is known as the 'Internet of Value' (The Internet of Value, 2017; Consultant, 2019) where value is 'to be exchanged as quickly as information' (The Internet of Value, 2017). IoV entails the digitalization of assets such as 'intellectual and digital properties, equity and wealth', as well as their transfer in an 'automated, secure, and convenient manner' (Truong, Um, Zhou, & Lee, 2018). Other views expand the asset category also to 'likes' and 'favourites', beyond the exchange of money and currencies (Skinner, 2016), which is made possible due to the creation of an ecosystem of

[1] Catalina Goanta and Marieke Hopman, 'Cryptocommunities as Legal Orders' (2020) Internet Policy Review, 9(2), retrieved from https://policyreview.info/articles/analysis/crypto-communities-legal-orders. For an expression of the cryptolibertarian ideology on the Silk Road, see for instance a forum post by Dread Pirate Roberts, the administrator of the first iteration of the Silk Road, about the platform's goal: 'Money is a tool, a means to an end. Our end here at Silk Road is not the accumulation of money, or the comfort and security it brings (not that there's anything wrong with that). Our end is freedom from tyranny, and secured basic human rights for the people of the world. As awesome as it is, Silk Road is just the beginning in what will likely be a long journey', <https://antilop.cc/sr/users/dpr/messages/20110727-0707-625-Re_SilkRoad_Fees.txt>, accessed 26 October 2019.

[2] Rechtbank Overijssel, 14 May 2014, ECLI:NL:RBOVE:2014:2667.

[3] Ibid.

blockchain-based applications and services facilitated by platforms such as Ethereum (Davidson, De Filippi, & Potts, 2018).

Illustrating the wide array of this ecosystem are decentralized applications such as Cryptokitties and Decentraland (Ducuing, 2019; Lee, Yoo, & Jang, 2019). In the case of a cryptocurrency like Bitcoin, 'the global log of transactions is jointly maintained by users' computers; distributed cryptography substitutes for centralized anti-forgery controls. The supply of Bitcoins is controlled by a function embedded in the cryptographic protocols, not by a single authority with the power to confiscate them or to make more' (Grimmelmann, 2014). In the case of both Cryptokitties and Decentraland, there is an underlying cryptocurrency (e.g. Ether or 'MANA'), but there is also something more, namely breeding and collecting digital cats as a non-fungible token (NFT), and buying 'LAND' in a virtual world. As the central example in this chapter, the latter is elaborated upon in the following section.

3 Decentraland

This section aims to give the reader an overview of what Decentraland is, how it works, and how the law categorizes the various transactions on which this platform rests.

As mentioned above, Decentraland is a virtual world built on the Ethereum blockchain. According to the platform, it is 'owned by its users', who can '[b]uild, explore, and earn money from [their] creations' Decentraland, a Virtual World on Open Standards, n.d.). Users can buy LAND (virtual content) using MANA, an ERC-20 token designed and used exclusively on Ethereum Decentraland, a Virtual World on Open Standards, n.d.), in this case to power the economy of the virtual world as a currency (Casper, 2018; Song, Chang, & Song, 2019; William, 2018). MANA was generated through an 'initial coin offering in August of 2017 and raised approximately $24 million worth of ETH, BTC, and other cryptocurrencies' (Buchko, 2018). Forty percent of the initial supply of MANA (a total of 2,644,403,343) was sold in the initial coin offering, with an additional 20% distributed to the community and partners, 20% to the founding team and 20% to the Decentraland foundation (Buchko, 2018). Users were then able to purchase LAND during two auctions, in December 2018 and December 2018, and once the purchases were made, the MANA spent on them 'was burned, meaning that the tokens were either deleted or sent to an empty, irretrievable address' (Buchko, 2018). In addition, users may sell LAND at their discretion. But what exactly is LAND? The present section tackles this question by looking into the Terms of Service and the Content Policy of Decentraland.

According to the Terms of Service, LAND parcels 'are intangible digital assets that exist only by virtue of the ownership record maintained in the Ethereum network. All smart contracts are conducted and occur on the decentralized ledger within the Ethereum platform. The Curator has no control over and makes no guarantees or promises with respect to the ownership record or smart contracts'.[4] The Curator is Metaverse Holdings Ltd., the company behind Decentraland, that provides platform users with the following 'Tools': the DCL (Decentraland) Client, the SDK (Software Development Kit) 5.0, the Marketplace, the Land Manager, the Command Line Interface, Agora, 'as well as any other features, tools and/or materials offered' by the Curator.[5] More technically, LAND is an ERC-721 token that associates 'each LANd parcel's x and y coordinates with a definition of a parcel's 3D scene that makes up the larger metaverse',[6] and LAND parcels 'exist only by virtue of the ownership record maintained on the Tools's supporting blockchain in the Ethereum network'.[7] Moreover, as 'any transfer of LAND parcel occurs within the supporting blockchain in the Ethereum network, and not within the Tools' Decentraland, a Virtual World on Open Standards, n.d.), the Tools mentioned above do not 'store, send, or receive LAND parcels' (Decentraland, a Virtual World on Open Standards, n.d.).

Metaverse Holdings Ltd. claims to not hold any ownership over Decentraland, as 'ownership is decentralized on the community', and the company's role is only to 'make available the Tools and the Site free of charge in order to allow different interactions with the Decentraland platform.[8] However, according to Article 12.1 of the Terms of Service, 'all title, ownership and Intellectual Property Rights in and to the Site and the Tools are owned exclusively by the Curator or its licensors', and the Curator's exclusive ownership shall include all elements of the Site and Tools, and all Intellectual Property Rights therein'.[9] These two statements, on the one hand that the company behind Decentraland does not own the decentralized virtual world, and on the other hand that it safeguards its intellectual property with respect to all the possible elements on the platform, including its architecture, are contradictory and

[4] Terms of Service, Article 10.6, (Decentraland, a Virtual World on Open Standards, n.d.). All terms of service cited in this chapter were in force in October 2019.

[5] (Decentraland, a Virtual World on Open Standards, n.d.), Terms of Service, Article 1.

[6] (Decentraland, a Virtual World on Open Standards, n.d.), Terms of Service, Article 5.2.

[7] (Decentraland, a Virtual World on Open Standards, n.d.), Terms of Service, Article 5.9.

[8] (Decentraland, a Virtual World on Open Standards, n.d.)Terms of Service, Article 1.

[9] (Decentraland, a Virtual World on Open Standards, n.d.) The elements of the site are further described in Article 12.1 as follows: 'The visual interfaces, graphics (including, without limitation, all art and drawings associated with Tools), design, systems, methods, information, computer code, software, 'look and feel', organization, compilation of the content, code, data, and all other elements of the Site and the Tools (collectively, the 'Curator Materials') are owned by the Curator, and are protected by copyright, trade dress, patent, and trademark laws, international conventions, other relevant intellectual property and proprietary rights, and applicable laws.'

add confusion to the perceived versus real set of rights that users ought to derive out of their transactions on Decentraland.[10]

In addition, the Content Policy is a 1279 word-long framework that details the rules applicable to content created by users who contribute to the development of the world. By definition, users cannot create LAND, as it is solely generated by the Curator, but they can, however, make additional content build on the LAND parcel.

The idea behind the (business) model of world-building is that, just as with the case of the Second Life game (Berger et al., 2016; Boellstorff, 2015; Gallego, Bueno, & Noyes, 2016; Locher, Jucker, & Berger, 2015; Malaby, 2011; Marshall, 2014; Partala, 2011; Shelton, 2010), users would increasingly take control of the world. In the case of Decentraland, this would occur not only through user-generated content, but also through the fact that this content is not created under the supervision of the Curator, but rather on the Ethereum blockchain, which entails that the Curator does not have any control over the validity of these transactions. The intention of the Curator is to give users a 'social experience with an economy driven by the existing layers of land ownership and content distribution', where 'developers will be able to create applications on top of Decentraland, distribute them to other users, and monetize them'.[11]

The development of the platform was created by the Curator in the image of human history: it began in 2015 with a so-called 'Stone Age', Decentraland was nothing more than a 2D grid of pixels running exclusively on web browsers that had metadata describing the properties as well as the owner of the pixels. After that came the 'Bronze Age', launched in 2017, and instead of pixel metadata it started storing the full content description (e.g. models and textures for given plots of land) in the blockchains themselves. The next steps have been the 'Iron Age' and the 'Silicon Age', which users are to experience on the Ethereum blockchain, allowing the virtual world to nurture a more sophisticated ecosystem of decentralized apps (Dapps) which in-game developers would be able build on Ethereum as well. At the moment of writing, the 'Iron Age' is still in beta version, and access to the world is based on an invitation system R/Decentraland—ETA on Iron Age?, n.d.), with the company hosting various events to stimulate developers to generate interesting content for the world.[12]

---

[10] Additional conflicts exist between the articles of the Terms of Service and mandatory European consumer protection, such as the unfairness of consumer arbitration clauses, like the one in Article 18.1: 'If the parties do not reach an agreed upon solution within a period of 30 days from the time informal dispute resolution under the Initial Dispute Resolution provision begins, then either party may initiate binding arbitration as the sole means to resolve claims, subject to the terms set forth below'. See (Engelmann, 2017). The same can be said for the limitation of liability included in e.g. Article 4 of the Terms of Service: 'You and the third party private key manager you select are entirely responsible for security related to access of the Tools. The Curator bears no responsibility for any breach of security or unauthorized access to your account'.

[11] Decentraland, 'White Paper' <https://decentraland.org/whitepaper.pdf>.

[12] See for instance the Game Jam that took place between 16 and 30 September 2019, a 'two-week online competition to create awesome interactive content that will form part of Decentraland' <https://gamejam.decentraland.org>.

4 LAND Under the Digital Content Directive

After understanding how Decentraland works, as well as going through the company's perceptions of its rights and obligations, time has come to assess some of the features of this virtual world by looking into the applicable law. As a virtual world claiming to engage in and facilitate the sale of virtual property, Decentraland poses a lot of fascinating questions which have at their core property and intellectual property laws. Who owns what in Decentraland? Can the platform claim not to own its own world, so that it can propagate the idea that the world is owned by its users? Is that claim accurate, namely can individuals or businesses even hold real rights in virtual assets? If the answer to this question is in the negative, what is the scope of the intellectual property rights held by the Curator, and how do they affect the rights users may exercise in the long run on the platform? How are these rights affected by the fact that the transactions generating them are based on the Ethereum blockchain? These are all questions that make Decentraland an interesting case study which ought to be given more academic attention. However, the main question this chapter endeavors to answer is: is LAND digital content in the meaning of the Digital Content Directive, and if so, what are the main features of the legal regime applicable to LAND from this perspective?

4.1 LAND as Digital Content?

The Digital Content Directive was adopted in May 2019 to enhance consumer cross-border purchases on the Digital Single Market and to safeguard a high level of consumer protection in the process (Hoekstra & Diker-Vanberg, 2019; Lehmann, 2016; Sein, 2017; Warburton, 2016). The scope of the Directive is laid down in Article 1 to include issues dealing with the conformity of digital content or digital services; remedies for the lack of conformity; and modifications occurring to digital content. The definitions used by the Directive are outlined in the following Article, which specifies that digital content is 'data which are produced and supplied in digital form' (Article 2(1)), and digital services are services 'that allow the consumer to create, process store or access data in digital form', or services that 'allow the sharing of or any other interaction with data in digital form uploaded or created by the consumer or other users of that service' (Article 2(2)). Illustrations regarding what may be considered as digital content are offered in Recital 19 of the Directive's Preamble, and include: 'computer programmes, applications, video files, audio files, music files, digital games, e-books or other e-publications, and also digital services which allow the creation of, processing of, accessing or storage of data in digital form, including software-as-a-service, such as video and audio sharing and other file hosting, word processing or games offered in the cloud computing environment and social media'.[13] Just like Second Life, whose developers insist it is an open-ended world with no set objective (Kalning, 2007), Decentraland does not refer to itself as a game. However, there can be no doubt that Decentraland, as a virtual world, is based on digital content (Hoekstra & Diker-Vanberg, 2019; Lehmann, 2016; Sein, 2017; Warburton, 2016).[14]

Decentraland's sophisticated setup most likely combines digital content as output with digital services offered through its tools (Buchko, 2018), such as Agora, where the Curator hosts public consultations where users can vote on questions regarding whether parcel sizes should be increased or whether MANA inflation should be removed. Another example of a digital service offered by the Curator is the Builder, an interactive platform that users can employ to create content on their parcels, very much in the fashion of the Sims game series (Kayser, 2006; Lastowka & Hunter, 2004; Mistry, 2018). As a digital asset/token generated by the Curator, LAND most certainly fulfills the criteria described in the Directive's definitional scope, and can thus be considered as digital content to this end.

The Preamble to the Directive mentions that 'the legal nature of contracts for the supply of digital content or a digital service, and the question of whether such contracts constitute, for instance, a sales, service, rental or sui generis contract, should be left to national law' (Recital 12). In other words, understanding exactly how Decentraland functions in the eyes of the law is a matter which can only be thoroughly analyzed by looking at a particular jurisdiction. This is important to determine when and under which circumstances consumers enter into contracts with the Curator. Still, to the extent of establishing the applicability of the Digital Content Directive to transactions concluded between the Curator and users who act outside their craft, trade, business or profession, namely consumers, Decentraland certainly falls under the scope of the Directive.

4.2 *What Are the Main Features of the Directive's Legal Regime Applicable to LAND?*

This answer will be tackled from three perspectives: (1) the timeliness of the provision of digital content; (2) the conformity requirements; and (3) the modification of the digital content.

Regarding the timeliness of the provision of the contract, Article 5 of the Digital Content Directive states that '[u]nless the parties have agreed otherwise, the trader shall supply the digital content or digital service without undue delay after the

[13] See also Inge Graef, 'Blurring Boundaries of Consumer Welfare' in (Bakhoum, Gallego, Mackenrodt, & Surblytė-Namavičienė, 2018).

[14] In addition, there are considerable questions relating to private international law and the applicability of European consumer protection to international services. However, it is generally accepted that if providers of digital content or services target European consumers, they must abide by European consumer protection standards.

conclusion of the contract.' This is a highly relevant point for virtual projects which require an extensive time for development. As it has been shown above, Decentraland was launched in 2015, and has undergone significant changes ever since. As they become more sophisticated, these changes bring with them the uncertainty of when the world will be a finished product, or at least when it will reach a development stage where all LAND acquirers from the initial auctions will be able to exercise the rights attached to their purchase of this digital content, such as the transfer or further development of the plots of LAND. Threads on the Decentraland Reddit show that users report still not having access to the world, even years after purchasing LAND through the ICO R/Decentraland—ETA on Iron Age?, n.d.). A more specific illustration of delays which can appear in this industry is the virtual reality promise made by developers (Sergeenkov, 2019). If consumers create avatars, invest money in 'claiming names', or in other words spend real-life money to buy MANA and customize their avatars under the belief they will be able, at some point to use this avatar in virtual reality, yet the company is not ready to roll out its virtual reality platform, this can be an issue from the perspective of Article 5. Whether additional development time can be considered undue delay is uncertain. However, what is certain is that a lot of platforms, especially deploying technology which has not matured enough, may promise consumers products or services which they consider feasible to build, but may not accurately estimate the necessary time. In this case, consumers could end up investing real money in digital content which they would not have access to for a long time after the conclusion of the contract.

Moving on to conformity requirements, Article 6 of the Directive sets out a general obligation for the digital contract provided under the contract to be in conformity with the said contract. Articles 7–9 further explain how conformity is defined and applied to contracts for digital content. Article 7 specifies four cumulative conditions which ought to be met as subjective requirements for conformity: (a) that the digital content or service be of the description, quantity and quality, and possess the functionality, compatibility, interoperability and other features, as required by the contract; (b) that it be fit for the purposes required by the consumer and made known by the latter before or at the time of the conclusion of the contract, and which the trader agreed with; (c) be supplied with all accessories and instructions (including regarding installation and customer assistance) as agreed upon in the contract; and (d) be updated as agreed upon in the contract. In some cases, not all conditions may be applicable (e.g. (b)). Article 8 builds on these requirements to define the objective requirements for conformity. For example, Article 8(1)(a) refers to fitness for purpose through benchmarking, by referring to digital content or services of the same type; whereas Article 8(1)(d) speaks about compliance with potential trial versions or previews of the digital content or service. In addition, Article 9 covers integration issues arising under the trader's responsibility or due to faulty instructions given by the trader.

Taking the description as a central tenet of the hype around Decentraland, the company behind the project has gained a lot of traction and initial investment in the project due to its label of decentralization, which is supposed to be the core difference between Decentraland and other virtual worlds like Second Life or Eve Online.

However, while LAND ownership runs on blockchain and thus entails that each transaction needs to be validated on Ethereum and outside of the grasp of Decentraland developers, not the same can be said about a lot of the other elements on which Decentraland runs. For instance, as it was revealed in the Terms of Service, there is nothing decentralized about Metaverse Holdings Ltd. holding all the intellectual property rights for the architecture of Decentraland, including the tools it is being built with. The same goes for the storage of data, as all the data stored in relation to a parcel of LAND is currently stored on a centralized server (Schultz, 2019). This can lead to the very danger justifying the existence of Decentraland: that centralization is a risk for when virtual worlds shut down shop and leave their consumers without the fruits of their time, effort or financial resources spent in those worlds (Schultz, 2019). Under the current setup, Metaverse Holdings Ltd. has not hedged this risk, as without the infrastructure that it has clearly retained rights for, and currently operates centrally, there simply is no Decentraland.

Lastly, regarding the modification of the digital content or service, Article 19(1) specifies that such content may be modified under certain conditions: (a) if the contract allows and provides a valid reason for such a modification; (b) such a modification is made without additional cost to the consumer; (c) the consumer is informed in a clear and comprehensible manner about the modification; and (d) the consumer is informed reasonably in advance, of the modification as well as the right to terminate the contract, or the possibility to maintain the digital content or service without such a modification.

This is likely one of the crucial contributions of the Directive on Digital Content with respect to policing new business models which entail subsequent iterations and constant change. Decentraland set itself on a pathway of various historical 'ages' to map its transformation. Its earliest age consisted of a 2D map, similar to the Million Dollar Page The Million Dollar Homepage—Own a Piece of Internet History!, n.d.), where users were attributed pixels on the grid according to a proof of work algorithm Decentraland/Stoneage-Browser, n.d.). The subsequent ages marked fundamental changes not only in its 'touch and feel', or its functions, but more importantly in the business model used by the company, which aims to become an intermediary for peer-to-peer Dapps, exchanges, etc.

It is unclear if and how the company communicates with its consumers about these fundamental changes. Article 2 of its Terms of Service indicates that 'the Curator reserves the right, at its sole discretion, to modify or replace the Terms of Use at any time. The most current version of these Terms will be posted on our Site. You shall be responsible for reviewing and becoming familiar with any such modifications. Use of the Tools by you after any modification to the Terms constitutes your acceptance of the Terms of Use as modified'. Put differently, the Curator places the information duty for becoming aware of changes made in the Terms of Service on the customers, and does not acknowledge a need to disclose such changes. Should Decentraland fundamentally upon transitioning into the 'Silicon Age', Article 19(1) of the Digital Content Directive will become pivotal for the protection of consumer interests.

5 Conclusion

This chapter focused on closing a research gap regarding consumer protection and blockchain-based content and services targeted at consumers. It labeled how Decentraland uses non-fungible tokens such as LAND which may be considered as digital content, and looked into compliance issues arising out of the application of the Digital Content Directive to Decentraland in general, and LAND in particular.

Launched in 2008, the Bitcoin blockchain was the first distributed ledger technology to be officially called a cryptocurrency, namely a type of digital money sent via a series of computer-enabled actions based on sophisticated cryptographic protocols. With the rise of blockchain ecosystems like the Ethereum platform, which considers itself a virtual machine for Dapps, a lot of new meaning has been given to blockchain products. Both MANA and LAND, the tokes referred to in this chapter, are ERCs (Ethereum Request for Comments), namely 'technical documents used by smart contract developers at Ethereum', that 'define a set of rules required to implement tokens for the Ethereum ecosystem' (Agrawal, 2019). The fast pace at which these developments take place, and new meanings found for the tokenization system (Lee, 2019; Nadler & Guo, 2019; Savelyev, 2018) can be seen by merely looking at the standardization of known tokens, which can be divided into 'draft (opened for consideration, such as the ERC721 Non-fungible Token Standard), accepted (planned for immediate adoption), final (implemented, as the ERC20 Token Standard), and deferred (dismissed for now and may be considered in the future)' (de la Rocha, 2018). Non-fungible token standards such as those used for Cryptokitties or Decentraland are illustrations of the moniker 'Internet of Value', where it is not just cryptocurrencies that are traded online, but new forms of informational value.

However, this value can be stripped down to a more familiar concept, namely that of digital content. As data created by a platform and destined to be transacted to a user/consumer of that platform, parcels of LAND in Decentraland are nothing more than digital content, to which users may attach subjective forms of value, as well as objective financial expressions (e.g. when reselling). From this perspective, LAND parcels make up a fascinating case study for the application of the Digital Content Directive to a more sophisticated form of digital content.

After briefly examining some of the Directive's main tenets, namely the timeliness of the provision of digital content; the conformity requirements; and the modification of the digital content, it becomes increasingly clear that the Directive can play a central role in protecting consumer interests in the blockchain market, in more concrete situations not facing excessive legal uncertainty, as has been the case of, for instance, smart contracts, but in very specific transactions that are undoubtedly governed by European consumer protection rules. Absent market research to shed light on more factual details, such as how many European consumers have purchased LAND parcels, and out of those, how many are still waiting for their access to the Decentraland client, it remains to be seen whether there will be a practical need for consumer protection in these cases. However, it must be stressed that the Directive on Digital Content amply covers problematic situations which may arise out of consumer contracts for digital content such as non-fungible tokens, and its application to such circumstances will mark a momentous opportunity to bring more legal certainty to the space of blockchain governance.

References

Abrahams, N. (2007). Media laws from virtual words. *UNSW Law Journal, 30*(1), 295–306.

Adimi, G. A. (2018). How the new generation cryptocurrencies decoded the investment contract code: Analysis of US and EU Laws IV: Scritti in Tema Di Diritto Dell'Economia. *Bocconi Legal Papers, 1*, 313–346.

Agrawal, G. (2019, May 8). *All about ERC token standards*. Medium. Retrieved from https://medium.com/coinmonks/all-about-erc-token-standards-9c759efdc791.

Alvarez, M. (2018). A comparative analysis of cryptocurrency regulation in the United States, Nigeria, and China: The potential influence of illicit activities on regulatory evolution. *ILSA Journal of International and Comparative Law, 1*, 33–56.

Bakhoum, M., Gallego, B. C., Mackenrodt, M.-O., & Surblytė-Namavičienė, G. (2018). *Personal data in competition, consumer protection and intellectual property law: Towards a holistic approach?* Springer.

Berger, M., Jucker, A. H., & Locher, M. A. (2016, August). Interaction and space in the virtual world of second life. *Journal of Pragmatics, 101*, 83–100. Retrieved from https://doi.org/10.1016/j.pragma.2016.05.009.

Boellstorff, T. (2015). *Coming of age in second life: An anthropologist explores the virtually human*. Princeton University Press.

Buchko, S. (2018). What is decentraland? (MANA). *CoinDesk* (blog). Retrieved from https://coincentral.com/decentraland-mana-beginners-guide/

Casper, C. (2018). How to buy MANA (Decentraland) your top 11 options. *CoinIQ* (blog). Retrieved from https://coiniq.com/how-to-buy-mana/.

Chen, A. (2011). The underground website where you can buy any drug imaginable. *Gawker*. Retrieved from http://gawker.com/the-underground-website-where-you-can-buy-any-drug-imag-30818160.

Chesney, T., Chuah, S.-H., & Hoffmann, R. (2009). Virtual world experimentation: An exploratory study. *Journal of Economic Behavior & Organization, 72*(1), 618–635. Retrieved from https://doi.org/10.1016/j.jebo.2009.05.026.

Consultant, The Cryptocurrency. (2019). *What is the internet of values?* Medium. Retrieved from https://medium.com/swlh/what-is-the-internet-of-values-3f14b5d35a90.

Davidson, S., De Filippi, P., & Potts, J. (2018). Blockchains and the economic institutions of capitalism. *Journal of Institutional Economics, 14*(4), 639–658. https://doi.org/10.1017/S1744137417000200.

De la Rocha, A. (2018). *Anatomy of an ERC: An exhaustive survey*. Medium. Retrieved from https://medium.com/coinmonks/anatomy-of-an-erc-an-exhaustive-survey-8bc1a323b541.

Decentraland (n.d.). *Decentraland*. Retrieved from https://decentraland.org.

Decentraland/Stoneage-Browser (n.d.). *GitHub*. Retrieved from https://github.com/decentraland/stoneage-browser.

Storj (n.d.). *Decentralized Cloud Storage—Storj*. Retrieved from https://storj.io.

DTube (n.d.). Retrieved from https://d.tube/.

Ducuing, C. (2019). How to make sure my cryptokitties are here forever? The complementary roles of blockchain and the law to bring trust. *European Journal of Risk Regulation, 10*(2), 315–329. https://doi.org/10.1017/err.2019.39.

Engelmann. (2017). *International commercial arbitration and the commercial agency directive: A perspective from law and economics*. Springer.
Gallego, M. D., Bueno, S., & Noyes, J. (2016). Second life adoption in education: A motivational model based on uses and gratifications theory. *Computers & Education, 100*, 81–93. https://doi.org/10.1016/j.compedu.2016.05.001.
Garofalo, D. A. (2013). Make the connection: Posting on social media. In D. A. Garofalo, *Building communities* (pp. 107–159). Chandos Publishing Social Media Series. Chandos Publishing. https://doi.org/10.1016/B978-1-84334-735-4.50005-1.
Gikay, A. A. (2018). Regulating decentralized cryptocurrencies under payment services law: Lessons from European Union Law. *Case Western Reserve Journal of Law, Technology and the Internet*, *9*, 1–35.
Graphite. (n.d.). Retrieved from https://graphitedocs.com.
Grimmelmann, J. (2014). Anarchy, status updates, and Utopia. *Pace Law Review, 35*(1), 135–153.
Hansen, D. L., Shneiderman, B., & Smith, M. A. (2011a). Chapter 3—Social network analysis: Measuring, mapping, and modeling collections of connections. In D. L. Hansen, B. Shneiderman, & M. A. Smith (Eds.), *Analyzing social media networks with NodeXL* (pp. 31–50). Boston: Morgan Kaufmann. https://doi.org/10.1016/B978-0-12-382229-1.00003-5.
Hansen, D. L., Shneiderman, B., & Smith, M. A. (2011b). Chapter 9—Thread networks: Mapping message boards and email lists. In D. L. Hansen, B. Shneiderman, & M. A. Smith (Eds.), *Analyzing social media networks with NodeXL* (pp. 127–141). Boston: Morgan Kaufmann. https://doi.org/10.1016/B978-0-12-382229-1.00009-6.
Hansen, D. L., Shneiderman, B., & Smith, M. A. (2011c). Part I. Getting started with analyzing social media networks. In D. L. Hansen, B. Shneiderman, & M. A. Smith (Eds.), *Analyzing social media networks with NodeXL* (Vol. 1). Boston: Morgan Kaufmann. https://doi.org/10.1016/B978-0-12-382229-1.00016-3.
Hoekstra, J., & Diker-Vanberg, A. (2019). The proposed directive for the supply of digital content: Is it fit for purpose? *International Review of Law, Computers & Technology, 33*(1), 100–117. https://doi.org/10.1080/13600869.2019.1562638.
Hughes, E. (1993). *A Cypherpunk's Manifesto*. Retrieved from https://www.activism.net/cypherpunk/manifesto.html.
Kalning, K. (2007). *If second life isn't a game, what is it?* Msnbc.Com. Retrieved from http://www.nbcnews.com/id/17538999/ns/technology_and_science-games/t/if-second-life-isnt-game-what-it/.
Karniell, Y., & Bates, S. (2010). Copyright in second life. *Albany Law Journal of Science and Technology, 20*(3), 433–456.
Kayser, J. J. (2006). The new new-world: Virtual property and the end user license agreement notes & comments. *Loyola of Los Angeles Entertainment Law Review, 1*, 59–86.
Khan, J. (2016). To what extent can blockchain be used as a tool for community guidance. *Edinburgh Student Law Review, 2*, 114–133.
Klastrup, L. (2009). The worldness of EverQuest: Exploring a 21st century fiction. *Game Studies, 9*(1) Retrieved from http://gamestudies.org/0901/articles/klastrup.
Krzywinska, T. (2006). *Blood scythes, festivals, quests, and backstories: World creation and rhetorics of myth in World of Warcraft*. Retrieved from https://journals.sagepub.com/doi/abs/10.1177/1555412006292618.
Lastowka, F. G., & Hunter, D. (2004). The laws of the virtual worlds. *California Law Review, 1*, 1–74.
Lee, J. Y. (2019). A decentralized token economy: How blockchain and cryptocurrency can revolutionize business. *Business Horizons, 62*(6), 773–784. https://doi.org/10.1016/j.bushor.2019.08.003.
Lee, J., Yoo, B., & Jang, M. (2019). Is a blockchain-based game a game for fun, or is it a tool for speculation? An empirical analysis of player behavior in crypokitties. In J. J. Xu, B. Zhu, X. Liu, M. J. Shaw, H. Zhang, & M. Fan (Eds.), *The ecosystem of e-business: Technologies,*

stakeholders, and connections (pp. 141–48). Lecture Notes in Business Information Processing. Cham: Springer International Publishing. https://doi.org/10.1007/978-3-030-22784-5_14.

Lehmann, M. (2016). A question of coherence: The proposals on EU contract rules on digital content and online sales. *Maastricht Journal of European and Comparative Law, 23*(5), 752–774. https://doi.org/10.1177/1023263X1602300502.

Lidsky, L. B. (2009). Anonymity in cyberspace: What can we learn from John Doe publicity, privacy, and intellectual property meet the first amendment. *Boston College Law Review, 5*, 1373–1392.

Liedel, D. A. (2018). The taxation of bitcoin: How the IRS views cryptocurrencies. *Drake Law Review, 1*, 107–146.

Locher, M. A., Jucker, A. H., & Berger, M. (2015, September). Negotiation of space in second life newbie interaction. *Discourse, Context & Media*, Communicating time and place on digital media, *9*, 34–45. https://doi.org/10.1016/j.dcm.2015.06.002.

Malaby, T. (2011). *Making virtual worlds: Linden lab and Second Life*. Cornell University Press.

Manning, P. (2019, February). Free the code, free the world: The chronotopic 'worldness' of the virtual world of ryzom. *Language & Communication*. https://doi.org/10.1016/j.langcom.2019.01.002.

Marshall, A. (2014, January). Sensemaking in second life. *Procedia Technology*, SLACTIONS 2013: Research conference on virtual worlds—Learning with simulations, *13*, 107–111. https://doi.org/10.1016/j.protcy.2014.02.014.

McCullagh, D. (2001). Technology as security symposium: Is technology changing the law. *Harvard Journal of Law & Public Policy, 1*(2002), 129–142.

Mearian, L. (2019). *Global blockchain spending to hit $12.4B by 2022; Finance Sector Leads Growth | Computerworld*. Retrieved from https://www.computerworld.com/article/3356502/global-blockchain-spending-to-hit-124b-by-2022-finance-sector-leads-growth.html.

Mistry, K. (2018). P(L)Aying to win: Loot boxes, microtransaction monetization, and a proposal for self-regulation in the video game industry student notes. *Rutgers University Law Review, 1*, 537–578.

Mowbray, M. (2006). Implementing pseudonymity. *SCRIPTed: A Journal of Law, Technology and Society, 1*, 34–44.

Nadler, P., & Guo, Y. (2019, October). The fair value of a token: How do markets price cryptocurrencies? *Research in International Business and Finance*, 101108. https://doi.org/10.1016/j.ribaf.2019.101108.

Nakamoto, S. (2009). *Bitcoin: A peer-to-peer electronic cash system*. Retrieved from https://bitcoin.org/bitcoin.pdf.

Partala, T. (2011). Psychological needs and virtual worlds: Case second life. *International Journal of Human-Computer Studies, 69*(12), 787–800. https://doi.org/10.1016/j.ijhcs.2011.07.004.

Pearce, C. (2011). *Communities of play: Emergent cultures in multiplayer games and virtual worlds*. MIT Press.

Popper, N. (2018, December 21). Timothy C. May, Early Advocate of Internet Privacy, Dies at 66. *The New York Times*, sec. Obituaries. Retrieved from https://www.nytimes.com/2018/12/21/obituaries/timothy-c-may-dead.html.

R/Decentraland—ETA on Iron Age? (n.d.). *Reddit*. Retrieved October 27, 2019, from https://www.reddit.com/r/decentraland/comments/a4nnza/eta_on_iron_age/.

Savelyev, A. (2018). Some risks of tokenization and blockchainizaition of private law. *Computer Law & Security Review, 34*(4), 863–869. https://doi.org/10.1016/j.clsr.2018.05.010.

Schultz, A. R. (2019, May 22). *Blockchain-based virtual world decentraland will finally launch its public beta in june, but it won't be very decentralized (Yet) and it won't support VR*. Ryan Schultz. Retrieved from https://ryanschultz.com/2019/05/22/blockchain-based-virtual-world-decentraland-will-finally-launch-its-public-beta-in-june-but-it-wont-be-very-decentralized-yet-and-it-wont-support-vr/.

Sein, K. (2017). What rules should apply to smart consumer goods: Goods with embedded digital content in the borderland between the digital content directive and normal contract law. *Journal of Intellectual Property, Information Technology and Electronic Commerce Law, 2*, 96–110.
Sergeenkov, A. (2019). *Why blockchain and VR might be a match made in digital heaven*. Retrieved from https://hackernoon.com/why-blockchain-and-vr-might-be-a-match-made-in-digital-heaven-3b0c849978cf.
Shelton, A. K. (2010). Defining the lines between virtual and real world purchases: Second life sells, but who's buying? *Computers in Human Behavior, Online Interactivity: Role of Technology in Behavior Change, 26*(6), 1223–1227. https://doi.org/10.1016/j.chb.2010.03.019.
Skinner, C. (2016). *ValueWeb: How fintech firms are using bitcoin blockchain and mobile technologies to create the internet of value*. Marshall Cavendish International Asia Pte Ltd.
Song, J. Y., Chang, W., & Song, J. W. (2019). Cluster analysis on the structure of the cryptocurrency market via Bitcoin–Ethereum filtering. *Physica A: Statistical Mechanics and its Applications, 527*, 121339. https://doi.org/10.1016/j.physa.2019.121339.
Sundquist, M. (2012). Online privacy protection: Protecting privacy, the social contract, and the rule of law in the virtual world. *Regent University Law Review, 25*, 153–183.
Taylor, T. L. (2009). *Play between worlds: Exploring online game culture*. Cambridge: MIT Press.
The Internet of Value: What It Means and How It Benefits Everyone. (2017, June 21). *Ripple* (blog). Retrieved from https://www.ripple.com/insights/the-internet-of-value-what-it-means-and-how-it-benefits-everyone/.
The Million Dollar Homepage—Own a Piece of Internet History!. (n.d.). Retrieved October 28, 2019, from http://www.milliondollarhomepage.com/.
Truong, N. B., Um, T.-W., Zhou, B., & Lee, G. M. (2018). Strengthening the blockchain-based internet of value with trust. In *2018 IEEE International Conference on Communications (ICC)* (pp. 1–7). https://doi.org/10.1109/ICC.2018.8423014.
Warburton, J. M. (2016). An innovative legal approach to regulating digital content contracts in the EU special issue on law and governance in the digital era. *Journal of Intellectual Property, Information Technology and Electronic Commerce Law, 3*, 246–255.
Wein, K. (2001). Dendrite v. Doe: A new standard for protecting anonymity on internet message boards developments in science and technology law—Part I: Internet law. *Jurimetrics, 4*, 465–478.
William, M. (2018). ERC-20 Tokens, Explained. *Cointelegraph*. Retrieved from https://cointelegraph.com/explained/erc-20-tokens-explained.

Application of a Systems Engineering Approach as a Preventative Measure Against Disruptions to Real Estate Institutions

C. Kat Grimsley and Cody A. Pennetti

Abstract As technology changes at an exponential rate, business and development industries must prioritize investments to be prepared for disruptive technologies. Within the real estate industry, the influence of new technologies is readily apparent in areas such as design and construction with Building Information Modeling (BIM), the incorporation of smart and sustainable/energy efficient systems into new buildings, and a shared economy approach to space use (e.g. AirBnB). However, there is an extensive network of critical interrelated institutions connected to real estate that is often overlooked, making the effects of disruption less transparent in the context of the larger system. This chapter will emphasize the complexity of the system that supports real property and its relevance for infrastructure, humanitarian, and market interests. The chapter will then propose a systems engineering approach as the appropriate lens through which to view the "real estate system" to ensure projects are holistically envisioned and disruptions can be anticipated.

Keywords Systems engineering · Risk management · Multiple objective analysis · Complex systems · Real estate institutions · Real estate disruption

C. Kat Grimsley (✉)
Center for Real Estate Entrepreneurship, George Mason University, Fairfax, VA, USA
e-mail: cgrims@gmu.edu

C. A. Pennetti
Department of Engineering Systems and Environment (ESE), Center for Risk Management of Engineering Systems, University of Virginia, Charlottesville, VA, USA

A. Lehavi, R. Levine-Schnur (eds.), *Disruptive Technology, Legal Innovation, and the Future of Real Estate*, https://doi.org/10.1007/978-3-030-52387-9_9

1 Introduction: Complexity of the Real Estate System

Real property assets are important in infrastructure, humanitarian, and market contexts, with specific areas of concern varying between different sovereign states depending on country-specific factors. Generally, the humanitarian perspective is concerned with improving conditions for vulnerable groups, such as those living in poverty, as well as ensuring the overall sustainability of the built environment. The focus of contemporary aid programs related to real estate often includes a connection to the Sustainable Development Goals of the UN's 2030 Agenda and themes related to ensuring security of title and tenure, including the provision of adequate and affordable housing, and eliminating social inequalities propagated by existing land use patterns and/or land rights regimes (UN Habitat, 2016; United Nations, 2015). Indeed, there is a compelling link between equitable improvements in title and tenure security and several critical measures for human wellness, such as improvements in women's rights, levels of educational attainment, and increased food security through gains in agricultural production (Bambioa & Bouayad Aghab, 2018; Higgins, Balint, Liversage, & Winters, 2018; Lawry et al., 2017; Muchomba, 2017). Among these themes, there is extensive overlap in underlying issues that are equally important for real estate markets. For example, while preventing energy poverty (Habitat for Humanity International and USAID, 2017) is a growing concern from a humanitarian standpoint, energy efficiency is also paramount from a for-profit investment/development perspective when cost savings are substantial. Similarly, security of title and tenure is also an important foundation for efficient property markets as a precondition to allow for the development and transfer of real estate assets (UNECE, 2019).

Regardless of the dominant underlying interest, real property considerations rely on an extensive array of supporting institutions. For the purpose of this chapter, institutions are considered to be organizations and their associated systems and capacity that are integral to a particular function or outcome. The connection between certain institutions and real property is obvious, such as the need for a land records office; however, other equally critical institutions may be less apparent. Examples of critical institutions include (1) legislative bodies (2) court and police systems (3) land records offices, (4) planning and zoning offices, (5) banking and other lending systems, (6) national data systems, (7) educational institutions, and (8) taxation authorities. Depending on state regulations, each different institution may operate at a national/centralized, regional, or local level. Each institution will also typically include sub-divisions or functional units, which are critical to the overall functionality of the institution. Further, different institutions, or even different divisions within a single institution, often have different capacities and access to human and financial resources. Figure 1 describes the institutions listed above in greater detail.

Note that the list in Fig. 1 is not exhaustive and is presented to highlight the dependency of real estate functions on an entire, interrelated system of supporting institutions. For example, an unsuccessful tax policy may have direct consequences

	Institution and function	Example Infrastructure / Market considerations	Example Humanitarian considerations
1	Legislative bodies - create clear and coherent legal/regulatory frameworks, including rights to property and contract law.	Must be sufficiently developed to enable sophisticated transactions and development projects.	Political forums must be inclusive; resulting policies must be equitable in practice, not formalize inequality, and must address tradtional and non-formal tenure.
2	Courts and police - able to resolve disputes and enforce the rule of law, including both property rights and contract law.	Disputes must be resolved in a timely and effective manner or else project risk/cost variables increase.	Outcomes cannot be biased in favor of those with means or education.
3	Land records office - establish transfer process and provide accurate and reliable evidence of title (or national equivalent, sometimes including recorded leases) to real property, as supported by registration, surveying, and record keeping actives.	Failure to maintain accurate and reliable records introduces risk that can limit investment and development activity.	Participation can be impacted if the office imposes high costs in the forms of fees or lengthy, complex registration processes may result in non-compliance and encourage informality.
4	Zoning / planning offices - implement planning and zoning controls to allocate appropriate land uses and approve development.	High costs in the form of fees, proffers, or lengthy, complex approval processes introduce risk and can limit investment/ development activities, or will impact affordability as costs are built into asset pricing.	Must produce results free from discriminatory policies and outcomes; must ensure a sufficient supply of affordable housing for vulnerable groups.
5	Lending / banking - provide funding resources dedicated to real estate investment.	Must be efficient so as not to impede transactions; must be reliable, accessible, and agile enough to support unique or complicated projects.	Free from discriminatory lending practices.
6	National data systems - the country's computing/ technological capacity is sufficient to manage the number of land records, banking transactions, etc.	Investment and development may be inhibited in jurisdications using only paper title records due to risk of fraudulent claims and lack of security/certainty.	Technology infrastructure should benefit all people and include service to remote and economically challenged areas.
7	Education institutions - sufficient education to produce both competent land users (owners, tenants, licensees, etc) and real estate professionals capable of serving the industry through surveying, brokerage, legal services, and other professions.	Availability of professional surveyors, attorneys, etc is necessary for efficient transfers and new development; the quality of a school system can incentivize or deter people from moving to a particular area, which can impact levels of local retail, office, and residential investment.	Groups without basic education are vulnerable to corrupt and predatory practices and/or may not be able to participate in formal transfer and ownership systems.
8	Taxation authority - set appropriate property tax policy and deliver public services of value in exchange for taxes collected.	Inadequate public services can limit demand and may restrict development, particularly if tax rates are disproportionately high.	Inappropriate tax programs or inadequate public services can incentivize tax evasion through unregistered property transfers, which can undermine formalization programs.

Fig. 1 Summary of critical institutions

for real property, but is also tied to the delivery of education as a public service, which has separate implications in the context of real estate. Similar connections exist between banking, land records, and data systems. This reveals a multi-layered, interdependent system, any part of which may be susceptible to disruption wherein institutions can impact real estate individually or in unforeseen conjunction. Within this complex environment, the influence of individual policies or programs as well as the impact of disruption by new technologies on the underlying real estate is not immediately apparent.

It bears noting that, in addition to disruptions to or through institutions, the real estate system can also be influenced by movements, conditions, and phenomenon that are external to a sub-system (e.g., a single development project). Examples include phenomenon such as environmental change, conditions such as food scarcity, or disruptive technologies. This chapter evaluates how real estate developers can prioritize investments to serve multiple objectives while considering how disruptive technologies may influence priorities and decision-making.

2 Discussion: Identifying Disruption with a Complex System

Tracing the potential for disruption is nearly impossible without (1) initial recognition of the wider real estate system and its influence, (2) appreciation for the importance of the benefits of tracking system influences, and (3) a framework to guide the exercise capable of identifying susceptible areas and testing causal connections. The challenge of anticipating disruption is intensified, although arguably even more important, in a global context where an estimated 7.7% of the population, or more than 582 million people, live in extreme poverty, facing tenure insecurity, unsanitary and/or unsafe housing, and food/water scarcity (World Poverty Clock, n.d.). Institutional challenges in developing nations are often exacerbated by limited capacity and varying levels of sophistication. Even so, global examples of efforts to accommodate complex systems do exist in a real estate context. These often take the form of efforts to set global standards, systems, processes, or as tools intended to address complex conditions related to title transfer, recordation, and tenure security, both with humanitarian and market interests. Specific examples include:

2010: the Social Tenure Domain Model (STDM).
2012: the Land Administration Domain Model (LADM).
2014: the New Continuum of Land Rights Model.
2018: the International Land Measurements Standards (ILMS).
2019: the Theory for Change/Logic Model for Land Tenure and Governance.

Most, although not all, of these models attempt to address the radically different experiences and conditions in different countries. However, they face a fundamental limitation in scope by focusing on relationships relevant for land governance and administration institutions (Augustinus, 2019; Grimsley & Kavanagh, 2018; ISO, 2018; Lemmen, van Oosteromb, & Bennett, 2015; UN Habitat, 2017, 2019; Whittal, 2014). As a result, they do not account for the greater real estate system and the potential for causal relationships or disruptions in other institutions. To strengthen and build upon these current tools, a fundamentally new approach is necessary to address limitations, both in domestic and international contexts.

The necessary sophisticated, multidimensional approach exists in the study of systems engineering. In the context of real estate, preliminary applications of systems engineering are being made in infrastructure development to account for the complexity of the factors involved. These initial considerations can be expanded to help prepare different sectors of the real estate industry, ranging from individual real estate development projects to global policy development, to withstand unexpected disruption. The following sections identify systems engineering methods and technologies that can assist developers, designers, and the community in program management by considering multiple objectives of stakeholders, temporal analysis of decisions, and scenario planning.

2.1 Systems Engineering Background

Systems engineering has emerged in the last 100 years and is inclusive of technical, managerial, and philosophical applications of a project (Haimes, 2019; INCOSE, 2007). This section provides a brief overview; however, systems engineering is a vast and complex field that encompasses a range of topics beyond the purview of this chapter. From the technical perspective, systems engineering investigates the applied mathematics of topics such as optimization and statistical modeling. Decision and risk analysis can fall under the managerial content of systems engineering. Perhaps most importantly, the philosophical element of systems engineering considers how multiple systems, objectives, and stakeholders are interconnected and interdependent. The philosophical perspective acknowledges the inherent challenges associated with models, risks, and decisions for systems with noncommensurate variables (e.g., financial investment costs versus risk of life) and multiple objectives. These topics are not independent within the realm of systems engineering and must also consider the shifting base of the system across time (Haimes, 2012) (Fig. 2).

The application of systems engineering is not prescriptive or uniform across domains, geographies or projects. It would be impossible to create a systems-based process or model that could appropriately represent the complexity of the built and natural environments. Instead, systems engineering is a catalyst for stakeholders to be engaged in the evaluation of multiple objectives, perspectives, tradeoffs and risks associated with development.

Applied to real estate development, systems engineering can function as a tool to investigate the challenges associated with the risk, uncertainty, and shifting conditions that are inherent to development projects. Real estate projects seek rapid design and development while attempting to consider long-term conditions with deep uncertainty. Specifically, three critical practices of systems engineering can be applied to real estate development processes:

1. considering *multiple objectives* and perspectives
2. evaluation of systems across a *temporal* domain, and

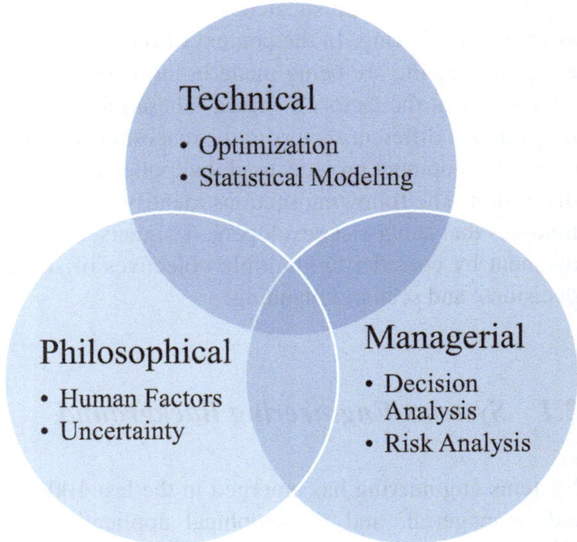

Fig. 2 Illustration of the interconnected systems engineering domains

3. *scenario analyses* to investigate possible outcomes associated with future conditions.

In this way, the multiple objective temporal scenario analysis (MOTSA) provides a framework that benefits developers, stakeholders, land owners, and decision makers.

The MOTSA process supports developers and stakeholders in decision-making. The approach demonstrated in this chapter describes a philosophy of planning that considers the complex interconnected and interdependent conditions of real estate development, with implications for different market-rate product types, infrastructure, and humanitarian initiatives. While it is impossible to find an optimal design solution when attempting to identify optimality from multiple perspectives, the intent of the MOTSA process is to introduce necessary actions into traditional land development planning in order to minimize regret. In this case, regret is measured as a function of what was completed when compared to what should have been completed (Ram & Montibeller, 2012). It would be unreasonable to assume that regret could be accurately measured except by a post-facto analysis; instead, the MOTSA process is meant to inform stakeholders of conditions that may not be self-evident and uses the concept of regret to evaluate the consequences of current actions on future decisions.

2.1.1 MOTSA Overview

The MOTSA process is a tool for resilience analytics. The term *resilience*, as defined by the International Council on Systems Engineering (INCOSE) is a system's ability "to adapt to changing conditions and prepare for, withstand, and rapidly recover from disruption" (INCOSE, 2007). When evaluated with real estate development projects and disruptive technology, a resilient project would maintain value under disruptive conditions and regret would be minimized. The disruptions may come as technological discoveries but in many cases it is the policies and social perspectives that establish the influence of technology (Maier & Rechtin, 2009).

Prior work has applied resilience analytics to infrastructure systems as a means of ranking and prioritizing investment initiatives (Collier & Lambert, 2018; Connelly, Colosi, Clarens, & Lambert, 2015; Quenum, Thorisson, Wu, & Lambert, 2019; Thorisson, Lambert, Cardenas, & Linkov, 2017). To consider the rapid emergence of disruptive technologies, this work introduces a temporal evaluation to evaluate how the timing of technology adoption will influence investment priorities. The prior work has established methods for evaluating the resilience of different initiatives by applying stressors and investigating the numerical rank of each initiative as evaluated under different perspectives (or conditions) (Thekdi & Lambert, 2015). This framework has been defined to investigate the ability for various project investment initiatives (p) to withstand different disruptions (d), where one or more disruptions are defined by scenarios (s). Each project is evaluated and ranked by a set of multiple objectives (mo) and then re-evaluated under different scenarios (Allen et al., 2018; Connelly et al., 2015; Thorisson et al., 2017).The variables are define by:

- Project Initiatives—different investment initiatives for a given project
  - $P = \{p_1,\ldots,p_n\}$, with n initiatives
- Disruptions—technological disruptions that could influence the ranking of initiatives
  - $D = \{d_1 \ldots, d_m\}$, with m number of disruptions
- Scenarios—one or more disruptions defines a scenario
  - $S = \{s_1,\ldots,s_k\}$, with k scenarios based on sets of disruptions
- Multiple Objectives—economics, environment, aesthetics, and others
  - Mo = $\{mo_1,\ldots,mo_m\}$, with m objectives based on multiple perspectives A weight value (w) is assigned to each objective (mo_m), where $\sum_{j=1}^{m} w_j = 1,\ 0 \le w_j \le 1\ \ for\ j = 1,\ldots m$.

In this way, the weight assigned to each objective is normalized. The weight can change for each scenario and temporal domain. For example, if the primary objectives are economy, safety, and environment, the weights might be 30%, 50% and 20% respectively. Then, the maximum score (z) for each objective is proportional to the weight (30, 50, and 20 from the prior example). Each project initiative (p_i) is scored (a_i) based on the ability to meet an objective, as measured with the associated weight (w_j). Continuing with the prior example, a project initiative might score 15 (of 30), 45 (of 50), and 20 (of 20) points (for a total of 80 out of 100 possible points). The evaluation and scoring of project initiatives is best performed by a group of stakeholders with multiple perspectives. Score values are based on relevant research and expert opinion. The scoring process is repeated across all projects. Mathematically, we can define this as shown in Eq. (1):

$$v_{s_k}\left(p_i\right)=\sum_{j=1}^{m} w_j^k a_{ji}^k \tag{1}$$

Equation (1) represents the project prioritization value (v) for a given project (p_i) based on the total value of each objective weight (w) and the assigned score (a) across all objectives (j) for a given scenario (s_k).

Resilience analytics traditionally begins with a baseline condition, in which there are no disruptions. Each scenario introduces one or more disruptions, often with a common (inevitable) disruption, that could modify the weight values of each objective. Each scenario also requires a new set of scores assigned to each project initiative to consider the effectiveness under the given scenario. For example, under a baseline (no disruption scenario), a site's surface parking may be designed to accommodate current transportation systems. However, under a disruption such as the emergence of electric vehicles, the investments in vehicle parking systems such as charging stations might be scored higher. Each stakeholder must evaluate the development program to determine a list of project initiatives that can be influenced by multiple objectives and disruptions. A sample set of project initiatives for real estate development projects is shown in Table 1 for reference.

Table 1 List of possible land development project initiatives that are influenced by disruptive technologies

P	Project initiatives
P_1	Provide infrastructure to support electric charging stations
P_2	Install electric charging stations
P_3	Provide infrastructure to support hydrogen vehicle fueling
P_4	Provide conduit, electrical systems and structural support for rooftop solar
P_5	Plan for surface parking redevelopment
P_6	Install additional (empty) communication and electrical conduits
P_7	Reserve building space for battery backup systems
P_8	Reserve site area for alternative transportation modes
P_9	Provide drop off and queuing areas for autonomous vehicles
P_{10}	Design roof layout (and structural support) to accommodate UAVs
P_{11}	Design structured parking with raised clear heights to accommodate future conversation to useable space (subsurface or above grade decks)
P_{12}	Design structured parking layout with side ramps to facilitate AV navigation
P_{13}	Change plenum depth to accommodate new sustainable heating/cooling mechanisms
P_{14}	Provide drone docking and delivery drop off stations (aerial or vehicular)
P_{15}	Increase building central computing capability and dedicated mainframe space for systems upgrades and/or to engage with future Smart City initiatives

The source of these initiatives may come from the developer, stakeholders, design team, academic works, or other sources. The list of project initiatives should consider similarities and the ability to disaggregate initiatives that may establish more resilient investments. For example, when faced with an unknown condition of the next dominant vehicle fuel source (e.g., electric or hydrogen), a resilient project initiative would include the primary infrastructure elements (e.g., underground conduit and additional electrical capacity) that would support onsite fueling options.

2.2 Multiple Objectives

Despite efforts to streamline or simplify, there is no complex system with a single objective. The *multiple objective* component of MOTSA acknowledges that stakeholder objectives will face competition between project priorities, available resources, community support, and other conditions. For example, water infrastructure projects compete on objectives of supply, hydropower and replenishment of natural systems (Siddiqi, Ereiqat, & Anadon, 2016). As another example, businesses located along a highway may compete for customer access to promote economic development, but transportation agencies may seek to minimize access points to reduce vehicle conflicts (Thekdi & Lambert, 2015; Thorisson & Lambert, 2017). A residential developer seeks to maximize profits while considering the physical and political boundaries of development, but public authorities will also consider the humanitarian responsibilities of providing affordable and accessible housing.

Hierarchical holographic modeling (HHM) is a framework to consider multiple perspectives and objectives of a system (Haimes, 1981, 2019). Originally demonstrated with large-scale complex infrastructure systems (energy distribution and water resources), the development of an HHM requires the decomposition of a system into multiple subsystems that expands across multiple models to consider different structures associated with political, economic, environmental, and functional conditions across time (Haimes, 1981). While HHM fundamentally relies on a mathematical representation of a complex system, the development of a schematic representation of the HHM will promote active discussions about a project's objectives, risks, stakeholders, and perspectives.

As an example, we can consider the complexity of evaluating some of the multiple objectives involved in a large-scale residential community development project. This includes both private actors and public institutions (Dewberry, 2019a). Private actors include the developer, investors, and consumers. As a private, for-profit entity, the developer will be focused on decisions that control expenses, maximize returns (for investors and itself), and meet consumer demand (Dewberry, 2019b). The developer's ideal project, however, may conflict with existing zoning and/or public sector goals outlined in the Comprehensive Plan. Consumer objectives can also conflict with public sector goals. For example, a municipality's transit division will be focused on the proposed new residential community's connectivity with the larger transportation network and may promote the inclusion of wide "complete streets" (parking, bike lanes, multiple vehicular travel lanes) through the neighborhood; however, consumers may prioritize walkability and ensuring the safety of children, leading them to prefer narrow, low-speed streets with traffic calming measures to reduce vehicle speeds. Further, despite the seemingly cohesive ideals often included in Comprehensive Plans, the various institutional components of the public sector will each have their own objectives, which may be contradictory. For example, service-related institutions, such as the school system and police and fire departments, may want to limit growth that strains their existing capacity and budgets; however, the housing board may be interested in pursuing density to meet housing goals and address affordability issues. Separately, the budget division may want to the inclusion of specific types of commercial space to increase the tax base. Regardless of municipal objectives, project design and delivery must comply with the objectives of relevant State and Federal legislation, for example environmental or fair housing policies.

A schematic representation of the HHM for a development project would investigate how each stakeholder is represented in the hierarchy of project decisions. The developer may believe they have the authoritative role in the project, but the from the perspective of community members the developer is subject to planning regulations established by the local jurisdiction and public opinion. The HHM introduces additional perspectives to identify new sources of risk for a system. This provides a more realistic, resilient, and robust model of the system. As HHM is applied to a development project, each perspective will likely have different measures of cost, benefit, and expectations that shape the evaluation of multiple objectives.

Clearly identifying the existence of multiple objectives requires a diverse group of stakeholders engaging with mutual respect. Each stakeholder (or stakeholder group) must also recognize that communication, objectives, perception, and priorities will vary between individuals (or groups). There is no single method to ensure inclusive design practices—each project requires a determination of the appropriate processes and technologies. Most importantly, an accurate representation of multiple objectives (and associated perspectives) requires a common language of understanding.

Table 2 provides a list of several stakeholders that contribute to the multiple objectives of a development project. These objectives are listed to mirror the multiple stakeholders outlined in Fig. 1.

Note that the stakeholders given in Table 2 are meant to provide a familiar example of groups that may have competing objectives in a common development context. These concerns will, theoretically, be addressed through existing development approval processes. In productive, although often lengthy and expensive, participatory planning exercises, it is possible to achieve comprehensive results leading to desirable outcomes. However, such results are not guaranteed as levels of sophistication and commitment vary between developers and jurisdictions. The objectives, and the associated weight of each objective, must be evaluated under various disruptions to achieve a resilient system. New technologies, policies, environmental conditions and other factors will influence the weight of objectives. To evaluate multiple objec-

Table 2 Sample list of the stakeholder sources of multiple objectives

M_o	Stakeholders representing multiple objectives
MO_1	Developer (private stakeholder)
MO_2	Investors (private stakeholder)
MO_3	Consumers (private stakeholder)
MO_4	Federal and State Legislative Bodies (institutional stakeholder)
MO_5	Police and Fire Departments (institutional stakeholder)
MO_6	Land Records Office (institutional stakeholder)
MO_7	Zoning and Planning Office (institutional stakeholder)
MO_8	Transit Office (institutional stakeholder)
MO_9	Education Department (institutional stakeholder)
MO_{10}	Taxation and Budget Authority (institutional stakeholder)

tives through a systems engineering approach, particularly for investments considered at the project-level, each stakeholder's objective(s) should have a maximum score that can be achieved with different project initiatives (p_i) and each project is scored (a) with respect to the a given project meeting each objective (mo). The weight (and maximum possible score) of each objective is determined by the stakeholders and revaluated based on scenarios that consider system disruptions.

2.3 Temporal Considerations

The development of real estate is often disproportionally focused on immediate needs and costs. While important, focusing only on the current conditions, particularly during the design stages of a project, fails to adequately address the uncertainty and challenges associated with the requirements of future timeframes. It also jeopardizes the ability to account for the impact of current decisions on future operations by taking a short-term view. Land development is especially challenged by the timeframe considerations of a project because of the long-term horizon for the design, construction, and use of real estate projects, during which time technology, policies, and market conditions continue to change, often without being accounted for in the project. When decisions are not evaluated across the temporal domain, parties fail to anticipate how current actions can limit future options and the associated long-term costs. This variability creates vulnerability for projects.

Infrastructure projects provide a unique demonstration of temporal influence. The political conditions that bound infrastructure development are subject to change across the temporal domain of the project as existing policies change with new environmental discoveries, the shifting vision of a community, and new technologies in design and construction. Additionally, changes to exogenous factors such as technology, weather, sea level, and population growth create deep uncertainty for infrastructure planning (You, Connelly, Lambert, & Clarens, 2014). Inadequate development of future capacity in critical infrastructure systems will lead to operational challenges and limit growth, while over-investments in infrastructure will create unnecessary operations and maintenance burdens. Infrastructure projects are built to last for decades and the design and material choices for infrastructure construction will influence the future social, environmental, and financial costs of both the operators and the community. Yet critical decisions related to the materials, design, and capacity often rely on current technologies, policies, and market conditions. For example, the eventual arrival of fully autonomous vehicles will dramatically change future transportation infrastructure needs, but current policies and development decisions are made based on traditional transportation requirements and, therefore, may not be able to serve future needs. Note that temporal considerations should not be limited to future conditions but should also investigate historic and concurrent influences on project requirements.

These temporal conditions provide an additional dimension to the scenario planning associated with the MOTSA process. For many of the scenarios the question of "when" is more important than "if" a disruption will occur. When prioritizing investments, a stakeholder must consider when a disruption will occur, how stakeholder objectives may change over time, and how current actions can limit future decisions. The process of temporal decomposition is an extension of resilience analytics and considers the time frame associated with each disruption. The original framework, as referenced in Eq. (1), can be expanded to consider different planning horizons associated with a scenario. A technological disruption might be inevitable, but other disruptions could be prioritized based on immanency of the disruptions.

To consider the planning horizons and temporal domains, a new temporal weight (τ) is introduced to the resilience analytics, where $\{\tau: 0 < \tau \leq 1\}$. The temporal weight modifies the ranked value for scenarios based on when they are anticipated to occur. The timeframe of the scenario must be less than the life expectancy of the project, or else it is not deemed relevant to the project. Based on a planning horizon in years (T), the anticipated timeframe of a scenario (t_{sk}) is evaluated as shown in Eq. (2):

$$\begin{gathered} \theta = \sum_{k=1}^{s} \frac{\left(T - t_{sk}\right)}{T} \\ \tau_k = t_{sk} \times \theta^{-1} \\ \left\{t_{sk} : 0 < t_{sk} \leq \mathrm{T}\right\} \end{gathered} \tag{2}$$

Each scenario (s_k) holds a temporal weight (τ_k) associated with the expected timeframe of the disruption. The variable τ represents a proportional weight of a given scenario to all other scenarios evaluated across the temporal domain. The variable θ represents the sum of all temporal values of the project. As an example, if the planning horizon of project infrastructure is estimated at 50 years and the disruptive scenarios are expected to occur 15, 25, and 40 years from project origination, then θ would equal ($1.0 + 0.7 + 0.5 + 0.2 = 2.4$). Each value of t is then evaluated as a proportional weight to calculate τ_k, such that $\tau_k = \{0.42, 0.29, 0.21, 0.08\}$. The temporal weight is assigned to the original Eq. (1) as defined by Eq. (3).

$$v_{s_k}(p_i) = \tau_k \sum_{j=1}^{m} w_j^k a_{ji}^k \tag{3}$$

As shown in Eq. (3), the temporal weight does not influence the score (a) or weight (w) assigned by multiple objectives, and instead applies an adjustment to the entire project initiative value (v) for each scenario. In this way, scenarios that are anticipated to occur later in the planning horizon will carry less weight than those in the near term. These temporal weights should not preclude an investigation into which decisions could obfuscate future project initiatives, such that a project in the future is no longer an available option. The value of t_{sk} does not reference the time of invention of a relevant technology but instead evaluates the expected timeframe of market penetration such that it would influence project initiatives.

Further note that this introduction of a temporal element does not account for the cost component of future improvements undertaken as part of a particular project scenario. If such costs are anticipated to be incurred within the investment horizon, they can be accommodated through an addition in the pro forma line for capital expenditure reserves if a scenario is deemed likely. Alternatively, the future value of the cost for required improvements can be calculated and introduced as a "shock" to test the resiliency of financial projections should the scenario occur in year t_{sk}.

2.4 *Scenario Analysis*

Scenario analysis is a method to consider that the future time frames will change with the exogenous and endogenous conditions of the system. Changes to policies, environment, community, and technology will all influence the timelines and effects of the decisions. By accepting the uncertainty, scenarios inform the current decisions with an investigation on a variety of effects across different time frames. These scenarios are key to the temporal considerations of MOTSA and are based on prior work that demonstrates the value of scenario-based planning (Bostick, Connelly, Lambert, & Linkov, 2018; Leung, Lambert, & Mosenthal, 2004). While the scenario development is meant to inform stakeholders, it is not reasonable to assume the scenarios are inclusive to all possible futures. Instead, the development and analysis of scenarios should prompt discussions about possible futures and the prioritization of initiatives that establish resilient designs, The determination of the appropriate metric of resilience should be prompted by the multiple objectives of stakeholders and informed by the scenario planning and analysis. A scenario analysis begins with identifying a list of disruptive conditions, as shown in Table 3.

The disruptions in Table 3 are provided as an example and should be developed by stakeholders and state of the art research. Based on a set of disruptions, a sce-

Table 3 Sample list of disruptive technologies that would influence the ranking and resilience of development project initiatives

D	Disruptive technology
D_1	Blockchain
D_2	Autonomous ground transportation
D_3	Artificial intelligence (building systems)
D_4	Drone delivery systems
D_5	Electric vehicles
D_6	Hydrogen-powered vehicles
D_7	Smart building materials (flooring, walls, sensors)
D_8	Enhanced communication (5G)
D_9	Autonomous air transportation
D_{10}	Renewable energy production (cheaper systems or policy requirements)
D_{11}	Robotic delivery or assistant services
D_{12}	Biometric security
D_{13}	Unknown unknowns

Table 4 Sample list of scenarios that group various disruptions by similar technology conditions or anticipated timeframes

S	Scenario disruptions
S_0	*No disruptions*
S_1	D_1
S_2	$D_1 + D_2, D_4, D_5, D_6$
S_3	$D_1 + D_3, D_7, D_8, D_{10}, D_{11}, D_{12}$
S_4	$D_1 + D_9$

Each scenario may have a common disruption or represent independent disruptions

nario will consider one or more disruptions. A base disruption (e.g., an inevitable condition) can be used across all scenarios. Similar disruptions can be grouped into a single scenario, as shown in Table 4, which considers a (0) baseline, (1) consistent disruption, (2) transportation technologies, (3) artificial building intelligence, and (4) energy technology scenarios as reference from the disruption in Table 3.

Scenario analysis can be used to prioritize different projects based on a defined set of objectives through various futures that consider emergent conditions (Karvetski, Lambert, & Linkov, 2009). Each objective has different weights assigned, which can be modified across various scenarios. Each scenario prompts a new assigned score on how well a project meets objectives given the disruptive conditions of a scenario. The scenarios can be opportunistic or disruptive and are meant to inform decision-makers (Karvetski et al., 2009). The development and analysis of scenarios promotes conversations across subject matter experts with different perspectives and objectives. Scenarios are best authored by a diverse team based on technical review of potential disruptions. Initially, each stakeholder may lobby for a set of project initiatives to meet one objective; however, scenario-based planning evaluates how the initiatives rank when considering all objectives. The resilience of each project initiative is evaluated by the scenarios that can disrupt the system. There is a growing recognition of the applicability of this technique and the American Planning Association (APA) supports scenario planning methods as a complimentary framework for traditional planning processes (American Planning Association, 2019).

2.5 *Example Demonstration*

Consider a basic scenario in which a developer is evaluating the infrastructure requirements for the expansion of an existing facility. The expansion will require a surface parking facility, which would traditionally be designed based on current parking requirements and vehicle modes. In this example, several transportation project investment initiatives can be identified and ranked with the MOTSA framework. Relevant transportation-related project initiatives are shown in Table 5. These initiatives represent different investments that can be made by the developer but are also susceptible to technology disruptions.

In this example, the developer is evaluating initiatives that warrant upfront investments in hopes of meeting multiple objectives while considering possible technological disruptions. The initiatives are developed with expert input from a variety of stakeholders and the relevant objectives evaluated for each project initiative also consider different stakeholder perspectives. An objective weight is assigned to each objective by the decision-makers for a baseline scenario (s_0) with no technological disruptions, as shown in Table 6.

As required by the MOTSA framework, the weight (j) of each multiple objective (m) sum to one, as indicated with $\sum_{j=1}^{m} w_j = 1,\ 0 \le w_j \le 1\ \ for\ j = 1,\ldots 5$.

Each stakeholder may assign different weights (likely biased towards their objectives), which can influence the final weight value selected for each objective. Anticipated technological disruptions are developed to evaluate the resiliency of different project initiatives. This sample demonstration references disruptive technologies (Table 7) applicable to site transportation project initiatives (Table 5).

Table 5 Project initiatives for example demonstration

p	Project initiatives
p_0	No additional transportation investment
p_1	Provide infrastructure to support electric charging stations
p_2	Install vehicle charging stations
p_3	Plan for surface parking redevelopment
p_4	Reserve site area for alternative transportation modes
p_5	Provide drop off and queuing areas for autonomous vehicles

Table 6 Multiple objectives (consolidated list) for sample demonstration with weights applied to each objective

MO_m	Applicable criteria	weight (w_0)	Max score (a_0)
MO_1	Initial costs (Developer)	0.40	40
MO_2	Parking requirements (Zoning and Planning)	0.25	25
MO_3	Electric power policy (Legislative body)	0.05	05
MO_4	Marketability of site (Technology Policies)	0.20	20
MO_5	Financial incentives from local government (Economy)	0.10	10
Σ		1	100

Weights represent a maximum score that can be assigned to each objective based on a project indicative's ability to meet objective criteria

Table 7 Sample list of disruptive technologies relevant to site transportation project initiatives

D	Disruptive technology
D_1	Autonomous ground transportation
D_2	Electric vehicles
D_3	Hydrogen-powered vehicles

The disruptions are grouped into scenarios, which may include more than a single disruption. Starting with a base scenario (with no disruptions), each disruption has an anticipated timeframe (t_k) that represents when the scenario will influence the project. The anticipated timeframe, along with an established planning horizon (T = 20 years) provides a temporal weight value for each scenario. The scenarios and temporal values are shown in Table 8.

Each scenario requires a reevaluation of the weights and maximum scores, as originally defined in Table 5. Modifications are made to each weight value based on whether the importance of the objectives will increase or decrease during various scenarios. For example, under a mostly autonomous transportation environment (S_1) the parking requirements (MO_2, w_2) would be less significant. The potential for reductions in parking requirements would reduce the weight and increase the values of all other objectives. Table 9 provides different weights for each objective across multiple scenarios.

The list of project initiatives for the development are scored based on the ability to meet the multiple objectives across the scenarios developed. The assigned score is associated with the weighted value for each objective. All quantitative results for each initiative are assigned a rank value based on highest to lowest scoring project initiatives for each scenario. The range and median of each project are listed for reference, and then a new comprehensive ranking can be determined based on median values (or other quantitative metrics) as shown in Table 10. The results are shown graphically in Fig. 3.

These results have considered the temporal domain of each scenario. Based on the planning horizon and the anticipated scenario timeframe, the temporal values can be assigned to the original results documented in Table 10. The new ranking of each project initiative will consider the anticipated timeframe of the scenarios as modified by the temporal weight variable as $\tau_k = \{0.4, 0.3, 0.2, 0.1\}$ from Table 8. A new set of calculations and resulting rank of project initiatives is shown in Table 11.

Table 8 Sample list of scenarios that group technological disruptions

S_k	Scenario	Anticipated timeframe (t_k)	Temporal weight (τ_k)
S_0	No anticipated disruption	0	0.4
S_1	D_1, Autonomous ground transportation	5	0.3
S_2	$D_1 + D_2$, dominance of electric vehicles	10	0.2
S_3	$D_1 + D_3$, dominance of hydrogen-powered vehicles	15	0.1

The anticipated timeframe and the associated temporal weights are calculated for each scenario

Table 9 Sample list of weights associated with each project initiative during each scenario

S_k	w_1	w_2	w_3	w_4	w_5
S_0	0.40	0.25	0.05	0.20	0.10
S_1	0.45	0.05	0.05	0.30	0.15
S_2	0.30	0.05	0.15	0.20	0.15
S_3	0.60	0.05	0.05	0.20	0.10

The weight values can change across scenarios if the criteria is deemed more or less relevant to development goals. The weights represent a maximum score value as each project initiative is evaluated

Table 10 Based on the score values assigned to each project initiative (not shown in this demonstration) the initiatives are ranked based on the highest scoring project initiative (rank of one) to the lowest scoring initiative (rank of six)

S_k	p_0	p_1	p_2	p_3	p_4	p_5
S_0	*1*	*5*	*6*	*3*	*4*	*2*
S_1	*6*	*4*	*5*	*3*	*2*	*1*
S_2	*6*	*2*	*1*	*5*	*4*	*3*
S_3	*4*	*5*	*6*	*3*	*1*	*2*
Med	5	4.5	5.5	3	3	2
Low	1	5	6	2	2	1
High	6	5	6	5	4	3
Rank	**5**	**4**	**6**	**2**	**2**	**1**

Across all scenarios, each project initiative has a representative range of values and a median score. The median score references the comprehensive rank

The temporal weights shift the comprehensive ranking of the project initiatives, as shown in Table 10. Evaluating the prior rank (without temporal considerations) and the adjusted rank value demonstrates how the anticipated time frame and planning horizon will influence the prioritization of initiatives.

The demonstration is provided to inform stakeholders of methods to prioritize land development project initiatives based on disruptive technologies and the anticipated timeframe of the technologies. This approach extends prior methods of resilience analytics by considering the temporal domains of inevitable technology disruptions.

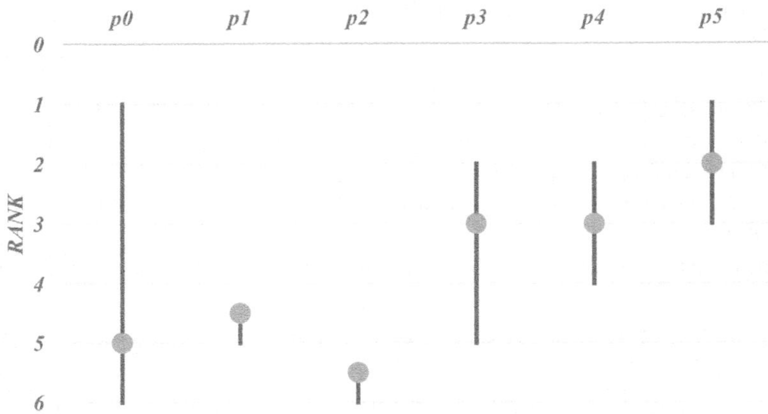

Fig. 3 Chart depicting the range and median (circle) of each project initiative (p) rank based on various scenarios

Table 11 Temporal weights assigned to ranked values to provide a new series of rankings

$\tau_k \times S_k$	p_0	p_1	p_2	p_3	p_4	p_5
$\tau_0 \times S_0$	0.4	2	2.4	1.2	1.6	0.8
$\tau_1 \times S_1$	1.8	1.2	1.5	0.9	0.6	0.3
$\tau_2 \times S_2$	1.2	0.4	0.2	1.0	0.8	0.6
$\tau_3 \times S_3$	0.4	0.5	0.6	0.3	0.1	0.2
Rank	**3**	**4**	**6**	**5**	**2**	**1**
Prior Rank	5	4	6	2	2	1

The bottom row referenced the original rank value without the temporal weight considerations

2.6 Broader Application to Real Estate

Real estate development is challenged by limitations in resources and the uncertainty of future conditions, including disruption from technology. It is further bounded by political and physical conditions that must consider the long-term operational requirements and the continuous shift of social, environmental, technological, and economic conditions. Improved decision making within this complex environment can be served by systems engineering. While the potential applications of systems engineering to real estate are extensive, this section will briefly highlight conceptual examples in infrastructure development, humanitarian aid endeavors related to titling projects, and market-based project decision-making.

2.6.1 Infrastructure

With the rapid emergence of technologies, infrastructure planning is challenged to serve current needs while also being adaptable to future conditions. These challenges are especially prevalent in infrastructure design because (1) the planning, funding, design and construction of a project will span multiple years; (2) the technology, policies, economics and other factors change during the years of design and construction (and continue to change over the life of the development); (3) each project is unique; and (4) the scale of infrastructure projects prohibits testing, prototyping, and agile development.

The planning, design, construction, operations and maintenance of civil infrastructure is interconnected and interdependent within a community and the economy. Water, transportation, energy, and communication infrastructure are critical to the economic system (Haimes & Lian, 2006). The multitude of stakeholders and contending objectives are constantly negotiated between local, regional and global environments. This interconnected state is not restricted to the physical infrastructure of the built environment—the rapid and continuous emergence of technology and communication channels adds to the complexity and risks of community development. This complexity requires processes that serve, plan, and adapt to economic, social, and environmental objectives.

2.6.2 Humanitarian

Globally, large-scale aid projects concerned with improving title and tenure security are often geared towards titling programs, land administration reforms, and/or capacity building. Such solutions, aimed at the individual institutional level, fail to account for the complexity of the systems that support meaningful change and sustainability in results. For example, delivering a revised process and improved capacity in a land records office may result in an initial increase in the issuance of new title documents. However, such progress is unlikely to be sustainable if court systems do not efficiently support title related claims or if taxation policies create disincentives for formal property transfers to continue in the future. While independent capacity building projects may be simultaneously run in land administration and other institutions, education for example, deliberate efforts should be made at devising a single/joint coordinated and comprehensive exercise. Applying systems engineering principles can allow aid organizations to consider the entire spectrum of institutions relevant to titling outcomes. Doing so may facilitate innovation for reimagining titling programs to account for a more holistic, system-wide approach. Similarly, using a systems engineering approach can contribute to the development of more robust, equitable policies by helping policy makers anticipate possible unintended social consequences before instituting new policies, regulations, or processes.

2.6.3 Market

Once developed, real estate projects are expensive and difficult to modify. In some cases, extensive retrofitting or rehabilitation is simply not possible due to design or site constraints. Unanticipated future changes in space use, technology, or other areas can limit functionality, increasing operating costs, or impact demand, leading to increased vacancy, slower rental/sales rates, or the need to discount prices. Thus, it behooves private sector developers to account for future disruptions that may impact their projects before each asset reaches its natural point of functional obsolescence. A well-known contemporary example of a future disruptive threat centers around the eventual impact of autonomous vehicles on parking structures. Previously, changes to automotive technologies were less relevant to real estate. However, a rise in the use of autonomous vehicles may now change the way parking structures are designed and used. While autonomous vehicles are already a part of mainstream industry discussions, other potential disruptions have likely not yet received the same attention. Applying a systems engineering approach to evaluating projects during the design stage can help developers consider what unanticipated disruptions or unrelated technologies may become relevant in the future, allowing the developer to plan accordingly.

3 Conclusion

Systems engineering has a range of applications related to real estate, including infrastructure delivery, humanitarian projects, and private sector market investment and development. The use of a systems engineering approach can enable developers and policy makers to consider a more robust, holistic view of the real estate system rather than limiting focus to individual industry sectors, institutional objectives, or temporal conditions. The intentional application of the MOTSA process can support an analysis of potential disruptions to projects, build resilience against future threats, prevent or limit unintended policy consequences, and lead to early adoption of best practices.

Despite its potential, however, systems engineering is often poorly understood outside of the engineering profession and military applications. This inherently limits its value to members of the real estate community who might otherwise benefit from its use. Thus, further development is required to increase the approachability of the MOTSA processes in order to support the engagement of non-engineering stakeholders. This includes the need to build a framework tailored for different real estate applications. Such a framework would guide users through an outline of considerations with prompts for defining and considering multi-objectives, temporal factors, and scenario analysis components. A fully developed MOTSA tool could become, in its own way, a type of disruptive technology used to improve the results of real estate planning and projects.

References

Allen, C. R. et al. (2018). Tiered approach to resilience assessment. *Risk Anaysis, 38*(9), 1772–1780.

American Planning Association. (2019). *Scenario planning*. Retrieved from https://www.planning.org/knowledgebase/scenarioplanning/

Augustinus, C. (2019, March 25–29). Using a multi-lateral organization to catalyze institutional innovation at global scale: Evidence from the work of Global Land Tool Network Partners. In *World Bank Conference on Land and Poverty, Washington, DC*.

Bambioa, Y., & Bouayad Aghab, S. (2018). Land tenure security and investment: Does strength of land right really matter in rural Burkina Faso? *World Development, 111*, 130–147.

Bostick, T. P., Connelly, E. B., Lambert, J. H., & Linkov, I. (2018, March). Resilience science, policy and investment for civil infrastructure. *Reliability Engineering and System Safety, 175*, 19–23. https://doi.org/10.1016/j.ress.2018.02.025.

Collier, Z. A., & Lambert, J. H. (2018). Time management of infrastructure recovery schedules by anticipation and valuation of disruptions. *ASCE-ASME Journal of Risk and Uncertainty in Engineering Systems Part A: Civil Engineering, 4*(2):04018012.

Connelly, E., Colosi, L., Clarens, A., & Lambert, J. (2015). Risk analysis of biofuels industry for aviation with scenario-based expert elicitation. *Systems Engineering, 18*(2), 178–191.

Dewberry, S. (2019a). In S. Dewberry & C. K. Grimsley (Eds.), *Development of the built environment: From site acquisition to project completion*. New York, NY: McGraw Hill Education. ISBN: 978-1260440737.

Dewberry, S. (2019b). In S. Dewberry, C. Pennetti, & C. Guyan (Eds.), *Land development handbook*. New York, NY: McGraw Hill Education. ISBN: 978-1260440751.

Dewberry, S., Pennetti, C., & Guyan, C. (2019). *Land development handbook*. New York, NY: McGraw Hill Education. ISBN: 978-1260440751.

Grimsley, C. K., & Kavanagh, J. (2018, March 19–23). Modernizing land service delivery through the application of a continuum approach: Examining the appropriateness of the international land management standard (ILMS). In *World Bank Conference on Land and Poverty*, Washington, DC.

Habitat for Humanity International and USAID. (2017). *How to improve residential energy efficiency in South Eastern Europe and CIS: Policy Discussion Brief for national governments and international organizations*.

Haimes, Y. (1981). Hierarchical holographic modeling. *IEEE Transactions on Systems, Man, and Cybernetics, 11*(9), 606–617.

Haimes, Y. (2012). Systems-based guiding principles for risk modeling, planning, assessment, management and communication. *Risk Analysis, 32*(9), 1451–1467.

Haimes, Y. (2019). *Modeling and managing complex systems of systems*. Hoboken, NJ: Wiley.

Haimes, Y., & Lian, C. (2006). Managing the risk of terrorisim to interdependent infrastructure systems through the dynamic inoperability input-output model. *Systems Engineering, 9*(3), 241–258. Wiley Periodicals, Inc.

Higgins, D., Balint, T., Liversage, H., & Winters, P. (2018). Investigating the impacts of increased rural land tenure security: A systematic review of the evidence. *Journal of Rural Studies, 61*, 34–62.

INCOSE. (2007). *Systems engineering handbook*. Seattle, WA: International Council on Systems Engineering.

ISO. (2018). *ISO standard 19152:2012, Geographic information—Land Administration Domain Model (LADM)*. Retrieved from https://www.iso.org/standard/51206.html

Karvetski, C., Lambert, J., & Linkov, I. (2009). Emergent conditions and multiple criteria analysis in infrastructure prioritization for developing countries. *Journal of Multi-Criteria Decision Analysis, 16*, 125–137.

Lawry, S., Samii, C., Hall, R., Leopold, A., Hornby, D., & Mtero, F. (2017). The impact of land property rights interventions on investment and agricultural productivity in developing countries: A systematic review. *Journal of Development Effectiveness, 9*(1), 61–81.

Lemmen, C., van Oosteromb, P., & Bennett, R. (2015). The land administration domain model. *Land Use Policy, 49*, 535–545.

Leung, M., Lambert, J., & Mosenthal, A. (2004). A risk-based approach to setting priorities in protecting bridges against terrorist attacks. *Risk Analysis, 24*(4), 963–984.

Maier, M., & Rechtin, E. (2009). The Art of Systems Architecting, Third Edit. Boca Raton: CRC Press.

Muchomba, F. (2017). Women's land tenure security and household human capital: Evidence from Ethiopia's land certification. *World Development, 98*, 310–324.

Quenum, A., Thorisson, H., Wu, D., & Lambert, J. H. (2019). Resilience of business strategy to emergent and future conditions. *Journal of Risk Research, 0*(0), 1–19. https://doi.org/10.1080/13669877.2018.1485172

Ram, C., & Montibeller, G. (2012). Exploring the impact of evaluating strategic options in a scenario-based multi-criteria framework. *Technological Forecasting and Social Change, 80*, 657–672.

Siddiqi, A., Ereiqat, F., & Anadon, L. (2016). Formulating expectations for future water availability through infrastructure development decisions in arid regions. *Systems Engineering, 19*(2), 101–110. Wiley.

Thekdi, S., & Lambert, J. (2015). Integrated risk management of safety and development on transportation corridors. *Reliability Engineering and System Safety, 138*, 1–12. https://doi.org/10.1016/j.ress.2014.11.015

Thorisson, H., & Lambert, J. (2017). Multiscale identification of emergent and future conditions along corridors of transportation networks. *Reliability Engineering and System Safety, 167*(September 2016), 255–263.

Thorisson, H., Lambert, J., Cardenas, J., & Linkov, I. (2017). Resilience analytics with application to power grid of a developing region. *Risk Analysis, 37*(7), 1268–1286.

UN Habitat. (2016). *Urbanization and development: Emerging futures, world cities report.* Nairobi. Retrieved from http://wcr.unhabitat.org/main-report/#section_eleven

UN Habitat. (2017). *Global land tool network, social tenure domain model—History*. Retrieved from https://stdm.gltn.net/history/

UN Habitat. (2019). *Guidelines for impact evaluation of land tenure and governance interventions, developed through a joint initiative of GLTN and IFAD*. Nairobi. Retrieved from https://gltn.net/download/guidelines-for-impact-evaluation-of-land-tenure-and-governance-interventions-2/?wpdmdl=14808&ind=1555494305960

UNECE. (2019). *Policy framework for sustainable real estate markets*. Geneva.

United Nations. (2015). *Transforming our world: The 2030 Agenda for Sustainable Development*. New York. Retrieved from https://sustainabledevelopment.un.org/post2015/transformingourworld/publication

Whittal, J. (2014). A new conceptual model for the continuum of land rights. *South African Journal of Geomatics, 3*(1), 13–32.

World Poverty Clock. (n.d.). Retrieved from https://worldpoverty.io/index.html

You, H., Connelly, E., Lambert, J. H., & Clarens, A. (2014). Climate and other scenarios disrupt priorities in several management perspectives. *Environment Systems and Decisions, 34*(4), 540–554.

Index

A. Lehavi, R. Levine-Schnur (eds.), *Disruptive Technology, Legal Innovation, and the Future of Real Estate*, https://doi.org/10.1007/978-3-030-52387-9

The manufacturer's authorised representative in the EU is Springer Nature Customer Service Centre GmbH, Europaplatz 3, 69115 Heidelberg, Germany. If you have any concerns regarding our products, please contact ProductSafety@springernature.com

Printed and bound by CPI Group (UK) Ltd, Croydon, CR0 4YY
28/09/2026
02224089-0001